PENGUIN BOOKS

The Diary of a Submissive

Sophie Morgan is a journalist working in South East England.
She lives with her boyfriend.

The Diary of a Submissive

SOPHIE MORGAN

PENGUIN BOOKS

PENGUIN BOOKS

Published by the Penguin Group
Penguin Books Ltd, 80 Strand, London WC2R 0RL, England
Penguin Group (USA) Inc., 375 Hudson Street, New York, New York 10014, USA
Penguin Group (Canada), 90 Eglinton Avenue East, Suite 700, Toronto, Ontario, Canada M4P 2Y3
(a division of Pearson Penguin Canada Inc.)
Penguin Ireland, 25 St Stephen's Green, Dublin 2, Ireland (a division of Penguin Books Ltd)
Penguin Group (Australia), 250 Camberwell Road, Camberwell, Victoria 3124, Australia
(a division of Pearson Australia Group Pty Ltd)
Penguin Books India Pvt Ltd, 11 Community Centre, Panchsheel Park, New Delhi – 110 017, India
Penguin Group (NZ), 67 Apollo Drive, Rosedale, Auckland 0632, New Zealand
(a division of Pearson New Zealand Ltd)
Penguin Books (South Africa) (Pty) Ltd, Block D, Rosebank Office Park,
181 Jan Smuts Avenue, Parktown North, Gauteng 2193, South Africa

Penguin Books Ltd, Registered Offices: 80 Strand, London WC2R 0RL, England

www.penguin.com

First published 2012
007

Copyright © Sophie Morgan, 2012
All rights reserved

The moral right of the author has been asserted

Set in 12.5/14.75 pt Garamond MT Std
Typeset by Jouve (UK), Milton Keynes
Printed in England by Clays Ltd, St Ives plc

All names, places and situations have been changed. Any resemblance
to actual events, locales, or persons, living or dead, is entirely coincidental

Except in the United States of America, this book is sold subject
to the condition that it shall not, by way of trade or otherwise, be lent,
re-sold, hired out, or otherwise circulated without the publisher's
prior consent in any form of binding or cover other than that in
which it is published and without a similar condition including this
condition being imposed on the subsequent purchaser

ISBN: 978-1-405-91063-7

www.greenpenguin.co.uk

ALWAYS LEARNING   **PEARSON**

Prologue

You might have slipped outside to take a call on your phone when you first saw us, or, if you're so inclined, have been finishing a crafty cigarette before heading back into the warmth of the bar. Either way, we draw your attention, standing in a gap between the buildings, across the street and along a little way from where you're standing.

Don't get me wrong, that's not to say I'm especially stunning, or that he is. We look like any other couple on a night out, neither unusually dressed nor especially loud, not even remarkable in our unremarkableness. But there's an intensity, something brewing between us that stops you short, making you look in spite of the fact it's bloody cold and you were actually getting ready to go back inside and rejoin your friends.

His hand is clenched around my upper arm in a grip so visibly tight even from this distance that you wonder fleetingly if it's going to bruise. He has pushed me up against the wall, his other hand tangled in my hair and holding me in place, so when I try and look away – for help? – I can't.

He isn't particularly big or broad, in fact you'd probably describe him as nondescript if you were to bother describing him at all. But there's something about him, something about us, that makes you wonder for a minute if everything is all right. I can't take my eyes off him and the obvious depth of my awe means for a second you can't either. You stare at him intently, trying to see what I see. And then he tugs on my hair, pulling my head closer to his in a sharp movement that makes you instinctively step a bit closer to intervene, before those stories in the papers about good Samaritans meeting sticky ends flood your brain and pull you up short.

Closer now, you can hear him talking to me. Not the full sentences – you aren't that close – but enough words for you to get a sense. For these are evocative words. Vicious words. Ugly words that make you think perhaps you really might have to step in at any moment if this escalates further.

Slut. Whore.

You look at my face, so close to his, and see fury glittering in my eyes. You don't see me speak, because I don't. I'm biting my lip, as if I'm restraining the urge to respond, but I remain silent. His hand tangles tighter in my hair, and I wince but otherwise I stand there, not passive exactly – you can feel the effort it is taking for me not to move as if it were a tangible thing – but certainly self-controlled, weathering the verbal onslaught.

Then a pause. He is waiting for a response. You move closer. If someone asked you'd say it was to check I was all right, but in your heart you know that actually it's curiosity, pure and simple. There is something feral, primal, about the dynamic between us that draws you closer even as it almost repulses you. Almost. You want to know how I am going to respond, what happens next. There is something dark and yet compelling about it that means while normally you'd be horrified, instead you're intrigued.

You watch me gulp. I run a tongue along my bottom lip to moisten it before trying to speak. I start a sentence, tail off, eyes flickering down to break from his gaze as I whisper my response.

You can't hear me. But you can hear him. 'Louder.'

I'm blushing now. There are tears in my eyes, but you can't tell if they are of anguish or of fury.

My voice is clearer, even loud on the night air. My tone is defiant yet the flush on my cheeks and running along the collarbone visible under my open jacket betrays an embarrassment I can't hide.

'I am a slut. I have been wet all evening thinking about you fucking me and I would be very grateful if we could go home now and do that. Please.'

My defiance cracks by the last word, which comes out as a soft plea.

He runs a finger idly along the edge of my shirt – low cut enough that there is a hint of cleavage, but not exactly slutty – and I shiver. He starts to speak and the tone of his voice makes you restrain the urge to shiver too.

'That almost sounded like begging. Are you begging?'

You see me start to nod, but I get pulled up short by his hand in my hair. Instead I swallow quickly, shut my eyes for a second and answer.

'Yes.' A pause, turning into lengthening silence. A breath which might almost be a quiet sigh. 'Sir.'

His finger is still running along the curve of my breasts as he speaks.

'You look like you'd do pretty much anything right now to be able to come. Would you? Do anything?'

I stay silent. My expression is wary, which surprises you bearing in mind the obvious desperation in my voice. You wonder what 'anything' has encompassed in the past, what it's going to mean now.

'Will you get down on your knees and suck my cock? Right here?'

Neither of us speaks for long moments. He removes his hands from my hair, steps away a little. Waiting. The noise of a car door slamming a distance away makes me flinch, and I shift to glance nervously up and down the street. I see you. For a second we make eye contact, my gaze widening with shock and shame before I look back at him. He is smiling. Utterly still.

I make a sound in the back of my throat, half whimper, half plea, and swallow hard, gesturing around vaguely. 'Now? Wouldn't you rather we –'

His fingers press against my still-moving lips. He is smiling, almost indulgently. But his voice is firm. Imperious even.

'Now.'

I cast the quickest glance possible your way. You don't know it, but in my head I'm playing a very adult version of a childish game – if I don't look at you directly you're not actually there to witness my humiliation, can't see it because I can't see you.

I gesture nervously in your general direction. 'But it's still quite early, there are people walking –'

'Now.'

You are transfixed watching the battling emotions flit across my face. Embarrassment. Desperation. Anger. Resignation. Several times I open my mouth to speak, think better of it and remain silent. Through it all he just stands there. Watching me intently. As intently as you are.

Finally, face crimson, I bend at the knees and drop down to the wet cobblestones in front of him. My head is bowed. My hair falls in front of my face and makes it hard to tell, but you think you can see tears glistening on my cheeks in the light of the street lamp.

For a few seconds I just kneel there, unmoving. Then you watch me take a deep, steadying breath. I square my shoulders, look up and reach for him. But as my shaking hands make contact with his belt buckle, he stops me, patting me softly on the head the way you would a loyal pet.

'Good girl. I know how difficult that was. Now get up and let's go home and finish there. It's a bit cold for playing outside tonight.'

His grip is solicitous as he helps me to my feet. We walk past you, arm in arm. He smiles. Nods. You half nod back before you catch yourself and wonder what on earth you're doing. I am looking studiously at the ground, my head down.

You can see I am shaking. But what you can't see is how aroused this whole experience has made me. How hard my nipples are in the confines of my bra. How my trembling is as much from the adrenaline high of everything that has just played out in front of you as it is from the cold and humiliation. How I thrive on this. How it completes me in a way I can't fully explain. How I hate it yet love it. Yearn for it. Crave it.

You can't see any of that. All you can see is a trembling woman with dirty knees, walking away on wobbly legs.

This is my story.

I

The first thing to say is that I am not a pervert. Well, no more than anyone else. If you came to my flat you would be more struck by the piles of washing up in the sink than my dungeon – not least because the cost of living in the city is such that I'm lucky to have been able to find somewhere with a living room which I could rent alone within my budget. Let's just say a dungeon wasn't really an option.

So, to address some of those pesky stereotypes, I am neither a doormat nor a simpleton. I don't yearn to spend my day baking while someone hunts and gathers for me and I keep the home fires burning, which is just as well as apart from a decent Sunday roast I'm a bit of a crap cook. I also don't look like Maggie Gyllenhaal in *Secretary*. Alas.

I just happen to be, at points when the urge takes me and I have someone I trust to play with, a submissive. Not that you'd know that if you met me. It's just one facet of my personality, one of the plethora of character elements that make me, well, me – coexisting with my love of strawberries, compulsion to continue arguing stubbornly even when I know I'm wrong and tendency to heap scorn on 99 per cent of television programmes and yet become obsessive about the other 1 per cent to a level that frightens even me.

I work as a journalist on a regional newspaper. I love my job, and – not that it should really need to be said – being submissive doesn't impact on my work. Frankly, if it did I'd get lumbered with tea making and picture stories about infant-school book weeks, which really is a fate worse than death. Also, newsrooms are bantery places. It's a dog-eat-dog world and you need to give as good as you get. I do.

I consider myself a feminist. I'm certainly independent. Capable. In control. To some that might seem incongruous with the choices I make sexually, the things that get me off. For a while it seemed jarring to me. In fact, sometimes it still does, but I've come to the conclusion that there are more important things to worry about. I'm a grown woman of usually sound mind. If I want to relinquish my personal control to someone I trust so that they can lead us somewhere which proves thrilling and hot for both of us, then as long as I'm not doing it somewhere where I'm frightening small children or animals I think that's my right. I take responsibility for my actions and choices.

It has taken a while for me to get to this stage though. I would, if the word hadn't been appropriated by reality television and turned into something that sounds both nausea-inducing and in need of a soft-rock video mont-age, go so far as to say it's been a bit of a journey, which is really how this book came about. This isn't a manifesto or a 'how-to' book, although I like to think if you're into this kind of thing and wanting to explore you might get some ideas. It's just what happened to me, how I discovered and explored this side of myself, my experiences, my thoughts.

Ask another sub their thoughts and what being submissive means to them and you'll get a whole other book.

Looking back on it now my submissive tendencies started young, although I wouldn't have called them that then. I just knew there were certain things that made me tingle, that I would find myself thinking about wistfully without ever really being able to put my finger on why.

Of course I was oblivious to all of that as a kid – mostly I was just going about my business growing up in a nice middle-class home in the Home Counties. I hate to bust myths here, but there's no deep-seated trauma in my past or anything missing in my formative years that has exacerbated my love of filth now. I have no daddy issues, there was no angst in my home life, and my childhood was – happily for me but probably not that exciting for book writing purposes – a happy, loving and simple one. I was, and remain, very lucky indeed with my family – we are all quite different to each other, but the bond of love and a shared sense of the absurd sticks us together through thick and thin, and I feel genuinely blessed to have them all.

I grew up in a nice house with my mum, my dad and my brother.

My mum, an accountant before she had me, devoted her life to bringing up my brother and me, and is very much the heart of our family. She spent a lot of time with us, nurturing us into little people whether that involved helping us with homework or flinging herself around the garden with us. She didn't believe in sitting on the sidelines; if we were going roller skating she was going roller skating with us. Her other passion was doing DIY in every room of the house in rotational turn, the home improvement equivalent of repainting the Forth Bridge, albeit with Laura Ashley wallpaper.

My dad runs his own business and is the most hard-working man I know, a provider through and through who ensured our childhoods were filled with whatever new bike or gadget we wanted (thankfully mum was around to ensure such goodies were bestowed in sensible fashion lest we get too unbearable), opportunities for travel and a wonderful home life. Funny and clever, he has a sense of adventure that I think I inherited, along with an independence of spirit and unapologetic sense of 'this is who I am' that he encouraged in his children, having occasionally clashed with his own parents' views of what he *should* do in life, as opposed to what he wanted to do.

My brother is in lots of ways the polar opposite to me. Where I am generally fairly quiet and more comfortable around a few close friends, he is the life and soul of the party, the one whose energy lifts up the room, who gets things done. Despite our differences he is the person I would call first at 3am if I was in trouble, not least because he is practically nocturnal. I feel incredibly lucky that this man, who is likely to be alongside me in life for longer than anyone else, is someone so amazing – although, hilariously and despite this ringing endorsement, give us three days together in the family homestead over a Christmas holiday and we will have reverted to our teenage selves, bickering over who's spending too long in the bathroom (usually him).

Our comfortable semi was also shared with a menagerie

of animals, ranging from Goldie the Goldfish – don't judge, I was three when I named him – to Cheesy the hamster and Barry the dog – named during my 'why shouldn't dogs have human names?' phase (a question answered fairly quickly when my poor dad was running round the park bellowing 'Barry!' in a way that undoubtedly perturbed other dog walkers). I've always loved animals and one of my strongest childhood memories is of burying a dead bird I found in the garden expressly against the wishes of my mum who, understandably, was concerned about hygiene issues. When she discovered I had not only gone against her wishes by picking up said bird to move it to its final resting place but was presiding over a burial service attended by my brother and our next door neighbours' children – in for a penny in for a pound – I was sent to my room in disgrace. Usually for me such a punishment, despite being my parents' main tactic for misbehaviour – no corporal punishment in our house – was no punishment at all. My room was one of my favourite places to be as it was filled with the books I spent all my pocket money on and I spent happy hours sat on the window ledge reading and watching the world go by. But in this instance I felt the injustice was too much to bear. I wrote an outraged letter to David Bellamy telling him about the oppressive anti-conservationist regime I was forced to live under, where dead birds were cast aside by uncaring adults. He never replied, which is probably for the best because I fear if he had he might have told me to listen to my mum, which would only have made me more irate. The fact that this is the closest I can think of to a clash with my mother while growing up is testament to the fact I was never a natural rebel. I went quietly about doing my thing, but I wasn't busy testing boundaries, mostly because I was allowed to do pretty much everything I wanted to do, and otherwise wasn't bothered about arguing in principle. That, admittedly, did change as I got older.

My interest in writing started young – I remember writing and illustrating stories in little A5 booklets tied with treasury tags. My stories were usually based around children's TV shows, books and films I enjoyed. The standard of my writing was considerably better than my drawing, although at that point that really wasn't saying much. I dabbled in art at an early age, having seen something on the news about some precocious child somewhere whose art was selling for thousands. Sadly, when I knocked up a couple of coloured pencil and felt tip mixed-media works my mum was pleased to accept the first picture I gave her, and even stooped to giving me 50p for a second original. But when I upped my price to a tenner – I felt this was reasonable under the circumstances – she gave me a firm but kind 'no', scuppering any further plans for a life in the arts and returning me to producing my mini books and comics. Given half a chance I would pull myself, my friends and family into the worlds of Narnia, Middle Earth or, slightly closer to home but somewhat more obscurely, having discovered it via cable TV, the city of Newcastle as depicted in *Jossy's Giants*, a TV show about a school football team.

My love of *Jossy's Giants* and football in general came

very much from a tomboyish streak a mile wide. I was – and still am – quite a way from the girlie stereotype. I have a pathological dislike of pink and never developed a love for make-up, expensive clothes or fashionable shoes – to this day put me in a pair of heels and I walk not unlike Bambi trying to get across the ice, although what I don't spend on shoes I more than make up for with nail varnish and handbags. Growing up I definitely didn't have much interest in worrying about boys, a fact which, ironically, meant I had lots of male friends at school as I'd quite happily play football with them in the lunch hour and didn't bother with anything much like small talk. If you asked me my favourite things when I was ten, I'd have said reading, roller skating, riding my bike and climbing the tree at the end of our garden, which gave me a view of the nearby allotments – a source of endless fascination for reasons that seemed very important at the time. The tree was my private place – my brother had no interest in the inevitable scrapes and dirt borne of making the initial jump up, even with my cunningly engineered skipping rope pulley system, which provided a boost to the first climbable branch. I was quite a solitary child in lots of ways, very comfortable on my own, reading or daydreaming, which is probably a bit unsurprising bearing in mind the picture I've just painted of myself as a bit of an antisocial bint.

Of course, no woman is an island – even if they do spend time hiding up a cherry tree given half a chance. My brother was a constant companion and co-conspirator at home, while at school – a mixed primary school until I was eleven and then an all girls' school after that – I had a mixed circle of friends, many of whom I'm still close to. While I wasn't one of the popular group – I tended to veer towards the geeks, of music, drama, technology – I got on with everybody, using humour to smooth over any problems when they did occur. I was, by the time I'd settled into secondary life, very much a mid-range student. It took a while to find my feet as I'd gone from being one of the cleverest of my primary school class to mid-class at most subjects in secondary, which suddenly meant things weren't coming so easily and took effort. It was a culture shock in lots of ways, but probably not a bad thing in that it burst any precociousness that might have seeped in from having the kind of supportive home life where everyone thought I was some kind of genius because I liked reading. I wasn't the prettiest or the brightest in the class, although I soon realized this worked in my favour because it seemed to me that the smartest and prettiest girls were the people who attracted the most bitchiness. Instead, I was conscientious and worked hard, a by-product of an inherent need to please. Despite occasional worries at letting either my teachers or parents down, I, for the most part, really enjoyed school. I know, it's sickening.

Somewhat ironically, I was a bit of a late bloomer on the romance front. I had my first kiss when I was twelve or thirteen with a boy I knew through one of my friends and, if I'm honest, I wasn't that impressed by it. There was no thunderclap, no roll of romantic music, and a feeling of anticlimax – no pun intended – afterwards. I think one of us actually said, 'Well then.' Suffice to say no one's world was set alight.

That said, I read *Just Seventeen* and *Minx* magazine and I knew the mechanics of sex, although I had no interest in trying it at that point. I had however learned that when I couldn't sleep, rubbing my hand between my legs would bring a pleasure that made me doze off and when my mind wandered as I brought about this kind of pleasure it did always return to similar topics.

I've always been into myths and legends, and growing up, Robin Hood was a favourite. I watched the films, the TV show – we'll overlook the most recent incarnations before I start gnashing my teeth – and read all the books I could lay my hands on, fictional and historical. But through every medium I had a difficult time with Maid Marian. I hated that she was continually getting into peril for stupid reasons and then having to be rescued. That she didn't fight, wasn't even given the relative dignity of being a bona fide sidekick and seemed to spend most of her time patching up the wounds of the Merry Men and looking pensively into the middle distance as they disappeared off for adventure.

Despite that, my favourite parts of those stories involved her in the very peril I scorned her for. When she had been captured – as the inevitable bait in a trap to catch Robin Hood, seemingly her major purpose in life – her defiance of Guy of Gisborne and the Sheriff of Nottingham captured my imagination. She would be held in some dank dungeony place, with the pictures often showing her tied or in chains. Powerless. But she would be unbowed, dignified in her indignity, and somehow that struck a chord with me, made my heart race. You know how when you were a kid and something you read or watched caught your imagination so deeply that you were transported into it, it was you in that moment, living it, feeling it? (Actually, I say 'when you were a kid', but I still feel that now when I read or watch something amazing, it just happens less often). Well, all the scenes I replayed in my mind with me in the lead role were the scenes of Maid Marian, even if she was a bit rubbish and I tended to gloss over the dull stuff after Robin saved her and she had to go back to the camp and resume tending the fire. Those were the stories I used to think about lying in bed at night.

Well, at least until I discovered porn.

When I was about fourteen there was a brouhaha about a magazine that gave away an erotic book aimed at women with their issue one month. I didn't have the internet in my room and, frankly, while I knew if you wanted erotic inspiration that was the place to go, I had no interest in pictures of boobs because I had my own and didn't think they were that epic. This book though, this was different. Lots of talk of moral decay and the like meant that I spent most of the month desperate to get hold of a copy, in part because I'd started to suspect I was dirtier than my school friends, or at least dirtier than they dared to admit aloud. Even aside from getting to see exactly how scandalous this stuff was, it could, I reasoned to myself, act as a kind of smut barometer.

Except there was a problem.

My next door neighbour worked in the only news-agent big enough to sell the magazine in our small town, and not only would she not let me buy it as she knew I was a long way under eighteen, but she'd also be bound to tell my mum, which would leave me open to one of those conversations so hideous you want to pull off your own ears just to make it stop. Definitely a no go. So one afternoon I took a different bus home, one that took me to the nearest big town, and bought the magazine there, hands clammy, still wearing my school uniform, terrified at any moment that the disinterested woman behind the counter would realize I was underage and shamelessly buying what the *Daily Mail* had described as utter filth and demand I give it back before I ended up inadvertently corrupted forever. She didn't. I stuffed it in my rucksack and, my heart still pounding, walked the two miles home to explain to my Mum that I was late because of hockey practice.

Looking back at that book, which I can't bear to chuck away though it's now so well thumbed that the pages have started to fall out, the scandal and outrage at the time seems laughable. But reading it then was a revelation. My favourite chapters still have the tops of the pages folded over for ease of finding. One particular section involved a feisty yet vulnerable woman having a row with a man who she clearly fancied but also found herself continually clashing with. She ended up tied to a tree with ivy (I know, it's a bit lame, but go with it – it was special Greek ivy, which may have heretofore unknown bondage qualities) while he did whatever he wanted to her – running his hands over her body, viciously kissing her, verbally abusing her. She stood there, aroused in spite of herself and he made her come, all without her able to do anything but rest her head against the tree and moan out her pleasure.

It sounds quite cheesy indeed now, almost Mills and Boon-esque, but at the time it struck a chord with me. Suddenly that was what I was replaying in my head as I lay in bed at night, now accompanied by a hand between my legs rubbing myself to bring about blissful sleep.

Of course, there comes a time in every girl's life where actual boys overtake both books and the Guys of Gisborne of our imaginations (I was never really the Robin sort). My first serious boyfriend, older but not wiser, initially seemed somehow to pick up on signals I didn't even know I was giving out. Unlike other boys I'd kissed, he'd hold my head firmly in place, my ponytail twisted around his hand as we kissed goodnight, and I loved it. I loved feeling under his power, immobile as our tongues duelled.

I used to daydream about the possibilities of those kisses, what they could be a prelude to, the hint they gave of a different side to him, a side the world didn't see but which I could feel, as if that side of him was calling to a complementary side of me. And then one night, while kissing me goodbye, he bit my lower lip, so hard I whimpered into his mouth in a kind of surprised pleasure. Instantly he broke away, nearly taking a clump of my hair with him in his haste, and apologized for hurting me. It felt awkward to explain that actually I'd liked it, so I accepted his apology, said it didn't matter, and went indoors disappointed, with my nipples erect and my knickers moist.

I still didn't really know the significance of that kiss exciting me. All I knew was that nice girls didn't get off on such things, or if they did they certainly didn't talk about it. So I didn't. I went about my life, going through all the usual milestones. Eventually my first beau and I, taking advantage of his mum having to go into work to cover a poorly colleague's shift as a doctor's receptionist, did lose our virginity together, but the mixture of neither of us having done it before, feeling a bit self-conscious and keeping an ear out in case his mum returned home unexpectedly, meant it was perfunctory and, while perfectly pleasant, didn't rock my world. Afterwards I reflected that it didn't feel as pleasing as lying in bed touching myself – although at the time I didn't connect that with the fact that I hadn't orgasmed. Looking back on how naive and tentative our fumblings were, it seems a miracle we managed to have any kind of sex that first time at all. However, we found that practice made, if not perfect, then certainly 'good enough that we'd both grin giddily at each other for a long while after', although the lack of privacy meant we were constantly in fear of being discovered *in flagrante delicto*, and developed skills for a quick change that Clark Kent would be proud of, although possibly also slightly disturbed by.

2

My first youthful romance fizzled out as we both moved out of home and went off to university at other ends of the country. We missed each other to start with but, in that way of freshers everywhere, were both soon caught up in academic life and the extra-curricular fun it offered.

That said, for a fair while my extra-curricular fun mostly involved using the shared kitchen to bake bread – my mum didn't take kindly to people using her kitchen so I was enjoying finally being able to do some cooking for myself. There were also post-lecture drinks punctuated with the kind of discussions that in hindsight are pretentious tosh but that, when you're eighteen, you think are very important and show how grown up you are. It was during one of these drunken rows that I met Ryan. If Ryan didn't exactly lead me astray (by this point I was fairly sure I was capable of coming up with enough dodgy thoughts of my own, even without my burgeoning book collection and access to the internet in my room, another perk of academic life), he certainly opened the door to a world I hadn't fully realized I wanted to visit, even if I had been vaguely aware of its existence. So that makes at least a few of those hours debating Foucault, feminism and Chomsky (I told you it was pretentious) worthwhile.

I'd first seen Ryan in the library during my third year of

uni. His favoured corner to sit and work was opposite mine, which makes us both sound more diligent than we actually were. We were on polite nodding terms, even moving up to the 'would you keep an eye on my stuff while I nip to the loo?' level, although I'd still have taken my handbag with me. I'm not that much of a sucker for a handsome face. He was though.

My friend Catherine brought Ryan to the pub one night and he joined the melée of drunken burbling, although I noticed he mainly observed everyone, rather than getting involved in the discussion himself. When he did intervene to say something he said it slowly and carefully, he was articulate and would not be shouted down. I found him impressive and in sharp contrast to most of the other guys huddled round our table.

He was a little bit older than I was, an American gradu-ate student majoring in politics on a term's exchange at our university, and while he was kind and funny and good company he took his studies – and indeed most things – very seriously. I liked that though. College life was fun, but I was not into freshers' week and drinking until I puked. I was always mindful it was costing money for me to study so I should work hard. I liked his work ethic and that he felt the same. Plus, I couldn't help but note, he was sexy in a brooding and slightly geeky way, and had an accent that could seriously cause butterflies, assuming of course that he was moved to speech.

It took a little while. Debate was raging about a calen-dar being organized by one of the female sports teams to raise funds, which involved them posing naked but with a selection of random objects covering their modesty. Someone who lived on my floor was moaning about how demeaning it was, mostly it would appear because his girl-friend was appearing in one of the pictures. I was arguing that it wasn't demeaning, and wasn't actually his business as long as she felt comfortable doing it. The ongoing row got increasingly heated, which was inevitable since he was worried about people leching after his lady's ample charms, and what he lacked in articulateness five pints down he more than made up for in volume, wild flailing gesticulation and hyperbole. I couldn't help myself. I didn't actually care either way, but arguing was fun and frankly talking to him about it was like shooting fish in a barrel. Possibly one filled with beer.

It soon became clear that I wasn't the only one who saw debate as a kind of sport. Ryan weighed in on my drunken floormate's behalf, calling me anti-feminist, discussing the nature of intent and effect of pictures, via a discussion of old-style bawdy holiday postcards and landing squarely on a debate on the pros and cons of pornography.

After a while the circle of people talking tightened, with others moving away to buy more beer, mingle or – frankly – hide. But we kept arguing, him against any kind of pornography, me for it as long as everyone involved was there by choice and paid fairly, while Catherine's head moved back and forth like she was watching a game of particularly wordy tennis.

Part way through I began grinning internally. My theory on porn is very much (legality allowing) an each-to-their-own policy, and as such I didn't care that much either way, but I couldn't allow him to have the last word and wanted to see how long before he would run out of steam. Also, if I was being honest and a bit fickle, I kind of liked how the hot American's entire attention was focused on me, even if he had taken to occasionally putting his head in his hands in response to my debating intransigence.

It took a little while, but I saw in his eyes the moment he realized I was arguing for sport. His head was in his hands again, and he straightened his shoulders, took a long look at me, saw my smile twitching in a way I couldn't hide, and then leaned over to shake my hand.

'Well played, miss. Well played.'

I grinned at him and bought him a beer. It seemed only polite.

By the time the bar kicked out and we all began our stumble home, both Catherine and I were unsteady and a little giggly. He offered to walk me home, and as I put my scarf on Catherine leaned over and grabbed his arm.

'You can walk us both home. We live in the same halls.'
It might have been wishful thinking but he didn't seem thrilled by that as a suggestion. If I'm honest I wasn't either – the guy I'd been eyeing for weeks across the library had turned out to be rather fun, and I was hopeful he might feel the same about me. However, bearing in mind how buttoned up he was when he hadn't had copious liquid lubricant, I was unsure how I'd get the opportunity to find that out again.

All praise the in-room internet though. I woke the next morning, with a banging head and yearning for a bacon sandwich, to find an email asking me if I wanted to meet and see a film at the local cinema. I was so keen I replied before I even got up in search of a stomach-settling cup of tea.

We went to the cinema. He made the mistake of chivalrously letting me choose the film, which meant I inadvertently dragged a man who disliked the shocks and tension of horror films and the implausibility of sci-fi to a film that was both. Even in the darkness of the room I could see the slight look of disdain on his face in the flickering light from the screen – when his hands weren't over his face at least.

After the film we went out for dinner. The chat was spirited, not least because I was mocking him for being even more of a wuss than I was, while he was decrying how silly the whole thing had been and nitpicking plot holes in a way that made me laugh out loud. It was lots of fun and when he said we should consider doing it again I found myself agreeing without hesitation.

So we did. A trip to a comedy club, a band at the students' union, and then eventually he just invited me round to watch DVDs, which even in my relatively innocent ways I figured was make or break on the flirting front. I made chocolate brownies and, while I'm not sure how they compared to those from back home, he devoured them while we drank massive amounts of coffee and channel hopped. And then finally, after I'd pretty much given up trying to work out if he was interested in me romantically, he leaned over and made his move. Ostensibly he was brushing crumbs from the side of my mouth, but he quickly followed the touch of his fingers across my lips by pressing his mouth to mine. I smiled inwardly, but didn't feel the urge to quibble. By this point I'd been thinking about what this moment would be like for weeks.

He started tentatively, gently kissing my lips, pressing little kisses over and over against me, and then, braver, he pushed his tongue inside my mouth and kissed me properly. I wasn't disappointed. He tasted of chocolate and coffee, his mouth soft against mine. As he explored me, I opened my mouth eagerly, urging him deeper.

His hands slipped around me, stroking my back, pressing me closer. The feeling of his fingertips along my spine made me shiver with arousal, all my nerve endings on alert at his touch, at every whisper of a connection his body made with mine – his hands, his mouth, even his groin pushing insistently against me.

For a long time we just kissed, drinking each other in. He was a great kisser, leisurely and passionate, and while our hands roamed each other over our clothes he was happy to continue teasing me with his tongue in a way that broke my brain a little. A splintered, half-formed thought came somewhere through the haze: *If he can make me feel like this just by kissing what on earth will fucking him be like?*

As he leaned down and began unbuttoning my jeans I thought I might be about to find out. My hands moved to his own belt, but he stopped them, unfurling my fingers, bring them to his mouth and kissing them softly before moving them away and returning his hands to my own zip. He pushed my jeans down to my thighs, leaving my blue spotty knickers showing in a way that made me blush a bit.

He grinned. 'Nice.' I started stammering a justification for my slightly quirky choice in underwear, but he stopped me with a look. 'Just sit up for me for a minute.' I moved, and he pulled both my jeans and knickers down so I was properly bared to him.

For a long moment he just looked. I tried not to squirm, but it's always awkward having someone see your bits for the first time, especially when you're seemingly not playing the grown up version of 'you show me yours and I'll show you mine'. I watched him smile and then snuck a glance down at his crotch, relieved to see he seemed fairly pleased with what he was looking at. I moved forward again, putting my hands out to touch him, but he stopped me.

'It's OK. Just wait.'

'I'm not a patient person,' I growled.

'Consider this character building then,' he said, as he knelt down in front of me. I kicked his knee, albeit gently, with my bare foot and then moaned as he ran his finger along my inner thigh, so close to where I wanted him to be but not close enough. Two could play at this patience game though. I waited, my thighs barely trembling at all, as he stroked up and down either side of my lips, desperate for him to just move a few centimetres in, to touch me where I was aching for him now. I closed my eyes, fighting for control. I think I was just about managing it, at least until I felt his mouth on me, licking delicately against me, before sliding gently in to taste me. I moaned, but he did too, and his purr of pleasure as he tasted me intimately for the first time thrilled me. Then he began to kiss me, in the same meandering way he had plundered my mouth minutes before, and I shuffled along the sofa, edging myself closer as he made me writhe with his licks, alternating between light and teasing and more firm and forceful. My orgasm rose, abated, rose again, and finally, as he nipped my clit with his teeth and sucked it forcefully I came loudly, fulsomely and with the such force that I saw stars. It was a revelation and it made me laugh out loud with the sheer joy of it. I was desperate to catch my breath and then do it all again.

I looked down at him, still looking at me so seriously, and cupped the side of his face in my hand, stroking the down on his face. He smiled and turned his head to kiss my hand and I leaned down to kiss him before sinking down on the floor beside him, curling into him, close enough that he could feel my still-pounding heart. As I got my breath back and came back to earth, I felt his erection pressing against me, and this time when I moved my hand down he didn't stop me. I undid his fly and pulled him free and leaned down to take him in my own mouth but he demurred.

'Please, let me just be inside you.'

I nodded quickly and moved on to my back as he grabbed a condom. It seemed rude to quibble when my own orgasm was still dissipating after all. He pushed inside me and that first moment of connection made me clench. He moaned and buried his face in my shoulder. I moved my hips, pushing him deeper, but before he began to move he undid my top and pulled my breasts out of my bra with a groan.

His eyes were hungry as he stared at my hard nipples, but he couldn't restrain a comment: 'No matching spotty bra? I'm disappointed.'

I stuck my tongue out at him and began moving more insistently underneath him, inadvertently making my breasts bounce more. He leaned down and cupped them in his hands, stroking them and kissing them, taking each nipple into his mouth in turn as he began to – finally – move himself.

Our breathing grew ragged as we fucked. Everything else was unimportant but our movements, our connection to each other and our pleasure. Watching Ryan's face lose its seriousness, to see him completely with his defences down was incredibly hot, and watching him come made me so close that my fingers sliding between us to touch my clit for just a second pushed me over the edge too.

The next morning the only blot on the horizon was knowing that our relationship, even in these early stages, had a time limit. I was disappointed, upset even, but having spent the entire evening lying naked in his room, watching TV and drinking with pauses to kiss, grope and then fuck, I was absolutely adamant I was going to make the most of every moment he was here. Making hay while the sun shines.

We began dating casually, although with his return to the States always hanging over us we had no plans for it to be a serious thing. He was a considerate lover, infinitely patient both when giving and receiving pleasure.

He patiently let me explore him and I grew confident as I licked and sucked his cock, stroking him for as long as I wanted, learning how to please him, what I enjoyed doing. However, I would never in a million years have picked him out as being into anything remotely kinky, which made what happened next my first lesson on not making assumptions about people.

My first taste of kink, like many people's I suppose, came from a good, sound spanking.

I like to think I have a fairly good imagination. I certainly have, and I say this not so much with pride but as a statement of fact, a very dirty mind which means I'm more than happy to come up with alternate uses for innocent-looking objects. That, paired with my financial priorities at university – books and beer, not necessarily in that order – meant a lot of my favourite sex toys were repurposed household items.

So I liked to think that surrounded by my own stuff, in my own room, there was nothing which could be picked up and used for nefarious purposes against me that I hadn't already thought of and quite possibly played with, thank you very much. Which was why the hairbrush was such a big surprise.

I have very thick hair and a lot of it. Not in a werewoman way – at least not when I ensure my daily routine keeps all the key parts shaved bare – but in a way that means first thing in the morning, when I'm warm and sleep-flushed, my sartorial style often owes a little something to the wild woman of Borneo.

As it often does after a good fucking.

At that point though, we hadn't even got that far. We'd been kissing for what felt like hours, the kisses of two people wanting to tease out the tension a little longer, each kiss and movement of the mouth a prelude to and a promise of something more. Finally, we surfaced in an unspoken agreement to move on, my face raw from his stubble and nipples visible through my top, he with an obvious bulge in his trousers. As we broke apart he untangled his hands from my hair, with some difficulty.

As I tried to finger comb it into some semblance of order he pulled my hand away and kissed each digit, his dimple flashing as he gave me a smile which was on the very edge of wolfish. 'Forget it. We're just going to muss it up again anyway. And it's OK. I like to see you mussed.'

I stuck my tongue out at him as I began unbuttoning my shirt. 'I can't help my hair. And anyway, yours is looking pretty unkempt at the moment, too.' I gestured vaguely over my shoulder, gently mocking. 'There's a brush over there you can use if you need to.'

Ryan's hair was as dark and at least as unruly as mine – even before I had anchored my fingers in it while we kissed. It was significantly shorter, but the front continually fell in front of his eyes, causing him to do an unconscious ruffling thing to pull it away from his head when he was saying something important. I found it, and him, adorable.

I turned away and pulled down my trousers, bending down to pick them up from the floor where they were pooled around my feet. That was when he hit me.

It was the sound that did it I think. That and the fact

that I wasn't expecting it. When someone smacks you so hard on the arse that the room echoes with the noise of it and it's totally unexpected, it hurts. Even if in the back of your mind you're thinking, 'that was only one bloody slap for goodness' sake', you can't quite resist the urge to rub your arse. Or I couldn't, at least.

I turned round, my fingers still on my stinging arse, to see his eyes wide and innocent, his smile wider, as he waved the paddle brush in front of me. 'You said I could use it.'

Ah. The age-old caveat of being careful how you phrase things. Feeling like I was standing on the edge of something amazing that I had been waiting for years to experience, I smiled back at him, screwing up my courage, giving him the permission he was hinting for. 'You're right. I did.'

Serious hair needs a serious hairbrush and that is what it was. As he pulled my knickers down, pulled me across his lap and started smacking me with it, the noise ricocheted across the room, leaving me worried about what on earth my flatmate would think from next door, at least until he'd been going for a few seconds, after which point I really didn't give a toss.

I had often wondered what a good hard spanking would feel like. But in a million years I would never have expected it to feel like this.

It hurt, obviously. A lot more than I was expecting – you can tell I'm of the generation that didn't get corporal punishment in school. The air whooshed from my lungs with each impact for the first few hits, and all I could think

of was how much it hurt – definitely not the sexy paddling of my secret fantasies. In a panicked inner monologue
I was trying to decide whether to put a stop to it proac-
tively or just try and withstand it until he moved on when,
suddenly, the sensation changed, blossomed almost. It
still hurt, but the sting of my arse melted to a pleasurable
ache in the seconds after the impact and, as the adrenaline
pumped through me, suddenly even the pain of the initial
hits was blurring with the warmth of the pleasure I was
getting out of it.

He'd started on my left cheek, hitting me in a regular
rhythm until my heart was practically beating in time with
his tempo, my body responding to the beats of him beating me. He varied where the brush landed until the whole
of my arse cheek was warm and I was squirming across
his lap in an incoherent bundle of nerve endings. In that
moment my world was him and me, the stinging warmth
of my arse, the wetness between my legs and the feeling
of his cock hard against my thigh as I squirmed against
him. If he'd asked me what I wanted him to do, if I was
capable of forming words, I'd have been begging him to
stop as the pain was on the edge of being too much. But
at the same time the warmth between my legs meant I
knew with utter certainty that if he had stopped within a
few seconds I'd have been bereft and pleading for him to
continue. I didn't actually get the choice, which to be honest is just as well as by that point there was no way in hell
I was capable of speech anyway.

He switched cheeks, and the process began again. But
as I tried to temper my reaction to the pain, I felt a finger

slide between my legs, and easily – so easily that I was glad I was facing away so he couldn't see the sudden blush on my face – he pushed inside me.

By this time I was practically writhing on his lap, my breathing heavy, tears behind my closed eyes. He didn't hold back on hitting my arse with the brush, and as I turned to look up at him, I saw the flush of exertion and excitement on his cheeks, and an expression that made me whimper. He looked so sexy. The look in his eyes, the way he held his head, had changed from the Ryan I had previously known. I couldn't take my eyes off him. He was power. Control. He made me feel warm and cold and excited and nervous and like the whole world was being turned upside down and all I could do was hold on for the ride and trust him to lead me through it.

As our eyes met it was like a spell was broken. We were both more than ready to fuck, and while he wasn't going to leave a job half done the last three smacks with the brush were at least quick, albeit hard enough that I gasped at the pain. My mind was spinning as I couldn't breathe enough in between hits to in any way prepare for them. I rode the waves of pain as best I could and was still gasping as he manoeuvred me on to all fours ready for – *please please please* – us to fuck.

He filled me and I moaned in relief. But relief turned to confusion when it became apparent that it wasn't his cock filling me. I turned round, eyes blinking and trying to focus, to see him smiling at me again and holding the brush from the wrong end so he could show me my juices glistening on the handle. He tucked a strand of hair behind his ear as his dimple flashed again, a glimpse of playful Ryan. 'Sorry, I couldn't resist.'

I harrumphed and opened my mouth to try and formulate a response, only to be stopped when he pushed himself deep inside me. As we fucked, me grinding down on him as feverishly as he pushed himself up into my wetness, the pain from the already forming bruising of my arse, the stinging heat of it, was a harsh reminder of the punishment.

He leant forward, frigging my clit as our movements got more frenzied and desperate, both of us close to coming. Just at the point where I felt like I couldn't go any harder, or take any other stimulus, he ran the brush, metal bristles side down, along the full length of my still-throbbing arse. It was like running needles across my flesh. I couldn't help it, I screamed. If I could I would have begged him to stop, purely because the sheer force of feeling was so much I thought I was going to shatter. But as fast as my brain shorted out, saying I couldn't cope with this and it was all too much, my orgasm came and with it the flood of warmth that makes me want to curl up and rest for ten minutes before doing it all over again because it feels so amazing.

We lay there, tangled in the sheets, the sweat from our exertions drying as our breathing returned to normal. And as I looked at him, his eyes closed and his long eyelashes making him look so angelic, it was almost impossible to reconcile him with the man who had just ensured I would be feeling the evening every time I sat down for days. I couldn't figure out how I'd never thought of a hairbrush that way before. Suffice to say I haven't overlooked its possibilities again.

I also never looked at Ryan in quite the same way again. As we both came down from our respective adrenaline highs there was a moment of embarrassment. He ran a gentle hand over my arse, assessing the damage and enquiring politely whether I was in a lot of pain. In a way that seemed very British somehow, I said I was fine, thank you, and then we fell silent. I think he felt disconcerted by how much he enjoyed hurting me – and looking back I wonder if he made a discovery about himself that night as he wielded the hairbrush.

He certainly helped fit one of the earliest pieces of the puzzle for me. By the time he was preparing to go back to the States a few weeks later my arse had become intimately acquainted with that brush – and his hand – several more times, including one notable occasion when he got so aroused punishing me he came across my buttocks and then rubbed his spunk into my still-stinging bum. We had danced the beginning of a dance of dominance and sub-mission but neither of us seemed quite sure what the next step was, or even knew to phrase it that way. During our last night together before he returned to the States I got a glimpse of what that next step might have been, and even now – years on and with the experiences I've had since – I still think our relationship had the potential to be amaz-ing. It was just one of those things that ended sooner than perhaps in hindsight I would have liked it to.

Before it did end, though, he really did pull out all the stops.

I wasn't a fan of outfits. I'd dug out my old grey gym knickers and netball skirt for a fresher's week school disco night and kept the peace for the occasional fancy dress party. But all in all I was still just too self-conscious to enjoy dressing up. I felt ridiculous and it's not rocket science to point out that when you feel ridiculous it's hard to feel sexy.

But the corset was different.

That last night, as I kicked my shoes off, chucked my keys down and headed into my bedroom to get ready for my farewell dinner with Ryan, I found the box on the bed. It was one of those boxes so understated and discreet that despite its lack of label it screamed 'ridiculously expensive boutique'. As I fingered the edge of cream ribbon bisecting it, Catherine, who had accompanied me down to reception to collect it when it was delivered earlier in the day, plonked herself down on the stool in front of my dressing table, mug of tea in hand, waiting to see its secrets. Ryan had told me he was giving me a goodbye present that he didn't want me lugging home from the restaurant, but I had no clue what it was.

Being both impatient and a big kid at heart when it comes to giving and receiving presents, there was no hope of me waiting till after the date to open it. And, as I rationalized to Catherine, he obviously wouldn't mind, or he wouldn't have brought it round. Well, that was my excuse and I was sticking to it.

When I first opened the box all I could see was tissue paper. And then as I pulled back the folds and pulled out the gorgeous corset nestled within I took a little breath of wonder. It was a rich vivid green. The kind of green that reminds you of lush countryside and summer and fucking outside amid the smell of fresh cut grass and sunshine.

'Soph, it's beautiful. Are you going to wear it tonight?'

It was a gift as surprising as it was stunning. Being a tomboy at heart it was not the kind of thing I would normally have chosen to wear and, if I was being honest, it seemed an unusually tender gift for him to give me.

But that was really by the by. As my fingers caressed the delicately finished edge I looked over at Catherine.

'How could I not?'

With forty minutes before I was due to leave to meet him, though, there wasn't much time for fussing. I picked a pair of tailored trousers which I knew flattered my arse, hopped in the shower and was back and ready to be laced up within twenty minutes.

The bodice was rigid and boned, with black ribbons running through eyelets down the back. Since there was no way I was going to be able to do it up myself, Catherine came in and, once I'd slipped it on and tried to adjust myself into it as much as possible, began the process of lacing me up. It was a very long process.

As her thankfully nimble fingers pulled the laces tight between each individual set of eyelets I felt my body – and my mindset – alter. My posture changed, my curves seemed to swell and contract into an hourglass figure unlike anything I could ever have imagined possible. My breathing became shallow, my movement was curtailed and my busy day, the hassles of the journey home, even the bitter-sweetness of the night ahead, all faded into obscurity. All I could feel was nerve endings tingling, and a roaring sound in my head. My nipples, pressed tight into the boned panels, were taut and aching and suddenly hard-wired to my cunt. I could feel myself getting wet just standing in the thing, and momentarily rued the fact I had gone for trousers since the seam betwcen my legs was only going to add to the distracting sensations.

There was no time to change though, even if I'd wanted to. Thankfully I'd sorted out my minimal make-up and hair beforehand, as Catherine had tied the laces off with an efficiency that meant my movement was seriously – and surprisingly – hampered. It had pulled me in and up in such a way that my breasts were spilling over the top of the bodice, pale and soft against the green. Suddenly I had a cleavage that was distracting to me, never mind anyone who was face-on to it. I made a mental note to throw on a jacket I could do up to the neck for the tube journey there.

As Catherine clasped my waist and turned me round to get the full view she unconsciously ran a gentle finger along the edge of the bodice above one of my breasts, only catching herself when I shivered slightly at the additional sensation. She blushed slightly and we both laughed.

'Sorry, it's the velvet. It's screaming out to be stroked.'

By the end of the night it wasn't the only thing doing that.

The journey to the restaurant was interesting. We met at Oxford Circus tube, and apart from a glance of appreciation as he saw me for the first time that was lustful enough to make me blush, Ryan didn't make a comment about my chosen outfit as we walked to the restaurant and got shown to our table. But as I tried to find a way to settle myself comfortably in the seat he bit back a smile. I realized that the corset wasn't as innocuous as it first looked. It was a beautiful and yet fiendish form of restraint.

Dinner was lovely but eating too much wasn't an option. As I excused myself for a loo trip he smiled at the way I moved, so different to my usual carefree, hundred-mile-an-hour dash through life. My movement was careful, slow, and I felt like a different person – more aware of my femininity, aware of every nerve ending, more submissive, more demure even – and that's not something I've ever really been big on.

It was also, unexpectedly, making me feel ridiculously horny. Well, honestly, it was just an outfit – you weren't seriously expecting me to say it changed my entire personality, were you? However, I was fast realizing this corset was a kind of subtle and totally unexpected bondage. Our dinner was one of the most sensual meals of my life, which is quite impressive for a small Italian with a student-friendly budget tucked behind Oxford Street. I spent the evening aroused and desperate to go home, my skin flushed and eyes sparkling in the candlelight.

We finally went back to mine. He stripped my trousers and knickers from me, tied my hands behind my back with the ribbon from the box, which I'd chucked on the floor in my haste earlier, and then we fucked. He sat on the stool and I rode him, grinding myself on to him until we were both gasping.

He pulled my breasts free from the constraints of the corset, but the respite was brief before he turned his teeth and fingers to my aching nipples. As I panted, my breathing shallow and constricted by the cruel beauty of the boning, he frigged my clit and sucked my breasts until I came, shuddering and whimpering in a hybrid of pleasure and pain.

With small tremors still reverberating through my limbs I sank to the floor and finished him off with my mouth, looking through my by-now wild hair into his eyes, watching him stare greedily at the anachronism of Merchant Ivory purity and slutty debauchedness I presented kneeling at his feet. As he tangled his hands into my hair and fucked my mouth for the final few thrusts I sucked him deep, drinking him eagerly.

We said goodbye the next day. We were both exhausted, sated and my body was covered with bruises, not only on my arse but also around my breasts and torso from Catherine's enthusiastic tightening of the corset and the harsh boning beneath it. The brush that had started it all (and with which I received my hardest punishment to date at the end of that last night) went back to the States with Ryan as part of his leaving present.

I've never met him again, although I often think about him. I wonder about looking him up on one of the plethora of social networking sites but then I think, 'well, he hasn't looked for me', and wonder if it's best to leave things be. I know this sounds like hippyish crap, but I do believe we meet people for a reason. Looking back on it now, what Ryan and I did together was relatively tame.

But it was my first taste of playing with someone who was a dominant foil to my submissiveness, who didn't judge me for what turned me on and let me see fully the depths of what did the same for him. I'll always feel gratitude for that, and smile at the fun we had together.

He also left me the corset, which I will concede is proof that some outfits can be fun. I still have it. I even wear it sometimes, although it is so tainted with memories of that night, even all these years later, that just slipping it on and beginning to get tightened up into it sees my juices begin to pool between my legs, my nipples harden and my breath catch.

The rest of my degree passed quickly. I realized once he'd gone that my feelings for Ryan were deeper than I had admitted even to myself. Feeling forlorn at the loss, plus grappling with pesky finals and a dissertation, left me the definition of all work and no play.

Even when I did find people who might tempt me away from my self-imposed exile, our interludes were veritably vanilla and attempts to try and make them otherwise ended in disaster. I asked one partner (Graham, Geography) to spank me while we were shagging and saw him look at me in horror before – if you'll forgive the pun – giving me a few half-arsed slaps and then resuming what he'd been doing before. He never called again.

Another time, when I asked another prospective date (Ian, Maths) in what I hoped was a coquettish fashion whether he fantasized about doing anything particularly kinky, he blushed slightly and told me he quite fancied having sex with me while he wore my clothes. I think I managed to keep my face from betraying any horror – goodness knows I have enough proclivities of my own for it to be churlish to respond negatively to anyone else's – but I didn't end up seeing him again, funnily enough.

It's fair to say I missed Ryan a lot. Although I did find it easier sitting on the wooden chairs of the lecture hall after he'd gone.

3

The end of my university life passed by in a flurry of deadlines – essays, work for the university paper, and then far too quickly and yet oh-so-inevitably, the avalanche of exams. I crammed desperately, focusing on the next exam, memorizing facts and figures, reading and rereading texts and then regurgitating them on endless blank sheets of A4 in, I hoped, a semblance of sense before moving on to the next subject to rinse and repeat. Three weeks after finals had finished I pretty much forgot everything I had ever learned, and while this would have horrified my parents, I didn't mind so much. The most important thing university taught me, I think, was confidence. Not necessarily confidence in myself over all things – who'd want to be that kind of ego on legs anyway? But more a sense that I could cope with anything life threw at me with a fairly calm head and a sense of humour. My next task was to find my place in the world. I knew I wanted it to involve writing, but I was realistic. People worked for years to try and become novelists, and since I had the attention span of plankton and the longest thing I'd managed to write was a dissertation I decided the first thing to do was get a job.

I moved back with my parents shortly after graduation and gave my CV to temp agencies for admin and typing jobs (a handy side effect of writing as much as I had through university was that I could type really fast). A recruitment consultant showed me how to use a foot-operated Dictaphone machine and tested how fast I could type things played back on it. When the results pinged back at 75 words a minute even with my clunky two-fingered typing she was thrilled, and over a period of months began sending me out to various places to work, typing, filing and generally being a professional office minion, all the while saving money as I figured out my next move.

Returning to my childhood home – with all the associated roast dinners and fussing that entailed – was a wonderful feeling, but by Christmas I knew that I needed to be making plans to move out. I'd become accustomed to my independence and despite the comfortable routine I'd fallen back into, I missed having my own space, eating cereal for dinner at 10pm if I fancied it, or having a bath at 3am if I woke up and couldn't get back to sleep. Around about the same time I began to find my temporary job was feeling distressingly permanent. I didn't mind the work, but there was a point where I worried it was just a matter of time before my brain would start seeping out from between my ears. It was repetitious, often dull, and at one particular office where I'd been asked to transcribe a letter that could only really be described as word-babble I found myself almost despairing. There had to be more than this. I needed to figure out what I was going to do and start doing it soon – and since my vows to start writing a novel had been scuppered by commuting, internet gaming and trips to the cinema it needed to be something achievable sooner rather than later.

I went to my local paper. I had a long and really helpful conversation with the news editor there about what life was like as a hack. Looking back without the wide-eyed optimism of youth, I realize now she was mostly warning me of the terrible pay, long hours and interminable council meetings. But then she suggested I go out on a job with the paper's photographer, come back and write it up. I stopped long enough to borrow a notebook before I was trotting down to the photographer's car.

No one has ever taken a primary school harvest festival picture story as seriously as I did that day. I wrote down the names and ages of all the children – it sounds simple but is akin to herding cats while keeping track of them all. I asked the slightly nonplussed headmistress probably a dozen questions, some of which seemed to actively confuse her. I was Woodward. I was Bernstein. I was both of them at once, albeit with a particular interest in tinned goods. As we walked back to the car Jim, the photographer, was grinning at me.

'You really enjoyed that, didn't you?'

I nodded, feeling a bit sheepish and hideously uncool.

'You did a good job. Nice one.'

I was pretty much floating on air as I got back to the office and prepared what was undoubtedly the most over-written piece about a harvest festival ever. The news editor nodded at me when I handed it to her.

'That's fine. Nothing else we need there.' Later I'd learn that newsrooms weren't places for effusive praise, but even a seemingly understated reaction – *fine? Just fine? What about the bit where I got the headmistress to talk about the most unusual thing that the children had brought in for the harvest boxes?* – couldn't dampen my enthusiasm. I'd written for school and university magazines and papers, but that wasn't the same. This was. It came through my parents' front door and everything. I was hooked. I was going to become a journalist. As soon as I figured out exactly how you did that.

Seven months later I moved out again, permanently. I'd done my research on respected postgrad journalism courses around the country, been horrified at the prices of courses in my immediate vicinity and come to the conclusion that a college around four hours' drive from my parents was the best option – it was almost a fifth of the price of nearby courses and as such with my savings and a bit of weekend work I'd be more than able to survive while I studied. My parents drove me to my new flat in convoy, with my most treasured belongings literally stuffed into every corner of the cars. They took me to the supermarket once we'd unloaded to buy me shopping to last well into the first term, and my mum insisted on a cafe lunch, seeming genuinely worried I wouldn't be eating, and – once my dad had checked the security of all the windows and doors, and had a mooch round outside to try and get a look at whether my neighbours looked suitably undodgy – they left me to unpack. I was living on my own for the first time, and I loved it.

The year flew by. Every week made me more sure I had

chosen the right course of action. I loved the challenge of interviewing people, the creativity of writing and even the more dry elements of the course – law and endless lessons about how councils worked – suddenly seemed fascinating, acting as a key to the door of my potential dream job. Our class had people from all over the county, ranging from those wanting to become broadcast journalists to a guy whose dream job was to be the football correspondent for Tranmere Rovers. We all wanted to be there though, and settled in as a fairly cohesive group, albeit tempered with a kind of friendly competitiveness which made for occasionally hilarious drunken chats about how particular assignments had gone. As suggested by our lecturer, we had all secured as much work experience as possible through the year, in the vague hope that it would lead to paid work as soon as we finished.

I hit the jackpot. The low-paid, unglamorous jackpot, admittedly, but a jackpot nonetheless. The paper I did most of my work experience at offered me a job. My dad was horrified when I told him what the starting salary was – definitely not a graduate wage, much less a post-graduate wage – but living so far from the city meant I could afford to survive, as long as I didn't worry too much about luxuries. Like heating. Or going out much. I didn't care though. I was an actual working journalist, with a byline. One day on the way home I even saw someone on the train reading a page with my name in the middle of it. I was so giddy I nearly missed my stop. I couldn't have been prouder if I was writing for a national newspaper. Plus restaurant reviews and theatre reviews meant I could still have a little taste of luxury every so often, even if because I was the newest I always got lumbered with the knuckle-gnawingly awful am dram.

The life of a junior reporter is a busy one. I was far from home and with very little opportunity for a social life, bar post-deadline drinks as we deconstructed how our stories had been subbed. My best friend from college, Ella, had found a job on a paper twenty miles away, so I saw her as much as possible, but with weekend jobs, evening jobs and everything else going on, I spent a lot of time alone.

But while switching on my little portable heater didn't feel like a necessity, an internet connection did. It provided me a way to email and social network with friends from uni and my journalism course, keep in touch with my family, play games, and then, when I was feeling lonely and like I wanted to flirt with someone, gave me a space not only to chat to people who were similarly bored and looking to talk but also to discuss things that I'd never dare broach in person.

I genuinely think that the internet has, for all intents and purposes, changed the landscape of sexuality. No matter how perverse your kink, you can bet there is someone out there on the web who shares it. Unfortunately, there's probably another three who actually think your kink is not perverted enough and given half a chance will tell you how the way they do it is more intense/sexier/just outright better than yours. Frustratingly enough, the most noticeable thing about dipping a toe into the BDSM subculture online is that there's as much judging of each other from inside the 'lifestyle' – I promise that's the last time

I'm using that phrase as I think it sounds pretentious in the extreme – as there is from the outside.

That said, there are some lovely people out there, once you look past the slightly odder ones. I've had some amazing, sexy and intelligent conversations with people I've met on various sites, who've sparked my imagination, reassured me, even become good real-life friends.

You do have to wade through some crap though.

I joined my first smut site the year I started work. Apart from those interludes with Ryan, which kept me in wank fantasies for years afterwards, I hadn't met anyone who'd interested me sexually at all, much less shown any obvious signs of being compatible with my burgeoning submissive tendencies. I was so focused on work and my day-to-day life that taking the effort to finding anyone felt too much like faff. That, paired with a penchant for *literotica.com* porn, which read as hot and yet very unreal to my ever-practical eyes, meant I figured my fantasies would stay just that. Over time I even wondered if perhaps I was romanticizing my experiences with Ryan. Could pain actually have brought me that much pleasure, or was I just looking back with rose-tinted glasses on a sexy time in my life?

Then, over a drink a friend told me about a site she'd stumbled across that was basically a chat and dating site for kinky people. The details she gave were vague – and heaven forfend I would ask her outright about it, thus betraying my interest – but there was enough info there that when I got home and did a bit of Googling I found my way to where I wanted to be.

Some people say that nowadays these kind of sites are

full of fakes, cliques and people wanting you to pay them. I didn't notice many pros but, fresh out of uni and on a trainee reporter's wage, if someone was looking for someone to fleece it was never going to be me. It felt like a whole new world full of people who knew each other and were talking a language that I didn't quite grasp, with many using an elaborate form of pronouns (always capitalized for the dominant, always lower case for the submissive no matter whether it was the start of a sentence or the word 'I'), which I found ridiculous. I decided quickly that committing crimes against grammar was a hard limit for me.

The message boards were filled with people talking about events they'd been to, things they'd bought, stuff they'd done, some of which made me wet, some of which made me shudder. I read people discussing the art of shibari rope bondage, St Andrew's crosses, needle play, ponygirls and a thousand other things that had never entered my world before. And for a while I lurked in a virtual corner, quiet and unsure, like the country mouse if he'd pitched up at the town mouse's for the weekend to find him wearing rubber, holding a crop and hosting a play party. It was surreal and yet intoxicating. Could these people be for real, doing this stuff while holding down jobs, making sure they paid their council tax on time and all the other little complexities of life? It seemed a million miles away from my existence. I was intrigued.

Having set up my account and put in some brief details about who I was and why I was on the site (I went for a vague 'dipping a toe' message, a generic picture with no distinguishing features and a brief note to say that I was looking for friends or possibly even an online relationship although I didn't see myself meeting anyone in real life any time soon), I started getting messages in my inbox every time I logged in. When people could see you were live on the site they'd message you straight away, often it appeared without reading your profile or taking time to bother with quaint concepts like punctuation.

– RU *feeling horny filthy bitch? Do U want to kneel before you're master?*

– No, because you talk in text speak and don't know the difference between 'your' and 'you're' and I'm enough of a grammar fascist that on that basis I don't think I could submit to you, sorry.

– *I think I have use of a slut such as you. Present yourself at my house in Bournemouth to see if you meet my requirements.*

– Firstly, I don't like Bournemouth. Secondly, do you really want someone you know nothing about to meet you at your house? Honestly? Cause if so you're a bit bonkers and I think I'd best pass. Thanks anyway.

– *Are U online now? Do you want to talk dirty?*

– Erm, yes I am. But no, not so much. Thank you.

Don't get me wrong, there were intelligent, articulate, interesting people to meet, but overall the overwhelming majority were disappointingly a bit mad or full on. Yes, I liked the idea of someone spanking me, even fantasized about it going further and letting them hurt me more. But, well, I don't think it's unreasonable to want to make sure they're not a nutter first.

I got the odd email which I replied to rather than just auto-deleting, but overall it was all a bit disappointing.

And then I started chatting to Mark.

We first started talking because I bookmarked him. I'd read his profile, found him interesting, but it was late and I wasn't sure whether I should mail so I bookmarked him, meaning to mail him later. I didn't think anything more of it.

Well, not until he mailed me, saying: *Favouriting me is lovely. But what's the point if you're too shy to say hello?*

I was mortified, having not realized the site software showed someone people who had expressed interest in them that way. The first few messages we sent were me apologizing for being a technotard, and him reassuring me. Well, that and laughing at the depth of my horror. And then we started talking generally. He was a techie type. Interesting. Articulate. We chatted slowly, not about kink initially, but over time things developed.

We were going quite slowly. Well, very slowly actually. While I liked Mark I was wary about meeting someone from the web without knowing them well enough to know I felt safe with them. Especially with this. I'm cynical and guarded in relationships at the best of times, even before you factor in the Dominant/submissive dynamic. But that didn't stop us having stupid amounts of fun online and on the phone. He had a filthy mind and a sexy voice and our chats often degenerated into phone sex with both of us reaching satisfaction while we chatted about what we could do to each other if we were in the same room together. But I had been deliberately aloof. I felt a bit uncomfortable at the thought of sending him pictures of me naked – even if there was a way of taking them that didn't make me look slightly deformed or like a secretary photocopying her breasts after too many lunchtime G&Ts, which, let's face it, with a camera phone with no timer and normal length arms isn't as easy as you'd hope. So ours was very much a meeting of smutty, kinky minds using words to weave various erotic scenarios round each other.

We never met. We lived relatively close to each other, but the timing was never right and, as often happens, connections forged intensely online flare and then die quickly, although not before he sent me a set of Ben Wa balls to wear during a long council election shift. I started work at 7am, meeting the head of the council to cover him casting his vote, worked through the day and then sat through the count after the polls closed, all with them inside me. It was a ridiculously safe council, with no upsets or changes of leadership, but I was excited through the whole process, albeit probably not for the reasons my colleagues imagined.

Over the next few months I chatted to various other people online. Some I was tempted to meet, others I'd have actively crossed the street to avoid if they'd appeared in front of me. I shared some amazing fantasies, got an idea of what I found erotic – and what I most definitely didn't – but still ended up too nervous to actually do anything in person, to take that final step.

For all that there are people that moan about the internet being full of fantasists who want to hide behind their computer screen and not try anything out in real life, for me it was a great place to start – somewhere which felt safe and gave me a chance to explore some of my fantasies and think through some of my feelings in an utterly secure, non-judgemental environment. But eventually thinking about or talking about being hurt or humiliated was going to be pushed into the background for something more hands on. And finally I met a three-dimensional, real-life man I felt comfortable enough to start exploring with in person.

4

I met Thomas in a queue. I know, it sounds ridiculous and oh–so-British, but it was a very long queue and we were in it for a very long time. And if you could ever call a queue serendipitous then in hindsight that's what it was, because when I first met him I thought he was an arse and if I'd had anywhere to escape to I would have wandered off and not spoken to him again, which with everything that's happened since would have been a real shame.

Ella and I had met at a cinema somewhere in between us to go to a one-off screening of *His Girl Friday*, journalism geeks to the end. We were chatting, waiting to go into the film, and he interrupted. He was alone and obviously bored and I remember thinking he was rude, arrogant and clearly thought a bit much of himself, although my irritation was tempered in slightly fickle fashion by my finding him attractive. After pre- and post-film chat – and a surprising amount of laughter – I had developed a grudging liking for him and when he suggested we go for coffee in the slightly pretentious cafe attached to the cinema afterwards Ella and I agreed, happy he wasn't an axe murderer and would be bearable company for a while – after that, who cared anyway?

Ironically enough, after a while I found I cared. He took our email addresses when he left, and we ended up having round robin email chats about films, current affairs and general life. He was funny, intelligent and had just come out of a long-term relationship. His ex had got custody of most of their friends and he seemed a little lonely. Sitting in my flat alone of a night sometimes I imagined him doing the same. The difference seemed to be that he wasn't as comfortable with his own company as me. Where I closed my door – and put the chain on immediately as per my dad's pleas – feeling as though I had come back to my sanctum where I could throw on PJs and just enjoy the peace, it seemed that he perhaps didn't feel quite the same. Ella and I met up with him a couple of times for drinks, dinner and cinema trips, but with Ella and I both working weekend shifts and Ella living considerably further away from him than I did, eventually we started meeting for cheap midweek films, just the two of us. He was a thoughtful person; he asked a lot of questions about me and remembered the answers, and I found myself confiding in him about my life. My instinct when something funny or interesting happened at work became to email or text him. We might have become friends out of a shared loneliness, but the more we got to know each other the more we had in common. I liked having a male friend who was straightforward and honest. This translated as bluntness sometimes, leaving me spluttering out my tea a couple of times when he was discussing women he fancied and how he was angling to ask them out, but I admired how articulate he was, and he made me laugh like few people I'd ever met. We quoted from the same films, liked the same bands, and soon I was spending a lot of time at his.

Why his, you ask? Well, winter had come. I earned enough to just about manage life in a tiny flat alone, but the lack of central heating became an issue very quickly. One weekend when he sent me a text asking me what I was doing and I told him I was hanging out in Starbucks to keep warm he suggested I just come round to his and stay in his spare room for the night. So I did. The next weekend I was working, but the weekend after that he suggested it again. I popped round on Saturday afternoon and left the next day after cooking Sunday lunch – thanks, Mum, your roast potato recipe does wonders. It was comfortable, lazy, fun. We walked his dog, I brought my laptop and hooked it up to his Wi-Fi so we could play co-op computer games, and we watched DVD box sets and films aplenty, all in the warmth. Simple pleasures, but it was wonderful and, as Christmas came and went and spring blossomed, I found myself going round to his more and more often, despite the weather no longer being an issue. Ella would come down too if she was free, but if she wasn't then we'd happily hang out alone.

It probably sounds naive now, but I didn't really think about having sex with him. He was a good looking guy, with dirty blond hair, glasses and a laid-back style that I approved of, but as he'd been keen to point out during that first invite, my visits were platonic with no expectations of sex on his side. I was fairly pragmatic about such things and just assumed he didn't fancy me, and I had no intention of scuppering our friendship by pushing things, not least because I knew he was still thinking about his ex. It was OK. I enjoyed his friendship without feeling the urge to jump him.

But then one night things changed. It all started pretty innocently. Thomas, Ella and I had booked tickets and hotel rooms to see a band together. But the week before the gig Ella suggested a change of plans. Another friend had got a ticket, so if I moved in with Thomas for the night this fourth person could join Ella, thus reducing all of our hotel costs. Practicality won out and, since we'd been seeing each other alone anyway for months by this point, why did it matter? It didn't really, and we had a fantastic night, enjoying the gig, giddy and excitable and a little hoarse by the time we got back to the hotel room, on an adrenaline high from the energy of the music.

We took turns in the bathroom, got changed and then climbed into bed. We lay talking in the darkness for a while, still too awake to sleep, talking about the night, the music, our weeks, life in general. And then, quietly in the darkness, he spoke.

'Sophie, have you ever thought of us sleeping together?'

Taken aback, the silence lengthened as I tried to formulate a reply. I decided to fudge it rather than inadvertently putting my foot in it by saying something that would either hurt his feelings or have him reassess my motivations for our friendship – did he actually *want* me to think that sort of thing? Or would it make him feel awkward knowing I felt that way? Vagueness was the plan.

'There's no point really, you don't fancy me.'

He laughed. 'What makes you say that?'

I threw a pillow at him. 'You've never tried to make a move. It's all platonic, remember?'

The silence lasted so long that I thought he'd fallen asleep. When he finally spoke, his voice was little more than a whisper. 'It doesn't need to be.'

'Oh.' Not my finest response, I'll grant you, but I honestly didn't know quite what else to say under the circumstances. Suddenly his hand was stroking my shoulder in the darkness, over the duvet, tentative and a little shy. I let it linger for a second or two, before finally succumbing, grabbing his wrist and pulling him over.

Our hands traced each other's bodies, firstly over our clothes – he mocked me for my pyjamas, being too cool for anything other than a t-shirt and boxers himself, and got a smack on the arm for his troubles – and then he slowly undid the buttons of my top, sliding his hand in to touch my breasts, moulding them and playing with the nipples. I whimpered quietly, enjoying the sensation, after so long, of someone touching me there, even before he slid his hand further down, into the waistband of my trousers, and under my knickers. As he touched me between my legs I moaned, spreading them wider, encouraging his fingers to continue their playful dance, thrilling at the sensation. Meanwhile I was sliding my hands into his boxers, taking his cock in my hand, echoing his movements with my own, and eliciting a similar moan from him. Our hands moved for a long time, back and forth, as we enjoyed the sensations we were evoking in each other. His hand, assured, pressed firmly against my clit, over and over again, until I couldn't restrain myself any more. The orgasm literally made my toes curl. My breathing returned to normal, and as I whispered to him I couldn't hide the need in my voice. 'Please, go get a condom.'

There was an abrupt pause. 'What?'

'What do you mean, what? A condom. Please. I want you to fuck me.'

'Fuck!'

'Yes, fuck.'

'No, that's not what I mean. Fuck!'

'What?'

His voice was so forlorn that in another situation I'd have laughed. 'I don't *have* a condom with me. I wasn't expecting us to do this tonight.' He paused. 'I don't suppose *you* have a—'

I snorted. 'I haven't had sex for over a year, and I definitely wasn't expecting anything to happen tonight.'

Now he sounded *really* forlorn. 'Oh.'

I definitely couldn't hide the amusement in my voice – or my urge to make mischief – then. 'Look, don't worry about it, let's just say goodnight . . .' His cock twitched in my hand as I spoke, and he made a strangled noise I assumed to be part outrage and part frustration. But then, I gave him a squeeze, and moved myself lower down the bed to take him in my mouth.

His groan as my lips encircled him was rich and made me feel not unlike a goddess. I licked him languorously, taking my time and enjoying the moment his hands clenched to grab the duvet, the way his body arched and stretched as I began to wring the pleasure from him. It had been a while since I'd had the chance to do this, and while I wasn't planning on being too mean on the teasing front, I had no intention of ending it too soon either. I took my time and, finally, when he came, stroking my hair and whispering my name, I felt a strange sense of achievement. Don't get me wrong, I wouldn't be putting it on my CV or anything, but it felt lovely, and I fell asleep with a smile on my face.

Of course the problem with nights like that is you have to wake up. I came back to consciousness to find myself pretty much nose to nose with him, our legs entwined. I opened my eyes, saw him staring back at me and shut them immediately, feigning sleep.

'Sophie? Are you awake?'

I stayed quiet. Fuck. What did I do now? 'Sophie? We need to go to breakfast soon. Are you OK? Talk to me.'

My eyes stayed closed. 'I'm fine. Great.' Too effusive? 'Fine.'

'Are you going to open your eyes then?' His voice was certainly starting to sound bemused.

'Yes, in a minute!' Mine on the other hand had a bright sing-song quality to it not dissimilar to my mum when she was being faux cheery. Which in hindsight is a mental image that didn't help.

His hand took mine. 'It's OK, you know. It doesn't mean anything.'

My eyes shot open and stared at his, reassuring, calm, oddly sweet. I couldn't decide whether I should be offended, but my glare must have given me away, because his hands came up in a gesture of surrender. 'Sorry, that's not what I meant. It was amazing, I enjoyed it, it was brilliant.'

'Damn right,' I said grudgingly, although a smile was starting to form at the edges of my mouth.

'All I'm saying is it doesn't have to happen again if you don't want it to, and it hasn't changed anything about our friendship.' I stared at him for a long time.

'You're sure?'

He nodded. 'Really.'

At that exact moment my stomach growled and I blushed. 'Right, time for breakfast then. I get the bathroom first.' I leapt up, grabbed my clothes from the side and headed for the shower, trying to act vaguely normally. He lay in bed, watching me move, not turning away or moving at all. I got halfway across the room before I couldn't restrain it any more. 'Stop checking out my arse!'

'I'm not, I'm admiring the pyjamas.'

By the time we had both washed and dressed and got ready to meet Ella and the friend who had inadvertently kick-started this turn of events things had returned to a kind of comfortable normality. We were bantering as normal, breakfast was as it would have been if I hadn't become intimately acquainted with his cock the night before, and no more was said about it, at least until later that night when I got a text.

> Glad you got back OK, I'm
> back fine now too. PS. Wish
> I'd had condoms.

Git.

It is, in hindsight, somewhat inevitable that not long after-wards we ended up sleeping together properly – ironically we both bought condoms that time. My visits were much the same as they'd ever been, it was just that over time I ended up sleeping in his bed rather than the spare room. We'd continued being friends first, talking frankly about everything, and that extended to our sexual relationship. We liked each other – a lot – but I was really not the woman for him, and as for him, he was wonderful, funny, clever, and I found him very attractive, but he didn't make my stomach flip when he walked into a room. I didn't put it that way to him – not least because I feared I'd sound like a naive fool – but in long chats walking the dog we came to our shared understanding of what this was, the terms of engagement for our relationship. It was fun, no expectations, no responsibilities. If either of us started seeing anyone else it stopped. Otherwise, as long as we were both having fun and one of us didn't have deeper feelings than the other, anything went. And, over a period of time, as we got to know each other, it really did.

I can honestly say though that, even bearing in mind our similarities, I never expected to find my wrists tied to Thomas's headboard with him looming over me with an evil half-smile that made me wonder for a second just what I'd let myself in for. Which goes back to the seren-dipitous nature of the queue, and – as my mother always said – the need not to judge a book by its cover (although this probably wasn't exactly what she had in mind).

We'd been fuck buddies for a while by that point, so it was inevitable we would end up having a conversation about long-term unfulfilled fantasies. But as I knocked back a glass of red, told him a vague summation of what had happened with Ryan and my foray into internet smut before shyly admitting I fancied unleashing – or should that be leashing? – my submissive side properly with some experimentation into BDSM, I really didn't see him as the guy who would take me there. And I wasn't even expecting him to become that guy – as far as I was concerned we were having a bit of horny chat as a prelude to a perfect end-of-week pick-me-up fuck. I'd come to appreciate his intelligence and his deliciously dirty mind, but little did I know I had crossed paths with someone who it would turn out was ying to my submissive yang.

Talking to him felt easy. Any worries I'd had about broaching my sexual turn-ons with a partner were negated by the very nature of our relationship. He was my friend, and I trusted him to be respectful and kind while we talked about such deeply personal and potentially embarrassing things, but because we weren't dating I didn't feel awkward telling him what turned me on, what I wanted to try. I wasn't worrying about him as a potential boyfriend who might think I was weird or twisted, or who might be unable to square the vanilla me with the other slightly rude aspects of my personality, because even if he did judge me a bit, it wasn't going to impact on any boyfriend/girlfriend relationship as a whole. Of course over time I realized he wasn't going to judge me at all, not least because he too had at least as many filthy thoughts as I did – and his inclinations complemented mine very well indeed.

He was fully clothed, which made me feel even more vulnerable as he knelt over my naked body to reach my nipple. To start with he was just playing, rubbing his fingers over and around it, watching it bud. I started to relax, my eyes drifting shut to enjoy the sensation, when he pinched it. Hard. I gasped at the sudden burst of pain and looked up to see him staring intently at my face. He released his hold for a second, but the respite was brief, as he adjusted his grip for a tighter one before beginning to pull harder, tugging my breast high.

The pain increased and my breath started to shudder. I bit my lip and arched my back to try and ease the tension, but with him kneeling across me and my wrists tied I couldn't move far, and having watched with amusement at my writhing, a slight move of his hand meant the full bittersweet pleasure of pain was back a second later. My moan filled the room and all that ran through my mind was the thought that it really was as arousing as I remembered, at least until the warmth of the pain in my nipple filled my mind and I wasn't thinking much else at all.

He turned his attention to my other nipple, licking delicately around it before sucking hard and grazing it with his teeth. I bucked underneath him at the pain. If my hands were free I'd have been running my fingers through his hair, but instead all I could do while he alternated between gentleness and cruelty was clench and unclench my fingers, unsure which it was I was actually craving at that moment.

Actually, I'm lying. The pain was turning me on more than I'd expected. More than my enjoyment at being spanked by Ryan had even hinted at. And as Thomas ran his hands down my body, I shamelessly spread my legs wider so he could see the glistening proof.

He chuckled and gently ran his fingers through my wetness towards my clit. In contrast to the treatment of my nipples, his strokes were light, frustratingly so, and I lifted my hips to encourage him to push his fingers deep inside me. But as I moved, he moved away. I looked up in frustration and he raised his eyebrows at me.

I knew what he wanted; I had spent a good twenty minutes blathering on about how I thought it would be sexy to have to do it. But somehow begging seemed so much easier in fantasy than in real life. What can I say? I guess I'm just contrary, but having spent years dreaming of properly giving up control, when the moment came to do it, in person, with a sexy man whose mind was a mystery to me, it felt like maybe I wasn't ready to give it up just yet after all.

As the silence lengthened it became a battle of wills, which was stupid since I knew him touching me would be a victory for both of us. His hand rested gently on my mound, one of his fingers tapping gently on my clit – one, two, three times – like he was drumming his fingers on a table while I decided what to do next. His calm infuriated me more. So I stayed silent. I was definitely more stubborn than I realized, a recurring theme that has gotten me into trouble in dozens of ways dozens of times in the years since.

A pause.

Tom moved his hand away and turned to face me, then ran a finger, slick with my juices, around my mouth. I sucked it deep, tasting myself, licking him clean, and trying to somehow reassert some semblance of control. And yes, I know that sounds contrary after having spent so long yearning to give it up, but let's just note it down as another recurring theme. As I pulled his finger deeper into my mouth, he smiled at my unspoken – and, admittedly, unsubtle – suggestion, pulled down his trousers and pulled his cock out. I strained forward, eager, and he fed himself to me. I sucked him, smiling around him as I heard him sigh his pleasure.

I've always loved giving blow jobs – but never more so than with Thomas. Even during the most vanilla of shags he seemed so in control, and I loved shaking that up a bit, seeing his reactions, hearing his breathing quicken, feeling him grow in my mouth, tasting him as he came. I may have been giving up my control, submitting to his power, but with my mouth round his cock I had a different kind of power and it made my heart sing and my cunt wet. And right then, tied down, his cock pushing between my lips as I lay on my back on his bed, that felt reassuring.

As I began to suck harder, he grabbed my hair. I moaned round his cock, glancing up to look at his face as I sucked deeper, moving eagerly, quickly, quickly, relentlessly, until I tasted him at the back of my throat. He sat back to regain his breath, running his hands lazily around my thighs. By then I was gagging for it. I'd learned that moving didn't work in my favour though, so I lay passive as he ran his fingertips up and down, coming closer and closer to where I was aching for him to be. If I hadn't been tied down I'd have been frigging myself senseless just to get some release, but instead I had to lie back, submit, as his finger slipped over my clit, an all-too-brief burst of pleasure, before going back to stroking meanderingly around my thighs.

Suddenly the whole issue of begging or not begging didn't matter. I was so desperate to come that I'd have said pretty much anything if it meant he'd let me. My hands were clenched into fists, I was biting my bottom lip and finally through a dry throat I was able to say, 'Please.'

His finger moved back to my core, gently stroking. He was definitely looking smug now. 'Please, what?'

The tone of his voice was different, darker, and it thrilled me and yet left me uncertain. This wasn't easy-going, laid-back Thomas. It turned out my fuck buddy was a man of surprises. But not a man of patience.

He pinched my nipple again, twisting it viciously. Tears filled my eyes and I gasped in pain. His voice was steely, not to be disobeyed and made me wetter, even as nervous butterflies moved in my stomach.

'Please, what?'

My brain locked. I'm someone who's never lost for words, but I had no idea what I was supposed to say and was terrified that if I got it wrong he'd draw it out even longer. Or, even worse, stop. In the end in spite of myself I went for every variation that might do it.

'Please, push your fingers inside me. Please touch me. Make me come, let me come. Please.'

As I finished on the final plea he began to frig me – strong, long strokes which I'd been yearning for. He slid two fingers inside me and began fucking me with them, rubbing, harder, faster, until I couldn't contain my cries. I shuddered, moaned, and came, pulsating around his fingers, my hands bashing against the headboard with the force of my orgasm.

As he pulled the knots so my hands fell free, he smiled. And as I rubbed my wrists I smiled back, knowing that I'd found a kindred spirit in the oddest place, that we'd be doing this again. That it was even worth begging for. What I didn't realize, not then at least, was that actually that was hardly begging at all, and only the beginning.

We still had no plans to date, but in a way that made discussing what turned us on easier – telling your boyfriend that you fantasized about him caning you until you were sobbing and then fucking you hard against the marks even as you fought to push him off could potentially be a bit awkward. But Thomas listened closely to everything I said and, although I didn't realize it at the time, was mentally making notes for things to do at some undetermined future point which would make me wet and my head spin.

It started on a Saturday night with punishment for a spurious host of reasons which, if I was feeling argumentative, I would have queried. Except, of course, when his voice and mannerisms changed from easygoing to implacable and it became apparent exactly where we were headed, I really wasn't going to quibble. I ended up naked with my arse in the air, bent over the arm of his sofa.

He began with a relatively gentle spanking, which left my arse tingling and warm. I'd learned early on that Tom was a fan of spanking, and he had soon developed a penchant for putting me over his knee to punish me relentlessly while his erection grew under my squirming body. My knickers half way down my legs felt somehow more embarrassing than if I had them taken off completely, and proved helpful for hobbling me a little if I couldn't stop myself struggling. Previously, once my arse was hot and stinging he'd push me to the floor and fuck me, his hips anchoring me hard to the floor as he pushed inside me, ensuring no respite from the rough carpet against my stinging arse, but this time things were different. He asked me a question which I didn't answer with what he deemed to be quite the correct level of respect and I heard the sound of his belt slipping through the loops on his trousers.

When you have spent so long thinking about something, fantasizing about it, the prospect of actually being on the receiving end of it is terrifying. Not just because it's going to hurt and suddenly lovely, kind, just-finished-helping-me-do-the-crossword Tom has shifted into an alternate-universe version of himself. Not just because I'm desperately trying to control my nerves, to ensure that I don't chicken out, that I can withstand whatever he doles out, please him and acquit myself with courage and stoicism – ah yes, Maid Marian would be proud. Not even because, having spent the best part of a decade lying in bed at night fantasizing about what it would be like for someone to give me a good old-fashioned thrashing with their belt, I'm concerned that in practice it might not be arousing and instead it might just hurt so much I have to get him to stop. It's terrifying because not only would asking him to stop be a disappointing enactment of a long-held fantasy, it would also be a form of surrender, a failure, a defeat too far.

I turned my head, which was dangling down towards the floor, giving me a headrush to add to the dizziness of my anticipation, to see him standing in front of me, still fully dressed, holding his leather belt in his hands, pulling it, looping it, getting ready to hurt me, and the look in his eyes made my stomach lurch with the same mixture of fear and excitement you get on a rollercoaster. And then he moved behind me and all I could do was wait and try not to tremble. I didn't have long to go.

The first strike didn't hurt that much; the noise was more of a shock than the impact itself. I felt a moment of relief that actually the pain was bearable, and then he hit me twice more in quick succession and I yelped loudly – it would appear he'd not got the aim or the strength of his swing right with the first hit as it was hurting a damn sight more now.

He told me the more I yelped the harder he would hit me, so I bit my lip to try and silence myself, until I was convinced I could taste blood in my mouth. The crack of each impact on my arse sounded like a gunshot and the pain after the impact was a wave of agony. If it wasn't for the arm of the sofa under my abdomen holding me in place my legs would have buckled till I was lying on the floor in front of him. As it was, when the flick of the end of the belt curved round to catch one of my arse cheeks in a place it had hit several times before the white hot pain caused me to wobble, sliding halfway to the floor anyway, until he grabbed a handful of my hair to encourage me – in unrelenting and rather painful fashion – to scrabble back into position.

My tiny gasps were almost sobs by the time he asked me to count the blows. The pain was so much more than I could ever have imagined, but it didn't occur to me to ask him to stop. Instead, my mental focus was on withstanding the impact, stifling the moans and whimpers bubbling up into my throat with every lash, although trying to control my breathing to work through the pain must have given away how much he was hurting me even if the angry red stripes on my arse, the tears streaming down my face and my shaking legs didn't.

After ten strokes he put his hand on my clit, frigged me hard and then pushed his fingers up inside me, laughing softly at how obviously, audibly, aroused I was.

'Oh yes. You are quite the little pain slut, aren't you, Sophie?'

I shut my eyes, even as the noise of his fingers moving between my legs proved his point.

As he rubbed me and I began to moan in pleasure, he explained to me the concept of the carrot and the stick – and how I wasn't in line for the orgasmic carrot just yet. He pushed me back up into position for punishment without removing his hand from inside me and I felt a moment of fury at being treated like a fucking hand puppet.

I could almost see his smile as I strained on tiptoe across the arm of the sofa, his fingers pushing cruelly up inside me. I counted another ten hits with the belt through my dry throat – plus 'one for luck', which I'm sure he inflicted just to amuse himself at seeing my visible relief at the end of the punishment be replaced with shuddering nerves as I waited for the final – and hardest – blow.

Before I could even gather my wits his fingers were back on my clit. He was frenetic, rubbing me so hard that even with the lubricant it was bittersweet pleasure. I came hard, and my legs gave out from under me, leaving me slumped across the end of the sofa.

After I'd recovered sufficiently, I knelt at his feet, sucking him until he spurted in my mouth and then slept the sleep of the exhausted, on my side because my arse had taken such a battering that even the whispering movement of a duvet on it made me wake in pain. It took days for the welts to go down and every morning, after my shower, I checked the changing colours of the bruises in the full length mirror, prodding to see how much it hurt and smiling to myself at the same time.

Yup, I was beginning to understand the full extent of my masochistic tendencies. And in Thomas I seemed to have found someone who not only recognized them too but enjoyed giving them a good workout, although I was soon to realize that it wasn't necessarily the pain that was the most challenging element of playing with my incongruous dom.

5

The day after my intimate introduction to his belt Tom and I headed into town for a spot of lunch and a trip to the cinema, experiencing the joys of a mid-week day off when it feels like everyone else has their nose to the grind-stone while you're bunking off.

We'd grabbed the papers and headed into a restaurant. As my bum hit the hard wooden bench – why are they so popular? They're horrible and the interior designer of Wagamama has much to answer for – I grimaced slightly. Tom noticed and smiled but didn't say anything until the waitress had taken our order.

'Is your arse sore?'

Pride? Stubbornness? An urge to wipe the undeniably sexy but still damn conceited look off his face? Probably. 'It's OK.'

'Really? You looked quite uncomfortable when you sat down.'

We shared a look that said he knew what I was thinking and I knew he knew but was going to do my best to ignore it anyway.

I didn't get much peace. We chatted about film possibilities for the afternoon, a woman at work I fancied, the latest in an ongoing love/hate saga between two mutual friends, and ate our lunches. Then once we'd finished he took a sip of his drink and looked over at me for long seconds without speaking.

'What?' I asked.

He put his drink down on the table. 'Nothing, it's just every so often you shift on that bench and when you do your face changes and I can see it hurts.' He smiled. Bastard.

I tried to act like it was completely normal to be discussing the thrashing he gave me over the remains of two club sandwiches. 'Actually, I thought the cane would have been more painful. But last night . . .' I shifted without thinking to find a more comfortable way to sit, only becoming aware of it when I saw him smiling at me. 'Well, the belt was a lot more painful. I don't know why really.' I raised my chin. 'But it doesn't hurt that much.'

He raised an eyebrow and I realized that I'd just unwittingly given him a challenge that would come back to haunt me.

'To be honest, I did hit you hard, because I knew you could take it, that you love it in fact. But I was only giving you about 75 per cent of what I could – because we were so near the wall I couldn't get as much swing as I wanted.'

My arse clenched at the thought of being beaten any harder with the belt, now an innocent fashion object round his waist once more. I suddenly couldn't drag my eyes from it.

'Of course I don't know if you'd be able to take much more. Your arse was looking pretty battered by the time I'd finished. And you could hardly stand to lean over the arm of the sofa, your legs were shaking so much. I'd have been worried except for the fact your juice was running down your thighs so I could tell exactly how much you were enjoying it. Dirty girl.'

I was lost for words. I think I may have managed a 'guh', but that's about it. As I looked round the restaurant – ladies who lunch with a gaggle of small children a table away, a couple of teenagers making a smoothie last while rummaging through a bag of purchases – I tried to regain some semblance of control and ignore the warmth pooling between my legs. It was working too, sort of, until –

'The thing I love with the belt is how it flicks round the side of your arse with each lash. I'm sure it's painful on impact but it's the last flick round the curve that seems especially harsh. The marks it leaves are great though. And I love how you shudder when I run my fingernails over them. I could wank just looking at your punished arse. Although that could leave you ultimately pretty frustrated.' He smiled in a way that showed he really didn't care. I aimed once more for the bantering coherent-ish conversation we'd been having a few short minutes ago.

'It'd be OK, I'm sure I could sort myself out if the need arose.'

Another wolfish smile. 'Ah, now there's an excuse to tie you down. Not that I really need one.'

My breath was getting ragged and I was definitely wet. I crossed my arms on the table in front of my breasts so no one could see my nipples, which were, inevitably, tight in my top.

I laughed quietly, with a faint air of desperation I couldn't disguise. 'We should stop talking about this now.'

He smiled. 'Why? Are you turned on?' As if he didn't

know. Except of course he did and was asking because he enjoyed seeing me blush as I answered.

My 'yes' was very quiet.

'Move your arms away from your chest.'

I muttered his name, the word both a plea and an exclamation of exasperation, my arms still firmly covering the evidence of my arousal.

Then the tide turned and his dom voice was right there, the bantering gone. 'It wasn't a request, Sophie.'

Slowly I moved my arms away.

'Move back in the seat a little so I can see you properly.'

My face was hot as I moved back.

He laughed softly. 'That really was a little. It's OK though, it was enough.'

He stared intently at my breasts, not breaking away when the waitress came to ask if we wanted dessert. He ordered for both of us, and when she'd gone and I pointed out she'd seen him doing it, he replied, 'Ah, I wasn't staring at them, I was just thinking what they'd look like naked.'

I gulped my drink. Oh, that was all right then.

As we waited for dessert, conversation reverted to the topic of the girl at work who might or might not be interested in me, but any hope I'd be given a chance to recompose myself from the incoherent puddle sitting in front of him was soon extinguished. Having met her briefly he'd decided she was a switch, someone who could be either dominant or submissive, depending on who she was playing with, and began explaining to me exactly how he'd go about showing her how to 'get the best' from me.

As he described tying me down, making me lick her,

showing her how to use the cane effectively on my arse and breasts, making me watch them fuck, and so much more, I was beginning to move on the bench for different reasons. My hand was shaking as I tried to eat my dessert.

All of which he noticed, of course.

By the time we'd finished and got the bill I had no interest whatsoever in going to the cinema. I wanted to go back to his house for rampant mid-afternoon shagging. When I told him this – OK, maybe not 'told', there may have been pleading on my part; I really was very horny by this point – he smiled.

'OK. We can go back. But not yet, I have some things I want to get first.'

He could see the frustration in my face but I wasn't going to complain as I knew he'd just spin it out longer. So we paid the bill and started walking. I was wearing jeans and no knickers at Tom's request, so walking around with a seam pressed along my slit drove me crazy.

By the time we'd been into a DVD shop, two book-shops and a supermarket, I wanted to scream with frustration. He wasn't even buying anything. I'd given up even pretending to browse and was just focused on not embarrassing myself in public either by begging him to take me home and fuck me or coming to a seam-related orgasm. Finally he walked up behind me as I stood staring vacantly at a display of magazines and slapped me hard on the arse, making me yelp and dragging me from my reverie.

'OK, I'm done. It's time to go home.'

Thank fuck.

*

We finally got back to the house and as soon as we got through the door I suggested a blow job. I was desperate and wanting to reassert a little control. Tom's ability to read me had left me on the back foot and I figured getting my mouth round him would redress the balance – blow jobs didn't make him any less in charge, but every so often he'd make a tiny noise in the back of his throat or clench and unclench his hand and I'd know that for once he was the one fighting for control and it was all because of me, a very satisfying thought. Almost as satisfying as feeling him respond to my tongue and thickening in my mouth, getting to swallow him, diligently licking him clean afterwards and the orgasm it usually guaranteed for me afterwards. Oh yes.

So on the way up the stairs I asked him if he wanted me to suck him. He smiled. 'I think I could be convinced by that. But I had something else in mind first.'

Before I could even begin to guess what he was thinking of, he'd grabbed my wrist and pulled me off-balance on to the bed. While I tried to right myself, or at least get myself in a slightly more comfortable position, he yanked my arm into the small of my back with one hand and began pulling down my trousers with the other. By the time I'd stopped struggling and become resigned to the fact I wasn't going to be able to move from the position he wanted me in he'd already grabbed the hairbrush off the side table and the sound of the first strike on my arse was echoing around the room.

The rhythm was relentless. Sometimes his punishments were light and playful but this was anything but, even though it was only a few hours after he had used his belt on me. I don't know how long it went on, I was just focused on riding the waves of pain.

By the time he paused to run his fingernails and then the bristles of the brush along the burning red marks of my arse, all I knew was that my face and my cunt were both wet. He pulled me back up, running his hand along my slit as I stood in front of him on wobbling legs. Chuckling, he pushed his finger into my mouth for me to suck it clean, pointing out that for all my tears and whimpers as he punished me I was now tasting the proof I enjoyed being treated that way. I blushed as I licked my juice from him, hating his smugness – and the fact he was right.

Once his finger was clean he ordered me to strip and then when I was naked he pushed me to my knees. He took one of my nipples in each hand and pinched them, mauling them between his fingers until I was biting my lip to avoid crying out. Finally he tired of the game and undid his trousers. I set on him like I was starving.

But he wanted control of everything. He tangled his fingers fully into my hair and began fucking my face at his speed, indifferent to my stinging scalp and struggle to breathe as he dragged me up and down his cock. Then suddenly, his hands tightened and he pulled me away from his crotch.

'I'm not coming in your mouth.' I looked up at him in confusion. 'I'm going to come on your breasts. And as soon as I have you're going to lie back on the bed and I am going to do what you've been gagging for me to do all day. I'm going to make you come.

'But there are rules. If any of my spunk drips off you and hits the bed I'm going to stop what I'm doing, immediately. I'll make you get dressed and you can go home wet, whimpering and unsatisfied. Do you understand?'

I nodded, watching intently as he ran his hand up and down his cock. And then he came, in long milky spurts across my breasts and stomach. Taking a step back he smiled at me. 'Well what are you waiting for?'

I sank carefully to the bed, gasping at the pain of lying on my still throbbing arse.

'Does it hurt?'

I nodded, any pretence at hiding it impossible.

He smiled again as he grabbed my arms at the wrist and moved them to make me hold the headboard of his bed.

'Shame. Just remember what happens if you spill any.' He ran a hand along my inner thigh and I trembled. 'I have a feeling you'd rather not go home frustrated.'

Then he started fingering me and I was lost. He ran his fingers along my slit and then pushed them deep up inside me. He finger fucked me relentlessly, while grinding my clit with his thumb. I was moaning and squirming in pleasure but every movement caused zinging pain as my arse brushed against the sheet. The sensations merged until the pain and the pleasure and the humiliation and the sheer sexiness of it was all one, my loud moans shattering the silence.

Tom stopped for a moment, taking a step back to look down at me, staring intently. I blushed, wondering what kind of picture I must make lying there, legs spread and begging to come. Then I realized he was checking whether anything had dripped off me as I writhed.

I was desperate. I went to move my hands but his 'tut' as I shifted halted me in my tracks. For a split second we looked at each other, my eyes no doubt narrowing as I realized exactly what this meant, while his twinkled, his lips widening into a smirk at my reaction when I understood what I needed to do if I wanted to ensure my orgasm.

Who am I kidding? There were no ifs involved. Even as my brain processed what he was expecting, and wondered if I would do it, I was already moving my body. I twisted awkwardly on the bed, each brush of the bedding against my welts making me suck air in through my teeth. One particularly forceful movement, made as I saw a droplet moving inexorably round the curve of my hip in a way which filled me with panic, saw me bashing the side of my arse against the bed hard enough that I whimpered. Still I kept moving, while he watched my inevitably futile attempt to thwart gravity.

Finally, he took pity on me. 'If you're having trouble, I'll let you use your hands.'

Thank fuck. Desperately I ran my hands along my rib cage and the sides of my breasts to catch his cum, greedily licking my fingers clean before putting my hands back on my now-glistening and also flushed chest. Feeding myself seemed to please him as – thank goodness – he started pounding his fingers inside me again.

It was like swimming against conflicting currents. The relentless frigging, fingers pounding into my cunt, the still raw pain of my arse pushing against the bed as I writhed. Feeling so many different sensations, all the while trying desperately to ensure I didn't spill anything, meant that it took me a long time to orgasm despite my desperation. Suffice to say, I was aching by the time the need to orgasm overcame any fears of failing at his challenge.

When I did come I came hard, my moans and eventual screams ringing loud in my ears. I trembled for a long time afterwards with the intensity of it all. He stroked my shoulder as the shudders subsided and as I looked over at his still fully clothed body I was reminded that even I could underestimate him sometimes. It was also one of the most memorable shopping trips I've ever been on, which is pretty bloody amazing when I didn't actually buy anything.

It was my first real experience of the challenges of a D/s that wasn't purely about pain, but also encompassed losing dignity and control. To my surprise I began to find those moments were the ones that made me blush the most, that I found most challenging. My pain threshold gave me a chance to withstand brute force, but the psychological side of being demeaned stayed with me long after the bruises had faded. The moments would flash into my mind and bring both a feeling of embarrassment but also arousal, along with confusion. Understanding the things that turned me on was at times difficult; accepting them even tougher when the intensity of the scene and the adrenaline high had faded and I was left remembering how far I had allowed myself to be pushed, had pushed myself. It was hugely exciting but sometimes a bit worrying – how would I know how to get the balance right? How would I know not to go too far?

6

The problem with being a masochist is that, when it comes down to it, if your dominant isn't an utter sadist then punishments in the usual sense of the word don't really work as a deterrent.

I know it's ironic, not least because, let's face it, we're not talking 'punishments' in the usual sense of the word anyway. I'm not a recalcitrant child, or a dog that needs training, and I'd be very uncomfortable being with anyone who felt that was an acceptable part of our dynamic – each to their own and everything and I guess as long as both parties are happy with it that's fine, but it doesn't work for me. Also, I'm forgetful, clumsy and very, very sarcastic – if someone were looking to train that out of me, firstly I'd be in trouble the whole bloody time, and secondly by the time they'd finished I'd be very dull and not much like me.

That said, I was fast realizing that in the right mindset I really did love pain a lot. The sting of it, the challenge of it, the adrenaline high it produced, the catharsis afterwards. And if Tom wanted to come up with arbitrary 'play' reasons to punish me, then I really wasn't going to quibble in the least.

After all, the ebb and flow of pain as a cane lashes the curve of my arse where it meets the top of my thigh makes me wet. Drugs aren't my thing but the high I get when the adrenaline is thrumming through my body is a legal (and free) equivalent to that rush. It stays with me for at least as long as the marks do, occasionally rushing to the forefront of my mind during the days after a session, catching me unawares as I grind through my vanilla, professional day. A flash of memory will make my nipples hard, my body ache, my eyes glitter in a way that might make my colleagues wonder exactly what I am thinking about in that moment where I seem elsewhere.

All in all, though, the pain was hardly a punishment and thus, it turned out, not that much of a challenge from Tom's perspective. Why have me endure that when he could have me do something else, something I'd never dreamed of, that broke my brain a little bit when he told me about it.

When you're playing with a dominant as irritatingly insightful as Tom, he watches to find out the thing that you don't find sexy. The thing you do at his behest while gritting your teeth, as an act of pure submission. The thing you hate, and do just to please, usually while pretending it doesn't bother you because you know if he realized just how much you hated it he'd make you do it more just because he could. The thing you don't want to do. Aren't sure you can do. Which leaves you with stormy eyes, flushed with anger and humiliation, wishing you could tell him to fuck off but knowing that you can't because in spite of yourself you crave this even if you can't explain why.

For me, that is the foot thing.

There are many amazing things about Tom, both in terms of character and appearance. He is intelligent, funny, has the most expressive, gorgeous blue eyes, a dirty smile and the ability to keep me on the back foot like few people I have ever met. Personally and sexually he challenges me in a way that makes life just seem that bit sharper, colours that bit brighter. There are many things I could tell you about Tom that are amazing, arousing, brilliant. But I really wouldn't say his feet are one of them. OK, two of them.

We'd been out with a group of friends and messing about, play-fighting and being silly. Our D/s relationship remained to the outside world a subtle and sporadic one, a dom/sub with benefits if you like, and our mutual friends knew nothing about it. However, when I tapped him on the head with the rolled-up magazine extolling the virtues of the latest releases showing at the cinema and caught his nose hard enough to make his eyes water things shifted. I dug a tissue out of my handbag, while apologizing for my cack-handedness. Taking it from my hand he smiled as he wiped his eyes. 'It's OK,' he said, loudly enough for everyone to hear, before adding, 'I'll punish you for it properly later,' in a voice meant just for me.

Suffice to say I spent a great part of the film wondering exactly what that meant. His tone wasn't unduly pissed off but it promised something out of the ordinary, so not his hand. The cane? The whip? His belt? A ruler? Would he punish me, fuck me until he came and then leave me unsatisfied, something he had done one memorable and hideously frustrating sleepless night a few months before when I had been left with my hands tied behind my back while he slept like a baby? God I hoped not. I was definitely up for something more satisfyingly fun.

In the end he chose something that made a night of frustration look like a walk in the park. In fact I think I'd rather have had a month of frustration. And I'm not really the chaste type.

I was on my knees, naked, on his bed when he explained to me what was going to happen. He was stroking the small of my back, running a leisurely finger up and down my spine in a way that – paired with the chill in the room and fierce anticipation – meant I was already distracted enough that for one hopeful minute I thought I'd misheard him. Definite wishful thinking.

'Do you understand?' he asked.

I stayed silent, hoping he'd actually say he'd changed his mind and instead was going to beat me until I cried and then fuck my bruised and throbbing arse without lube in recompense. That'd hurt like hell and definitely count as a punishment. Would that count? Could I suggest it? Would that count as topping from the bottom?

He stopped stroking my back and instead pinched one of my nipples. Hard.

'I said, do you understand?'

I swallowed hard, and – unable to speak – nodded. What is it they say? You can understand but not comprehend? That was me. He had just asked me to do something that I just didn't think I could do. I didn't want to do it. The thought of doing it made me feel sick with humiliation and anger. This was not in any way alluring to me.

Even the usual submissive satisfaction I get from knowing I'm pleasing someone by demeaning myself wasn't enough to make this seem in any way sexy. At all.

He moved and began pulling down his trousers. 'Well move over then. You can kiss your way down. Acclimatize yourself as it were.' The amusement in his voice was audible and it made me furious. He knew he had asked me to do something that every fibre of my being was saying I wouldn't, couldn't, do, and he was settling down against the pillow, arms behind his head, watching with a smile as I tried to process it. 'Why don't you start by running your tongue along my cock?'

OK. This I could do. This I liked to do. Great. I shuffled round on the bed to get into position. He was already hard, but as I began gently licking my way up his shaft he grew further, his cock pushing into my face, almost as demanding as its owner. I lapped at him, diligent and focused, losing myself in something I enjoyed. But suddenly I was dragged back to reality. Literally. Tangling his hands in my hair he pulled me up so abruptly a strand of saliva stretched from my lips to his tip and then broke before I could catch my breath and swallow it back. The lewdness of the visual made me flush with humiliation.

'Very nice, but that's enough of that.' He patted my head in the way you'd stroke a pet. 'Now why don't you move down and kiss my balls for a little while?'

Obediently I pushed my face fully into his groin. I suddenly had a flashback to the first time he told me to do this, and how I flushed scarlet with embarrassment and hesitated at doing something so obviously meant to demean me. As I gently sucked him now, I wondered what had happened to me. How did I go from tentative embarrassment to happy, even greedy, obedience? In a few months' time how much further would my boundaries have moved? How was he able to move me past my limits with such ease?

There wasn't time for self-analysis though, as he ordered me to kiss my way down his inner thighs, past his knees and shins and to the top of his feet. I did so, my kisses getting faster and lighter the further down I got in spite of my fears of admonishment. All too soon I was face to toes with him, the room completely silent as he waited. He was insouciant, everything about him screaming confidence that I would do what I'd been told to do eventually. I felt him shift behind me, moving position to better see the war going on in my head and on my face, missing nothing. No one was watching, it was just me and him.

I could have got up and left. I could have told him to fuck off. If I'd made enough of a fuss he wouldn't have made me do it. Probably. But somewhere along the way stubborn pride and a small corner of my brain were telling me I could do this. I should do this. Even that it's sexy to do it – after all submission isn't really submission if you only obey the stuff you like to do. It was a very small part of my brain and as I got closer to his feet it shrank further.

I couldn't begin to understand why this was affecting me so much. I knew his feet were clean – he wasn't evil after all – and they were just feet. No one was watching, it was just us and him. OK, in wider terms feet felt a bit taboo, demeaning, but trying to move past that shouldn't be this difficult, should it? *How is it any worse than kissing his hands?* I thought, trying to chivvy myself along, making my conscious thoughts more businesslike.

I lowered my head to his feet. *I can do this. It'll please him if I do this. If I get it over with quickly we'll move on to something else and it'll be sexy as hell.* I closed my eyes. *Do his feet actually smell? Am I imagining it because I can't see them?* I moved in even closer but I couldn't quite bring myself to take the final step. I took a couple of deep breaths and tried again. Still no good. My lips were dry, my mind racing. *I can do this*, I thought to myself. If I did it quickly he wouldn't realize how much it was bothering me.

'Did I tell you to breathe on my toes?'

He knew how much it was bothering me. Blatantly. My voice was small. 'No.'

'Well, what are you waiting for? Go on.'

Tentatively I shifted slightly on the bed and leant down to kiss his little toe. It was a feather-light kiss, I licked my suddenly parched lips and pushed my face back down, in opposition to every screaming instinct. He made a small murmur of pleasure as I connected with his toes again and I knew it was about my submission to his will rather than the sensation of my mouth on his foot. I could almost see him smiling behind me and it made me furious, at him, at myself and the part of me that craved this even while bridling at my own, at least partially self-inflicted, abasement. I kissed each toe, gently and respectfully and slowly – I wasn't going to have him make me do it again – finishing with a lingering kiss on his big toe. And then I turned back to look at him, breathing heavily, my face and neck red with embarrassment. I was trying not to glare but his smirk made me think I wasn't hiding my ire especially well.

Succinctness was what was going to stop me getting into more trouble, so I went for brevity even though my tone was mutinous. 'OK?'

He smiled at me. 'Not quite yet. You've got the other foot to do. Lean over me and suck my toes.'

I turned back quickly, wanting to face his feet rather than look into his eyes, which seemed to see too much. Tom was more experienced in D/s terms than me, and it was a constant source of wonder and irritation to me that he seemed to understand this part of my nature better than I did, leaving me scared and infuriated even while the intensity of the scene was making me wet. I veered between feeling so exhilarated it felt like flying and wanting to smack him about the head for being arrogant, even while a tiny voice inside me knew it was unfair to call him arrogant when most of the time he was actually right.

I moved over, straddling his outstretched legs to get to his other foot, thinking I could endure this last bit of grovelling. Just do it, don't think about it. I started by kissing the top of his foot, before screwing up the last of my courage and finally taking several of his toes in my mouth. It actually didn't taste bad, so I moved along his foot, sucking his big toe. Licking it. Worshipping it. My mind running a mental mantra – this will soon be over. This. Will. Soon. Be. Over.

Then unexpectedly he put his hand between my legs

and I moaned around his foot in pleasure and surprise. Typically he took the opportunity to push his foot further into my mouth.

'You're very wet. You're lips are puffy. You're obviously enjoying something we're doing right now.'

I closed my eyes and kept sucking, my body responding as he pushed his fingers further into what was – to my shame – my wetness.

The room was silent except for the sound of me sucking his toes, and his fingers leisurely frigging me. In spite of myself I was wet, horny and desperate to come, pushing back on his hand as he shoved his fingers inside me.

He chuckled. 'After all that glowering it turns out you like being made to lick and suck my feet. You actually like being treated like a slut, even in spite of yourself. Don't you, slut?'

I ignored him and his repeated use of what he mockingly calls 'the "s" word', knowing he was trying to get a reaction. I reddened even more, but with my back to him and my hair falling in my face I knew he couldn't see it. Instead I kept licking, thinking it was probably a good idea I was effectively gagged by his foot as otherwise I'd be bound to say something that got me into more trouble. Instead I tried desperately to focus on making him so happy he'd let me move on to something else. Which is very difficult indeed when you're so desperate to come that despite it all you'd pretty much do anything for release.

As he brushed my clit with his thumb I whimpered with excitement, so close to coming despite everything. I think that's when he came up with the idea.

'You seem to really be enjoying worshipping my feet now.' I huffed my annoyance through my nose, while pushing my tongue between his toes almost viciously. 'I think I should make you keep sucking them until you come around my hand. That would be amusing wouldn't it?'

Amusing wasn't the word. I closed my eyes, trying desperately to blink back tears of fury and humiliation, knowing that in spite of how much I hated doing this he was going to be able to manipulate my body into getting the utmost pleasure from it. He upped the tempo, pushing his fingers harder and further inside me, jabbing my clit with his thumb with every thrust until my face was buried in his feet, and I was whimpering round his toes. I was going to ache tomorrow but his vicious, insistent penetration was doing its job and despite it all my orgasm built, then ebbed as he slowed things down, enjoying the power he was able to wield so effortlessly over me, before building it up again. And again.

I don't know how long I licked him, although when I came my jaw was aching and my cries were almost croaky my mouth was so dry. By the end I had no awareness of anything but his hand and his foot. I was a primeval bundle of nerve endings, desperate to come, willing to do whatever he wanted, so long as he would let that happen and give me the release I craved. I'd have begged him for it, but instead I sucked his toes into my mouth as far as I could take them, licked the sole of his foot and wordlessly showed him I'd do anything for him, even something that an hour before I'd have said with confidence was a hard limit.

I once read somewhere that the key to sexual humiliation is not about making somebody do something they don't want to do, it is about leading them to do things they secretly dream about doing. I can honestly say I had never dreamed of debasing myself in quite such a humiliating way and still blush when I think of it. At the same time, when I came around his fingers my orgasm was one of the most intense I'd had for a long time. And even as he made me lick his fingers clean of the sticky juice which proved how much I had enjoyed the unusual punishment, before pulling me down his body by my hair to suck him, I couldn't help wondering what it would be like to have to do it again.

As was so often the case with Tom, he managed to stumble across something that affected me deeply, and that I thought about for a long time afterwards – why *are* feet such a big deal anyway? The thought of it made me flush, my body reacting like I was right back there in that moment.

7

Words are funny things. When I am in my submissive headspace I will grovel, I will beg, I will say whatever it is my dominant demands of me. True, some of the words will flow freely, while others will stick in the back of my throat. Pleading for him to fuck me, punish me, use me, are all things I used to find difficult, but now – thanks mainly to Tom's obsession with making me say things I find embarrassing for his amusement – my voice is assured despite my debasement, proud and wet at pleasing him by demeaning myself. Calling him sir is harder, my voice then is quieter, and if I can get away with it I hide the humiliation I can't quite overcome behind the curtain of my hair. But even though it chafes I can do it. I do. And my submission ultimately brings great pleasure and release to us both.

But the word that grates, no matter how often it is said around me, is *slut*.

I know. It's a little word. And in BDSM terms it is not even a derogatory one. I am comfortable with the dual nature of my personality, the fact that I am independent, capable and in control for most of my day, and yet crave giving power to my top for mind-blowing nights. And afternoons. Mornings too, actually. But there's something about the word slut that, even immersed in the most arousing scene, will jar me out of the moment like a needle scratching across a record. Men who like sex are studs. Women who like sex are sluts. I know this is the vanilla meaning. I know when I am kneeling naked in front of Tom, sucking greedily on his cock and he calls me it the context and thus the meaning is as different as night and day. But it doesn't stop my glaring up at him even as I suck him further into my mouth.

He laughs when he sees me bristle at it. I'm hardly a prude and there are so many other words which wider society as a whole would consider worse and which don't bother me at all, but slut is the one I hate. And he knows it, loves pushing me, making me explain to him exactly how much of a greedy, grateful, horny slut I am before he'll let me come. And while in the back of my mind there is a part of me bridling at the terminology and wishing I could tell him to fuck off, I obey. I obey in spite of every fibre of my being saying I don't need to do this, for the small voice which whispers that I do. It is not the most demeaning thing he makes me do but it is one that stings most. An act of pure submission.

So when I saw the paddle I had to buy it.

Tom's birthday was looming and while I'd bought a couple of great vanilla presents I was looking for something extra. Symbolic. Special. Sexy.

I was looking at crops when I saw it, pondering whether it was bad form to give someone a present which I was going to get at least as much pleasure from as he would. It was on the end of the shelf, beautifully boxed, and in the split second after I realized exactly what it was, I felt a flutter in the pit of my stomach.

SLUT.

Well actually TULS, cut into twelve inches of vicious-looking black leather attached to a sturdy handle.

I couldn't even look directly at it. I stared at the toys next to it, behind it, sneaking little glances. I knew he'd love it. Love marking me with it. But the thought of walking around with that word emblazoned across my arse like a brand made me shiver in revulsion. It was perfect. But I hated it. And I knew he'd love that even more.

I stood in front of the shelf for a good ten minutes until a saleswoman came over to ask if I needed any help, presumably fearful I was a demented potential shoplifter. Her approach was the impetus I needed. I reassured her I was fine, grabbed the box – heavier than I anticipated – and almost ran to the till to pay. I'd even stopped blushing by the time I was halfway home.

In the ten days between buying the paddle and his birthday I thought about it constantly, the carrier bag a permanent reminder on my desk. Half a dozen times I decided against giving it to him, not sure I'd be able to withstand the inevitably intense scene when he finally wielded it. But in the end, I had to wrap it up. I knew he'd love it. And I could withstand this. Right? I had time to get over it. Really. It'd be fine. Probably.

His eyes sparkled when I gave it to him. His fingers traced the stitching, flexing it and swiping the air in front of me in a way which made me restrain a shudder. He watched my reactions closely, and I did everything I could not to show him how much it bothered me.

Of course he knew how much it bothered me.

I'd got myself so wound up thinking about what it would be like to be on the receiving end of it that when he smiled and thanked me and put it on the mantelpiece it felt like an anticlimax. Then he started stroking my breasts, moved lower, and I got distracted with other things.

It stayed there for two weeks and two days, not that I was counting. Every time I walked into the room and saw it I felt a flutter in my stomach. I dreaded the thought of being punished with it but part of me wondered how I would respond. Would I be able to withstand it physically? How long would the marks last?

It was a Saturday night when I found out. We'd had a very lovely fuck earlier in the evening and crashed out pretty much instantaneously. I woke from an odd dream and then watched the red illuminated clock change for more than an hour courtesy of the kind of insomnia that leaves you feeling convinced that you're the only person in the world awake and incapable of switching off. In the end, I decided an orgasm was the only way to get back to sleep. So I shuffled away from him, put my hand between my legs and began touching myself.

It was a utilitarian wank, all about the release and, hopefully, the sleep that would come afterwards. My strokes were assured, my fingers working towards the delicious friction that would bring the orgasm I so desperately needed. I was quiet, close to coming and utterly focused, which is why when he spoke from the darkness it made me jump.

'What are you doing?'

My hand stopped abruptly between my legs. Ooops. Belatedly it occurred to me he'd probably find this bad form.

'I couldn't sleep.' My voice was croaky.

'I gathered that.' He was amused but his voice had the tone I jokingly refer to as his dom voice – although only when we're not actually playing, as when we are I wouldn't dare. 'What are you doing?'

Suddenly I was very glad for the darkness. It's easier to pretend indifference at being caught red-handed when you don't have to look anyone in the eye. 'I was having a wank. I couldn't sleep and I thought a quick orgasm would help me –'

I stopped talking as he moved across the bed to spoon behind me, his hand clamping around my wrist, still nestled – albeit now unmoving – between my legs. The warm breath of his 'tut' tickled my ear as he pulled my hand away, making me shiver against him.

'So, just two hours after I give you what, if your moans were anything to go by, was a very intense, very pleasurable orgasm, you're greedy for another one already?'

I shook my head. 'It's not like that, it's just –'

He pulled my hand up to my mouth, effectively silencing me with my own sticky fingers.

'I think it's best you stay quiet for a moment now. Don't you?'

Tom's tone was dangerous and made me wetter but a little fearful. I stayed quiet and still, not even risking a nod as I didn't want to do anything to displease him further.

My nipples were hard and my body was trying to process the fact that I had been so close to orgasm and yet apparently was going without for now.

'You are a greedy slut.' I could see where this was going and my heart was already starting to race. 'You woke me up with your bouncing because you're so horny you can't wait a few short hours before you get to come again.' I wanted to argue but I knew if I did it was just going to make things worse. 'You deserve punishment. Don't you?'

I was still silent, even in the face of the direct question. I knew what was going to happen now and part of me was thinking I was knackered and not ready for the inevitable intensity, that all I wanted was to go to sleep. But I didn't dare say that so I remained quiet. Until he pinched my nipple. Hard. I gasped at the unexpected pain.

'Don't you?'

I hate it when he does this. The act of submission is one thing, but admitting that I need this, yearn for it even, always makes me blush. Which of course he knows. I tried not to sound huffy as I responded. 'Yes.'

He slapped my breast. 'Some respect now might save you some pain later.'

I tried to restrain my tone. 'I'm sorry. Yes. You're right, I deserve punishment.' I hoped my penitent tone would work in my favour, although I didn't hold out much hope.

He was stroking my bare breast, running his fingers round in a very distracting circle. In spite of the tension running through my body I started to relax into the movement, enjoying the sensation, which made what he said next even more of a wrench.

'Go downstairs and get the paddle. Now.'

I was up, across the room and halfway down the stairs before my brain really began to process what this meant. The paddle. The. Paddle. Shit. Could I endure this? Suddenly I really wasn't sure, and I was hardly filled with confidence to start with. I should have been better prepared, not groggy from lack of sleep, sexually frustrated and with my head elsewhere.

I picked it up with shaking hands and headed back upstairs, mindful that keeping him waiting was just going to make it worse. Taking a couple of deep breaths outside the bedroom door, I pulled together my tattered courage. But before my hand could connect with the handle the door was pulled open and bright light flooded my eyes, leaving me half-blinded and disoriented.

By the time my eyes had adjusted he had plucked the paddle from my hands and manoeuvred me across the room to the bed. I knelt on all fours, waiting nervously for what happened next, suddenly wishing I slept in something more than a pair of knickers.

I was staring intently at the sheet, trying to prepare myself for what was to come, which would have been easier if I'd had any idea exactly what that was. He stroked my arse through my knickers, and the touch made me flinch. He laughed as I tried to regain some composure. His hand moved round.

'Your knickers are so wet I can actually see how much of a slut you are.'

I closed my eyes. He stroked me through the fabric of my knickers and I bit back a moan of pleasure, my body crying out for the orgasm it was so close to getting just a few short minutes before. As he ran his fingers up and down my slit, pushing the sodden material into my wetness, my breathing got harsh. I was so close to coming my legs started to buckle. I was suddenly hopeful – was he going to let me come after all?

Of course not. Wishful thinking. He stopped and I tried not to sigh in frustration. He moved up the bed and pushed his finger into my mouth. I blushed but sucked it deep, licking myself off him. He chuckled at my eagerness.

'You are a slut. We both know it and now I'm going to mark you in a way that anyone who sees you will know it too.'

He pulled his finger away abruptly and moved behind me, pulling my knickers down to bare my arse. I had spent so long worrying about how this would work that I was already trembling, trying desperately to stay in position and not give away the extent of my fear. I was mentally kicking myself for buying him the paddle, the idea of it was all well and good but the idea of walking around with SLUT emblazoned across my arse in purple bruises repulsed me. What was I thinking? What if I really couldn't do this and this was the first time I'd have to use my safe word?

My rising panic meant I heard the first strike before I even felt him move behind me. It sounded like a gunshot and made me jump. For a split second I didn't feel anything, I actually thought he'd missed. And then the pain, god the pain took my breath away. I gasped. I may have cried out. Tears filled my eyes. He might have asked me if

I was OK then. To be honest I'm not sure. There was a noise like rushing waves in my head. I couldn't really deal with anything, see anything, feel anything, except for that noise – and the pain where the paddle had connected. It hurt much more than I'd expected it to. More than his belt or the cane. I realized the full impact of what I'd given him.

The next blow came before I had time to blink away the tears from the first. I was trying to control my breathing, trying not to cry. I wanted to be able to withstand it, was definitely too proud to say I needed to stop. So I sucked in gasps of air and felt the tears running down my cheeks from behind my closed eyes as I tried to work through the pain of blow after blow.

After maybe a dozen blows he stopped. I tried to pull myself together, brought myself back to the present, was aware of him moving behind me. As I cowered slightly, anticipating more punishment, he moved his hand to my arse, stroking the punished cheek, even the relatively gentle touch leaving me quivering. I felt him move closer to see his handiwork, tracing the marks he'd inflicted on my pale flesh, like a painter looking at his canvas.

'Hmmm. I need to hit you harder I think. And make sure the strike connects squarely or I won't get the full effect. I think I might have to practice on one cheek to ensure I'm doing it right, and then when I feel ready I'll give you one last massive crack across the other one which should see you properly marked. What do you think?'

I tried not to shudder and closed my eyes so he couldn't see they were once more filled with tears. 'I think it's entirely up to you.'

I could hear the laugh in his voice as he patted me on the head. 'Good answer, my slut.'

He picked up the paddle again and I steeled myself for more pain, but instead he ran it up between my legs. I bit back a moan of embarrassment – the paddle slid easily along, betraying exactly how turned on I was. I could almost see his smile as he moved the paddle round in front of me.

'Kiss it and thank me for giving you the punishment you seem to be enjoying so much.'

I brought my mouth to the now glistening leather. My voice was small and I could bring myself to say nothing more than the barest minimum his order allowed. 'Thank you for punishing me. I'm sorry I woke you up.'

He began again.

I wish I could say that when it started again I withstood the punishment better. But the tears still flowed, although in spite of myself my juices did too. Eventually, by the time my arse felt like it was glowing with the agony, he stopped. I felt light-headed with relief, until I realized what this meant.

He let the tension lengthen before he gave me the final blow, on my as-yet-unblemished cheek. I was trembling at the prospect of it and when it finally connected and the noise reverberated about the room I cried out, my legs and arms buckling underneath me. He had put all his weight into it, swung hard, and it caught me perfectly across the vulnerable stripe of skin where my bum met my thigh. I was sobbing, in pain but also in relief that

I had withstood the punishment. He stroked my back, making soothing noises, telling me how I had pleased him by being brave, and how beautiful my arse looked, all red and hot.

Then he pulled me on to my back and gave me the kind of fucking which I normally yearn for, fast, hard, vicious, filling me up. Except of course under the circumstances it was just another torturous pleasure – every movement of my arse against the sheet made me cringe in pain as did his hands pinching my arse as he pushed himself deeply into me, pain tinging the pleasure of each thrust.

Eventually I came, spasming around his cock, my cries of pleasure overshadowing the previous cries of pain. He came inside me, then pulled out and I was finally able to get the sleep I craved.

My right arse cheek was a mess of bruises for about a week afterwards. My left was pale and pristine in comparison, except for the word SLUT emblazoned across it like a brand, which meant I had to take special care in the changing room at the gym.

I still hate the word slut, but unfortunately Tom loves it and he loved that bloody paddle. For ages afterwards he ensured that I was marked somewhere every time we played, whether it was my arse, my inner thighs – which bruise a lot easier and which, as he had to punish me with my legs spread, tended to show in embarrassing detail exactly how wet his punishments left me – or on one notable occasion a breast.

When I saw that paddle my heart started beating faster;

my body reacted in a way that proved that I am indeed a slut for the punishment – and pleasure – that it could inflict, although saying it out loud remained almost more than I could bear. They say a picture paints a thousand words though, and if you had seen my body once he'd finished playing with me then I don't need to say anything at all.

8

Over the months Tom and I kept playing. He kept pushing my boundaries, introducing me to new things. But then, as we got closer to the end of the year things slowed down a little.

Working in newspapers means Christmas and New Year is a busy and hideous time. While the paper's pagination gets smaller so the amount of news we have to write gets less, no one wants to work longer than necessary, and with schools closed, your local MP more often than not nowhere to be seen and businesses away for a break, it gets harder to actually find stories. Combined with the fact that early deadlines and all those bank holidays mean you're effectively writing two papers at once, filling them with the least lame features you can come up with and the much-loathed 'Review of the Year' when all you want to do is finish early and go to the pub, all in all it makes for a pretty stressful and annoying time.

By the time I've finished up at work and headed home for Noël en famille I'm usually ready for a rest, which is a bummer really, as a few days in close confinement with my nearest and dearest is many, many things, but restful is not one of them. After a lot of food, some great presents and a lot of trips round the various parts of my family, I was ready for a holiday from my holiday. And that was when Tom invited me to come and stay at his place for a while in the lull between Christmas and New Year.

Honestly, the idea of spending five days lounging around his house fussing his dog, reading, watching his big screen TV while he was at work (oh yes, he was even more unfestive than me), catching up on some reading and eating Quality Street – plus some inevitably stress-relieving sex – sounded brilliant to me, and I was in the car as fast as I could explain a hastily made-up work emergency, pack my stuff and kiss the family goodbye. I know, I'm a bad daughter.

When I arrived we hugged hello – we didn't tend to kiss, it felt wrong and too relationshipy somehow, which makes us both sound worryingly like prostitutes although it made sense to us – but as soon as I curled into him, relaxing into his familiar scent, he pulled away. Without speaking he pushed me to the floor, kicking the front door shut as he moved, undoing his fly.

His hands in my hair pulled me into position, I opened my mouth, and suddenly the thought of nativity play write-ups, Christmas party organization and anything other than the taste of him were far from my mind.

He moved to lean against the front door, and I crawled with him, unwilling and (technically, since his hands were in my hair dragging me along) unable to let him out of my mouth. As I sucked my way up and down his length, enjoying his reactions, he came hard, coating the back of my throat in a way that made me think he was looking forward to burning off some festive-season steam too. All too soon his breathing slowed and he pulled out of my mouth.

'That was great.'

I smiled at him as he zipped himself away and helped me up, pleased and aroused at how we – apparently – weren't wasting any time getting started on the amazing sex portion of the break.

He slapped my arse. 'Come on, let's go get some lunch.'

Oh. OK.

I was wet and my nipples were visible through my top, but I could see the glint of humour in his eyes and I wasn't going to give him the satisfaction of seeing how much I wanted to come. I could wait. I'm fairly patient. OK, who am I kidding, I'm not. But what's a couple of hours between friends?

The rest of the day passed pleasantly. We went into town and looked at the sales, and I bought books and a handbag which I loved so much I could barely restrain my glee. We had lunch, went to the cinema, walked the dog, crunching along in the frost. Generally it was wonderful, restful and everything that that time between Christmas and New Year should be – all with the additional sexual tension resulting from my awareness of the possibilities of what would happen when we got back to his house.

And then we did get back to his house. Drank tea. Watched telly. Cooked some supper. By the time we headed up to bed my patience had pretty much faltered. As we snuggled into bed he kissed me on the forehead. And then went to sleep.

Brilliant.

After the 'waking him wanking' debacle of a few weeks before there was no way I was going to risk that, so I lay quietly in bed, watching a chink of street light reflecting on the wall and listening to his soft, rested breathing, restraining the urge to smother him with a pillow. Finally I dropped off to sleep. My final thought was, *tomorrow morning.*

I woke up to feel Tom's erection pressing against my elbow. Hoo-blimmin-rah. Being the antithesis of a morning person, there are very few things that will cause me to smile early in the day but this was definitely one of them. I rubbed him tentatively, trying to ascertain how awake he was.

'Good morning. Is there something in particular I can help you with?' His voice was wry although a good indication he was actually awake, which was pleasing all things considered.

'Good morning. There might be something I'm in the market for.'

His chuckle vibrated his chest under my cheek. 'I can tell. I get the feeling you're a bit horny this morning.'

There really wasn't any way to deny this, so I didn't.

'Why don't you put your lips round me then?'

I didn't need asking twice, and turned round to lean over, licking his tempting tip before beginning to suck him properly.

He lay back, doing very little but moaning gently when my tongue touched a spot which felt especially good. I enjoyed having control of the pace and took the opportunity to tease a little. As he began to buck in my mouth I pulled back and licked and sucked his balls for a while, something he loves but which wasn't going to be enough to make him come just yet. I half expected him to complain, but – for once – he seemed happy to let me play, although he began stroking the curve of my arse, before running his fingers along the edge of my knickers. I felt myself get wetter, desperate for him to move his hand just the tiniest way, to slip in under the fabric and begin to finger me. It seemed he was good at teasing too.

Little did I realize how good.

As he began stroking me through my knickers I moaned round his cock, a wordless plea for him to stop playing with me. He ignored me, though, tracing my slit up and down the outside of my knickers until I was, admittedly rather unsubtly, pushing myself down on his hand to try and get him to give me the friction I needed.

In the end, I broke away from him for a second.

'Please, can you just touch me? Properly?'

He laughed, and kept on with his torturous almost-stroking. 'You are desperate this morning, aren't you, poor slut?'

I managed to withhold any response to his use of the 's' word, I was so desperate to come, although I couldn't hide the frustration in my voice. 'Well you did get to come yesterday. I didn't, remember?'

He laughed again, the kind of laugh that makes my stomach dance. 'You're quite right. And you will get to come eventually, when I'm ready for you to. In the meantime I suggest you go back to doing what you were doing.'

I harrumphed quietly to myself and obeyed. If he wanted a blow job I was going to give him the best damn blow job he'd ever had and then he was going to make me come.

I sucked him to the best of my ability. I used every trick I knew about his body, did all the things I know he loves, from gently stroking his balls and then kissing them to licking the length of his cock and then breathing on the wetness to make him tingle. I worshipped him. His cock was the focus of my world, and I was going to make him come and it was going to be great and then I was going to get my orgasm. Because, well, while it's not all about me, a woman has needs.

Suddenly his hand was pinching at my hip as he came. I let him rest for a moment in my mouth before licking him gently clean. And then he started to move. To get up.

I couldn't actually form words but there was a kind of grumbling noise in the back of my throat that I couldn't stop.

'What? I'm going to make us some coffee.'

'But you said –'

'I know, I said you'd eventually get to come. And you will. But not this morning.'

Don't get angry Soph. It'll just last longer if you make a fuss. Then I had a thought.

'Can't I just –?'

'No. You can't. I'll tell you when. For now you wait.' He tweaked my nipple. 'Now get up. Come on. If you're lucky I'll make breakfast.'

I got up. Grumpy.

*

Now the first thing to bear in mind is yes, I could have had a wank myself. But, well, what's the point of that? He obviously had something he was plotting and, well, as I've said before, only submitting for the bits you actively *want* to do is pointless really. I wanted to prove I could wait, and was curious as to what he had in mind for later when he would let me come. And I was stubborn. I know, I hide it well.

And so, after a breakfast that normally would have left me completely satisfied, the day unfolded. We pottered around. I did some writing and played some online poker, we walked the dog, I cooked a massive roast, we watched some DVDs, argued about the news. And through it all I didn't think at all about the fact I wanted to orgasm. OK, that might be a slight lie. Mainly I thought about not showing how much I wanted an orgasm and, for the most part, I think I managed it, except perhaps for the odd moments when Tom brushed my arse or the side of my breast accidentally. Actually, I wasn't sure it was accidentally, but I didn't want to draw his attention to it in case it was and I sounded like I was hyper-sensitive about it. My nipples were aching most of the day. But I absolutely was not going to show it. No way. Ha. That'd teach him.

I was fast realizing I wasn't the orgasm-denial type. Now, this wasn't a decision I had come to lightly. If the first night had been difficult, and the morning after set me up for a day of distraction, then that night – a lengthy blow job with me knelt on the floor between his legs while he watched the news and played with my hair like I was his pet, followed by him coming across my naked breasts, leaving me to go to sleep unfulfilled again – made me sure.

Don't get me wrong, I am definitely not averse to some anticipation. But two days of abstinence – made worse by the fact Tom was still taking his pleasure in lots of different tempting ways – was making me seriously grumpy.

I lay in bed waiting for sleep to claim me, which – let me assure you – is actually quite difficult when, barring the odd night in a room share, I have tended to fall asleep following an orgasm either at my own hand or someone else's every night of my adult life. I was a little sticky and so frustrated I was trembling, and pondering physical violence against Tom, who had tucked himself up happily and was laid on his side smiling widely at me.

'Are you OK?' he asked, knowing full well I wasn't.

'I'm fine,' I said. Usually when I say I am fine it means I am about as unfine as it is possible for me to be without me either bursting into tears or going postal with a cricket bat.

'So this whole orgasm denial thing isn't bothering you at all?' He knows it's bothering me. But he also knows I will chew through my tongue before I admit that.

'Nah.' I am a crap liar, and I'm hoping keeping my responses short will at least make it less obvious I am lying.

'Oh good. Because I thought it would be fun to explore this a bit while you're staying. I've decided, you can't come until the new year.'

As he turned over and went to sleep I felt my jaw drop

open like a cartoon character. When I worked out how many days that was – four more days of torture and unreciprocated play, assuming he let me come on New Year's Day – I wanted to despair.

'If it's not bothering you so far then I'm sure you'll be fine.'

He had his back to me but I could imagine his smile anyway and it made me want to push him on to the floor. I didn't though. I didn't say anything. I didn't trust myself. And as I – finally – fell asleep my last thought was, *He's joking. He's got to be joking.*

He wasn't joking. By the time I had spent two days trying not to think about not orgasming I was pretty much climbing the walls. I had never really understood how fundamentally important I held being able to come whenever I wanted to and, alas, to paraphrase the song, I really didn't know what I'd got till it was gone. Every casual touch felt torturous. Tom brushing my elbow with his arm as he walked past me made me wet. Showering was a kind of torment with the pressure of the individual droplets of water feeling both amazing and yet, well, frankly not quite amazing enough, thus ultimately just adding to the frustration.

Over the next days Tom came up with ever more exotic ways to orgasm. The amusement he derived from me giving him blow jobs while trembling in frustration seemed to pall a little after the first half a dozen times, so he moved on to different, more fiendish, plans. I was lying on my back on the bed, gagged with knickers wet because I'd been wearing them all day, glaring up at the sexy yet irritating view of him wanking in my face when I realized: I am not a naturally abstemious type. While I wouldn't call it a hard limit – mainly because I wouldn't give Tom the satisfaction – orgasm denial was not something that I was going to be encouraging as an ongoing part of our sexual repertoire. As he came across my face and in my hair, stroking my cheek in a gesture that would have felt tender at any other time but actually made me clamp my teeth down on the damp fabric in my mouth to try and restrain my inner fury, I made a decision that one way or another I was not waiting much longer to come.

I was also realizing that the thing about Thomas that made him simultaneously fun and irritating to play with was that he knew me so well, sometimes even better than I knew myself. He knew how far to push – usually just further than I would have been comfortable going – and he watched intently as I did every sexy, demeaning thing he demanded I do, to see the feelings playing across my face as I battled with whether to submit or not, secure in the knowledge that eventually I would. He could also read me better than most people I know. In part because I'm fairly forthright, although the fact I'm a terrible liar and find it difficult to hide my feelings at the best of times probably helped. So I should have known really that he was pushing me, raising the stakes. If I'd thought about it logically it made perfect sense. However, after four days without orgasm I was so distracted I had regressed to a sometimes-weepy, sometimes-furious bundle of nerve endings. Stringing a sentence together was difficult, something particularly embarrassing for someone whose job relied on just that. I was blunt to the point of rudeness, grumpy, and probably rotten to be around, but for all that Thomas kept smiling – and was blatantly enjoying having such power to mess with my equilibrium, which just made me more cross again.

Enough was enough. By the time we'd gone to bed after another perfectly civilized evening, spent eating a leisurely supper followed by me curling up to read with the dog sat on my feet while Tom pottered on the internet and MSN, I was ready to pretty much spontaneously combust. We lay in bed together, on our backs with Tom's arm around my shoulder and his finger tracing along the curve of my neck. Despite my best efforts even this most innocuous of touches was making my breathing ragged, a fact that – of course – he was more than aware of.

'You seem a little shivery there,' he said as one particular movement strayed close to the point on my neck where – if stroked – I purr embarrassingly like a rather contented kitten. 'Are you OK?'

I'm not an idiot. I knew that he wanted to hear exactly how he was affecting me, knew that the whole pretending-everything-was-fine thing was not going to cut the mustard and that, if I wanted to come before next year, I had to explain precisely how frustrated and desperate to orgasm I was before I had any hope at all of being able to do just that. I knew that. But it still chafed. Yes, I know, I had given him that power over me. Yes, I know he knew everything I was going to say. But even so. I swallowed hard.

'I'm fine. Just a bit sensitive.'

His teeth flashed in the dim light of the room. 'Really? How come?'

Huh. It'd be so much easier to say this stuff if he wasn't so irritating in victory. And yes, I appreciate effectively this is a victory I give him, but honestly, he was three steps away from a dance of joy.

My teeth were gritted. 'You know why.' Damn. I was going for suppliant, respectful and desperate. How had two sentences made me suddenly revert to grumpy, stubborn type?

'Humour me.'

This would be why I end up reverting to type. I closed my eyes, knowing I had to do this. That this was the least that I would have to do. Suck it up. Get it over with. I sighed.

'OK. You win. You know I've been desperate to come for days, right? All I can think about is you fucking me, your teeth nipping at my clit, your finger exploring my arse . . .' I tailed off, losing my train of thought as my throat went suddenly dry at the thought of everything we could do, my body aching with the need for release. Suddenly aware I'd stopped talking, I cleared my throat and tried again. 'I've been trying to hide it, but we both know that I'm desperate to come, that it is all I've been thinking about for days, that my body is crying out for it.' He trailed a finger along my collarbone and a deep and involuntary shudder of need passed through my body in a way that made my cheeks heat. My voice was tremulous as I continued. 'So, yes. I know we're still days away from your deadline, but I thought you should know that I'm pretty much begging you. I'm sure you must realize that I'd do pretty much anything right now if you let me come.'

He chuckled. 'Anything encompasses a lot of things, Sophie. And while that makes me tempted to play with you tonight and explore exactly what that means –' at this my internal monologue started singing the 'Hallelujah' chorus '– you realize that you're agreeing to let me push you completely out of your comfort zone? How desperate are you to come? Do you really mean anything?'

The small voice in the back of my head was counselling caution but frankly the rest of my body was desperate enough to agree to anything, although I still had to swallow my nerves before I could speak. I moved my hand down to begin stroking his already semi-hard cock. 'Within the things we've agreed previously, yes, I'm agreeing to anything.'

If my life had a soundtrack, there would have been a dramatic sinister chord there, but instead 'Song 2' by Blur began to play, which was a bit disconcerting until through my lust-addled mind I realized it was Tom's mobile phone ringtone.

And then I felt a surge of fury as he picked it up.

Don't get me wrong. I'm one of those irritating people surgically attached to their mobile, too. I like to pretend it's because I'm often on-call for work, but actually it's not. I like to be in contact with people; in control, if you like. My phone charges in the room where I sleep, is on my person when I'm awake, it comes on holiday with me, all that stuff. But I like to think if I had my arm round a semi-naked woman trembling with need who had her hand on my cock and had just told me she would do anything I wanted her to as long as I let her orgasm, and my phone rang, I'd let it go to voicemail. No. Not Tom. As he picked up and started chatting to whoever it was – the Charlie Brown-style murmuring emerging sounded female, but that was all I could tell – I felt a surge of fury and another of frustration. Tears filled my eyes in over-wrought, desperate annoyance as I lay against him, his free hand still tracing along the line of my shoulder even as he continued making small talk. Not only had I just begged him, something which – let's face it – still wasn't getting easier for me despite the fact he enjoyed it so much he was constantly making me do it, I had also just told him I would do anything he wanted, any bloody thing. The voice in my head told me to shove his arm off, get up, get my clothes on and get out, that this was not playing, this was disrespect pure and simple and a step too far, but I couldn't bring myself to move, which just made me feel weaker and more pathetic and even closer to tears.

And then he said, 'Yes, she's here right now, lying next to me, shuddering with need. As you rang she told me she'd do anything if I let her come this evening. Yep, anything. I know. Luckily I have some ideas for what anything could mean if you're interested in hearing them.'

I turned to try and look at him in the darkness. As I thought, he wasn't talking to me. At the realization of exactly what might happen next my stomach started to lurch. Playing with other people was something we'd said we would only do after extensive prior discussion, but this, this was within the limits. Just. Although, god, the idea of anyone else hearing how desperate I was right now made me flush with shame and horror.

Yup. I'd been well and truly stitched up.

Charlotte was someone Thomas had been talking to for a while. She was funny, sarcastic and exactly the kind of person you could imagine having a laugh with over a few drinks in real life. While they hadn't played together in person yet, I knew Thomas had been chatting to her a lot both online and on the phone, with a view to possibly meeting up to play and maybe even dating. This didn't bother me – we'd decided long ago we were never going to date each other, and that our arrangement was something that would come to an end when one or other of us met someone special. And to be honest, I had seen Tom date some truly rotten people in the past, so the idea that he could end up with someone who was his equal and who was also submissive was one I welcomed. Plus, I had chatted to her a fair bit myself and she seemed lovely, something he definitely deserved.

But none of this was particularly helping with my equilibrium as Thomas explained to her in explicit details exactly what had been happening over the last few days. Listening to him explain made me feel furious and embarrassed and then – worst of all and yet so inevitably – aroused.

'. . . Oh yes, she was sopping, she was so wet. No, I didn't touch her, I just made her take her knickers off so I could gag her with them . . .'

I could get up and walk out.

'. . . It was so cute, we were in the queue at the cash-point and I brushed a finger along the side of her breast. Yeah, accidentally on purpose.' I gritted my teeth. I knew it. 'You could see her nipples through her top within a second, and her eyes were all wistful. Yeah, she looks amazing – it's like she's glaring at me because she wants to murder me, but there's an undertone of lust that she can't shake that means she'll endure the rest in the hope I'll let her come . . .'

Actually I could just kill him now with a shoe. That worked too.

'. . . Yeah and she bites her lip. It's like she's trying to stop herself from speaking or whimpering or giving her-self away. She doesn't realize the little half sighs she can't suppress, or the little tremors of her body. It's amazing. Right now, I control every aspect of her. Even that . . .'

I was furious. But I stayed. Because even while I was embarrassed and shy and unsure about what was going to happen next, even as my mind rebelled against the idea of having given him such control, let alone him bragging about it to someone else, I began to realize he was right; I knew this could be something fun, something challen-ging, something amazing. He was listening to her intently. And then he chuckled and I zoned back into the conver-sation. 'That's a pretty evil idea, you know.' My stomach dropped and I huddled closer into him to try and hear what she was saying. I realised as I moved forward that I was also rubbing myself against him desperately, my hand still on his cock, albeit shaking slightly now.

He knew what I was doing, and his hand in my hair

pulled me away, making it clear it wasn't going to wash. His hand tightened into a fist and I began twisting my body to move the way he was urging me to, to minimize the pain in my stinging scalp. He pulled me until my head was level with his crotch and then pushed me down. He let go of my hair only to put a hand over the phone's mouthpiece to say, 'Come on. Suck me. I'm discussing with Charlotte how – or if – I'm going to let you come. Doing a good job is only going to work in your favour.'

As I obeyed and began sliding my lips up and down, enjoying the texture of him on my tongue, he moaned slightly. Charlotte said something and he replied, 'Yes, she's got her mouth round me now. It feels amazing. She's good, very enthusiastic.'

I blushed in the darkness, but irritatingly felt a surge of pride in spite of myself. I tried to brush it off by focusing on the task at hand, only half listening to his conversation until I heard him say, 'So, you're touching yourself now listening to this? That's very rude indeed. I don't know that you should get to come this evening either.'

I heard a plaintive tone from the other end of the phone and then – I swear – the sound of Thomas's brain ticking.

'In fact, I think maybe we should make it a bit of a challenge. Maybe I'll let one of you come. Just one of you. You can each try and persuade me as best you can and the winner gets to come.'

I could hear loud disagreement from the other end of the phone, although frankly I already felt a sense of injustice and fear – I knew if there was a choice between the two of us he would be more likely to let Charlotte come than me, and after all these days and the humiliation of this phone conversation, the prospect of spending another night unsatisfied was too much to bear. I began sucking him deeper into my mouth.

He laughed. 'Oh, Sophie's pulling out all the stops. I'm practically ball-deep now.' He murmured in pleasure and stroked my hair. 'Oh, that is very good indeed. You'd have to go some to beat that.'

My heart began to beat faster at his words, and at the feeling of his hand touching the curve of my arse, moving ever closer to where I was desperate for him to be. And then I felt him harden even further in my mouth. 'Oh Charlotte, I do love to hear you beg.' Shit. Begging? I had no hope. While his amusement at hearing me beg meant I spent way more time doing it than I ever anticipated, the fact remained I was not a natural beggar. In fact, if anything, I was a grudging and slightly grumpy one. Shit.

I began gently stroking Thomas's balls with my fingers while taking him further into my mouth. I'm always a keen giver of blow jobs, but even for me this was unprecedented. I could hardly breathe I was taking him so deep. His hand on my arse, stroking me gently, was both soothing and distracting. I could feel my juices pooling between my legs, hating to think what sort of picture I must have made.

He explained to Charlotte exactly what I was doing to him. At one point he interrupted his conversation to tap me on the arse and urge me to take him further into my mouth. I was so focused on doing the best I could that it was only when I heard him say, 'She is especially submissive tonight, actually. Normally I'd have expected her to disagree with some of this or at least glare as she obeyed me, but she's so desperate to come she really does seem happy to do anything,' that I zoned back into the conversation.

That's when he said again that Charlotte was evil. I soon found out why. And he was right, she was.

My jaw was aching by the time he'd been on the phone for half an hour. I could hear him teasing Charlotte, taunting her, making her beg, and in spite of myself it made me wet, made me wish I could hear the proof of her submission somehow in the same way she could hear mine. And boy could she hear mine.

Once Thomas had finished telling her how submissive I was being he held the phone out and had me tell her. I had to explain exactly why I was so wet, what a slut I was to enjoy being treated this way. And I did it all, with a throat clogged with tears of humiliation, although I didn't think to disobey. He made me tell her that I would do anything to get to come this evening and then, once I had and he had gone back to having the phone against his ear, he clarified it further.

'She said anything. Anything. And I think she'd obey anything pretty much now. Seriously. Listen.'

He ordered me to crawl down the bed to worship his feet. The toe thing was still the thing he made me do that I hated most but – heaven forgive me – I was so desperate to come that I began to move without hesitation, until he grabbed my hair to stop me.

'Actually Sophie, before you do that, beg me to let you lick my toes.'

'What?' I snapped. I couldn't help myself.

'Beg me. You're going to beg to lick and suck and worship my feet and if you do it well then I will let you. And when you put your mouth around my toes if you are a good girl I'll push a finger inside you. I wonder how wet I'll find you when I do.'

I whimpered. I knew the humiliating answer to that and both yearned for and dreaded the moment when he felt it for himself.

Thankful for the darkness in the room that meant I didn't have to look him in the eyes, I asked him if I could worship his feet. He pulled my hair back and demanded I speak up so Charlotte could hear clearly.

With a voice filled with loathing and tears I just about managed a second go. 'Please, I am begging you to let me suck your toes.'

'Just to suck my toes?'

God, I hated him. God, he made me wet.

'No, to kiss them, to lick them. I want to worship your toes. All of your feet.' I was hoping I'd got most eventualities covered, but every word was laced with aggression and frustration so I thought I'd better moderate my tone a little: 'Please.'

He patted the side of my face, a gesture of tenderness which made everything else seem a little easier to bear, for a second, until he spoke again. 'You may.'

Thank fuck. I crawled down and pushed my face into his toes, steeling myself for the first taste as I heard him give Charlotte a running commentary. As I pulled his big toe into my mouth and began running my tongue up and down it, he explained to her how greedily I was taking it, and pushed his foot in further. He told her how he was making me clean him up properly by wiping his feet on my face and demanding I licked his soles. I heard her shriek in disgust and then giggle at my predicament – her words indistinct but the tone of her amusement carrying loudly across the room.

Silent tears dripped from my eyes as I did what he asked, unwilling to show him how far he'd pushed me but still desperate to continue. As he pushed one finger up inside my knickers I gasped, and he took the opportunity to push his foot further into my mouth.

As I focused on the feeling of his finger between my folds I heard him say, 'She's dripping, she's so wet. It's not going to take much to push her over the edge.' And then, after the mumbling sound of Charlotte saying something at her end of the line he stopped and pulled his hand out. As I whimpered in frustration round his foot and he wiped his wet hand on my arse he said, 'That's a great idea.' My blood chilled.

'Sophie? You can stop now.'

Normally those words would fill me with joy. As it was I was filled with terror. Would I get to come? Would I be able to stop myself from bursting into tears if I was going to be left frustrated? What was a good idea? If they were going to let me come, what were they going to do with me that was worse than the foot thing? Would I be willing to let them to do anything? Would I rather go without? Could I rather go without? Almost-hysterical thoughts ran through my mind of all the horrible things they could do to me, could make me do. I knew, if there was anything utterly terrible I could refuse, end the game, except in that moment I had no intention of doing that. I was a hostage to my own desperate needs. The possibilities terrified me. And in the end what they came up with between them was something that hadn't even crossed my – let's admit it – pretty twisted mind.

It was Charlotte's idea, something that one day I will properly thank her for in person – preferably by watching her have to go through exactly the same thing. As Thomas told me what I was to do I shut my eyes and pressed my lips together, shaking my head in silent rebellion, unwilling and unable to consider doing it. As the silence lengthened I realized this was it, that if I didn't do this I wasn't getting to come. For long seconds I tried to think of another way. Anything else I could. But slowly, grudgingly, I accepted my fate.

And then I moved into position.

I knelt straddling one of his legs, looking through the darkness at him lying propped up slightly on the pillows with the phone to one ear, thinking that if I could only just see him then at least he would only vaguely be able to see me. I'd like to say that helped, but actually it didn't. I knelt there for a couple of seconds, unwilling to continue, even while in my head I had already surrendered to the knowledge that I would be doing so. That I was, right now, going to hump his leg like an animal to get my orgasm.

One of the things I find particularly interesting about the D/s dynamic is that it pushes you to do things that otherwise you might not do. Not because you don't want to do them – so often you really, really do want to – but because they're things that you think might be hot/fun/interesting/unusual but that a small part of your mind baulks at, for some reason – whether that's because you feel it's 'dirty', or it's too embarrassing, or you're worried your arse'll look like a small country or whatever. I love that I can be pushed past the small part of my mind that feels that to experience these amazing new things is wrong. And, no, that's not being pushed into doing something I don't want to do, coerced or whatever – my body simply reacts before my mind has a chance to catch up; my body betrays the fact that it's something I'm into even if my eyes or words might for a time not make that obvious, and even if I can't exactly explain why or how it's making me wet. It's more about someone knowing how far I'd like to go and helping me find the courage to go for it.

Thomas did that, often seemingly (and irritatingly) without effort. Mainly he made it happen by striking a chord with my stubborn side, where my response is to think, 'No, I *am* going to do this, you can't come up with anything I don't feel comfortable doing,' even while I feel hideously uncomfortable. Generally I enjoy that dichotomy, enjoy being pushed out of my comfort zone, doing things that make my stomach drop with nerves and make me blush with fury and embarrassment even as I get wet. But leg humping? Suddenly I was thinking fondly of his bloody feet. I hated it. Hated the idea of it. The indignity, the awkwardness of the angle I'd need to grovel at to actually do it, the fact I'd been fantasising about how he'd make me come for five fucking days and instead of it being any of the things I'd thought of, I'd have to do it myself. And not in a lovely way, not curled up with my hand between my legs, or with my favourite toy from the drawer, but humping him like a bitch on heat. I felt rooted to the bed. I couldn't do this. I couldn't.

'Are you feeling embarrassed? Like you don't want to do this?' His voice had a sing-song mocking quality which was blatantly due to him playing to our telephonic audience. It made me feel murderous. OK, more murderous.

I cleared my throat and started to answer, my voice stuttering and unsure, but he interrupted me. 'I don't care. I've ordered you to hump my leg. We both know you're going to do it eventually one way or another because if you don't then you're not getting another chance to come before New Year, so if I were you I'd make it easier for yourself and start.'

So. I humped him.

Fine, there's more to it than that. A lot more. And I'm not that much of a tease. But actually, honestly, even writing about it makes me feel prickly with embarrassment, a little sick with humiliation. And let's face it, I'm hardly shy about this stuff.

I hated it. Not in a 'pretending to hate it but secretly quite liking it' way but in an 'I actually hate it so much it is irritating and surprising to me that I might come doing this, bearing in mind how much it bothers me, how much it takes me out of the moment, how much it makes me want to tell Thomas to go fuck himself' way. As I said, I get that only submitting to fun stuff isn't submission and I agree, which is why I didn't push Thomas over and bugger off home to my comfy bed and full toy drawer. But humping his knee, trying to grind myself on it at the right angle to catch my clit and come and end the indignity, even while he was deliberately shifting slightly to stop that happening and prolong my agony, all while (of course) he sat there telling Charlotte how wet I was making his leg, how I was crying and yet my breathing was beginning to increase as I got closer to my orgasm, how desperate I was . . . It made me furious. Flashbacks-for-days-afterwards-and-I-couldn't-think-clearly furious. It wasn't painful, not even that humiliating on paper. It sounds like such a little thing. I humped his leg. But it wasn't a little thing to me, and I still can't get my head round why not, much less explain it. If I started writing about D/s in part because I enjoy the intellectual pursuit of trying to explain what I'm feeling and why the things that arouse me arouse me, then this is the thing that is so unexplainable to me that I may as well try and explain it in Flemish.

So I humped his leg, like an animal, while he gave Charlotte a running commentary of how I was grinding myself against his knee, using the friction to provide my clit with the sensation I needed to come.

I ground myself against him, thinking how low I had sunk, how degraded and humiliated I had become in pursuit of my pleasure. Tears streamed down my face, trickling down my chin to cool my chest. I was flushed with embarrassment, thankful for the darkness which hid the worst of it. Practically speaking, it was an awkward position to get any kind of stimulation from. Thomas was lying with his legs flat on the bed, and only by spreading mine widely around him and bending myself low to the bed could I even get close enough to his knee to push myself against him with the level of pressure I needed to get close to coming. I tried, oh how I tried, desperate to have this end, for me to have my orgasm and for this to be over.

Now you'd think that after five days of no orgasms, all that time I'd thought about sex, and how desperate and aching I was, that I would have come quickly. But, of course, the mind is a funny, twisted and occasionally horrible thing. Knowing Charlotte was listening to me doing this humiliating thing, hearing my moans and gasps of pleasure as – in spite of my humiliation and my horror – I became wetter and more aroused and vociferously, shamefully took pleasure from Thomas's knee, made me falter, as did hearing Tom tell her how he could hear the sound of me sliding against his knee, I had made him so wet. I tried blocking it all out, tried grinding harder, but I couldn't get the pressure I needed to bring myself off and end it.

'I can't –' I swallowed back some tears and some snot, cleared my throat and tried again. 'This angle isn't going to work. I'm not going to be able to come like this.'

'Well, what do you want me to do about that?' he sneered. 'You know what you have to do, and I'll be honest, I'm getting impatient now at having you grinding on me, making my whole leg wet. I'd hurry up if I were you.'

The thought of having gone through all this and still not getting to come made fear cramp my stomach.

'Your knee, if you could just raise your knee a little bit, that would make it easier. Please.'

I thought I saw his teeth flash in the darkness. 'Are you begging me to move my knee to make it easier for you to hump it now?'

There was a pause. I had to moisten my lips with my tongue before I could speak and even then my voice was wavering and filled with tears. Normally I'd have prevaricated, tried to avoid this, but frankly I was broken, desperate, haunted. Every fibre of my being was desperate to come. 'Yes. Yes, I'm begging you.'

'Good. Well beg me properly, louder, so Charlotte can hear exactly how desperate you are, so desperate you're rubbing yourself against me like an animal on heat.'

My hands were clenched tightly, my fingernails digging into my palms as my voice filled the room. 'I am begging you. Please, lift your knee a little bit so I can grind against it—'

He interrupted me. 'No, "hump it".'

I sighed but didn't even pause. 'Hump it until I come on your knee. Please.'

As he pushed his knee up, with force enough it bashed against my pubis in a way that zinged through me like a welcome electric shock, his voice was smug. 'There. That wasn't so difficult was it? Now make yourself come for me.'

The change in angle made all the difference. Suddenly the movement of my hips against the delicious friction of his knee was rubbing perfectly against my clit. I tried to block out as he told Charlotte how suddenly I had started bucking like a madwoman, more desperate than ever, tried to ignore the sound of my arousal as I slid up and down against his knee, tried to block out everything but the pleasure beginning to thrum through my body, tried to overcome all the obstacles between me and the release I had been craving for the best part of a week.

I was crying in humiliation and horror by the time my orgasm neared although, inevitably, it didn't slow me down. As the shudders began running through me my sobs got louder. I spasmed around Thomas's leg, like an animal, my high-pitched cries loud enough for Charlotte to hear down the phone. After days of pent-up frustration my release was body-juddering and intense. Never in my life have I felt an orgasm like it, and for a second or two afterwards my world went dark as I lay there, my limbs trembling with the force of it. Once I came back to myself, I became aware of Thomas wanking above me. I went to crawl up his body, but he stopped me with a tut.

'I don't think so. You need to clean your mess first.'

I knew what he meant and it should have filled me with fury but my head space was such that without demur I crawled over and began licking his knee, well, actually, most of his leg. I had managed to make him sticky from his mid-thigh down to his lower shins, much to my shame. I kept licking as he told Charlotte what I was doing. I kept licking as he rubbed himself, aroused by and enjoying this final humiliation. I kept licking as he came on the side of my face and into my hair. Finally, he dripped down my cheek, he held the phone closer to my ear and I heard Charlotte orgasm.

Yes. The first time I heard Charlotte on the phone she was coming. Even I will concede my world is at times an odd one. It was a bloody memorable Christmas holiday though.

9

Of course, if listening to someone you've never spoken to before orgasm on the phone is a slightly odd experience, then meeting her for a beer a few weeks later is, well, even more disconcerting really.

Thomas had been chatting regularly on one of the online communities and when they organized a 'munch' he was keen to go along and say hello to everyone. Once I realized that a munch was essentially a gaggle of people going out for drinks and possibly dinner, and that he wasn't signing me up to an evening strapped naked to a St Andrew's cross being flayed by random people as they walked past to go to the buffet table, I was happy to join him. Especially when I realized it meant I could meet Charlotte, and thank her for the whole humping thing, in person.

So one Sunday afternoon we went to a pub in a leafy suburb, and had a beer and a lovely roast dinner – there's nothing better than pork with crackling and home-made Yorkshire puddings – with a couple of dozen interesting and kinky people.

The first thing of note was that, well, most people weren't really of note. Now, I don't mean that it in a rude or disparaging way, but more that if I'd seen them walking down the street I would never have pegged them as being smutty types. They were all casually dressed (no gimp masks or PVC to be found), intelligent, articulate, warm people just having a chat and getting to know each other.

Being a people watcher, I enjoyed guessing where things would develop. Carol and Neil, a couple from up north who had moved down when Neil got a good job as a deputy head in a school just outside the city, were chatting animatedly and with a fair amount of dirty-sounding laughter with Bev and Ian, who owned a business importing sustainable furniture from China. Meanwhile Ciara, who had been single for a while and had spent months merrily telling everyone that, actually, she preferred it that way until she found someone special to play with, was fiddling with her glass and smiling widely while chatting to Jo in a way that made me hope she might have actually found what she'd been looking for. Thomas meanwhile was moving from group to group, chatting comfortably with loads of different people in the way he often does. I'm a little envious of his ability to chat engagingly with almost anyone; despite being able to hold up my end of polite conversations in work situations, I'm not naturally chatty and given half a chance would be sitting in the corner with a couple of people I know rather than, to use the vernacular, working the room.

Not that I was given half a chance to be anything even remotely resembling a wallflower. Charlotte made a bee-line for us when she entered the beer garden, and when she came over, took my hand and pulled me up and into a hug, my fingers tingled. Her touch was cool and firm. Her grip was stronger than I'd anticipated and she held my hand longer than expected as she looked into my eyes. Suddenly I was buzzing – and it wasn't from the glass of Shiraz I'd been nursing for most of the afternoon.

The spark surprised me. I'd had a bit of a bisexual phase at university and had slept with a few women since, but it was rare for me to feel such an intense attraction to someone I'd just met. I could see why Thomas was attracted to her. She was stunning. Elfin features, green eyes, a short haircut which showed off the nape of her neck.

I'm a sucker for the nape of the neck. There are other places you could stroke which would make me squirm faster and harder, but for my money the neck is an overlooked erogenous zone. I wanted to stroke her there and see if it made her squirm. I wanted to kiss my way down to her shoulders, pull open her shirt and work my way further down until I was in a position to find out whether her hair colour was natural.

As we sat making small talk I learned little things about her that made me like her more. She was intelligent and quick-witted and we had similar taste in everything from a love of cheesy popcorn flicks to a shared loathing of Dan Brown. She had a dirty laugh and the way she licked her lips every time she took a sip from her vodka and Coke made me think very rude things indeed. I had to restrain the urge to forget our surroundings and lean over to run my own tongue over her mouth.

By the time we'd eaten lunch we were firm friends, although I still hadn't forgiven her for the humping, much to her amusement. Thomas stopped mingling and came to sit with us in time for some dessert and a fair amount of smutty flirtation and mocking. The dynamic was fun, comfortable and – barring the teasing that saw me nicknamed Humpy for part of the afternoon and blushing accordingly – rather sexy.

Charlotte was unconsciously, unfussily, attractive, with the kind of carefree doesn't-give-a-shit attitude that was both refreshing and made her beauty all the more natural and appealing. Whether she was absent-mindedly playing with her hair as she talked or gesticulating wildly while doing an impression of her boss, everything she did was honest and raw and emotive – and, frankly, sexy as hell. As the wine flowed more freely, she told me exactly how things had felt from her end of the phone conversation, gnawing slightly on her full lower lip as she told me how hot I had sounded begging Thomas to firstly let me kiss his feet and then let me come.

I flushed as the memories of what I had said, how desperate I had felt, flooded through my mind, and suddenly the atmosphere round our table shifted imperceptibly. I felt my nipples harden, but seeing Charlotte's had done the same beneath her pale blouse made me feel slightly less self-conscious. We looked at each other, recognized our mirrored predicament, both moved to put our arms across our chests, and giggled, embarrassed co-conspirators. I shifted slightly in my seat, my hair falling in front of my face as I moved, hiding the worst of my blush, but she moved forward to tuck a strand behind my ear. She stroked my hair and I blushed harder, resisting the sudden urge to turn my head and kiss her fingers. Thomas watched our exchange intently, but said nothing.

Of course, Thomas not expressing an opinion on something is pretty much a sign of impending apocalypse and only lasts for a finite period of time. After we'd dropped Charlotte off at the station and were in the car heading back to his house he was more relentless than Jeremy Paxman after a bag of Haribo.

'You seemed to get on really well. Did you like her?'

'Did you find her attractive?'

'Did her touching your face and stroking your hair like that make you wet?'

'Did you want to kiss her?'

By the time we'd got back to his house I was ready to burst.

'Yes! I liked her. She was sexy and lovely and fun. Happy? Now will you shut up?'

I know. It was an uncharacteristically pissy response. The thing is, I bet you're thinking it's because I was jealous of Thomas turning his attention to someone else. In a way, that would make sense. But I wasn't jealous about Charlotte potentially getting to play with my dom-with-benefits; actually, I was a little grumpy about the idea of him getting to play with her. I liked her.

In the weeks that followed, Thomas continued chatting to Charlotte, and they met a couple of times. It gave me some pause for thought. Their relationship wasn't developing into a monogamous dating-type arrangement yet – the first giveaway was Thomas happily tying me down with a plug in my arse, caning me and fucking me a couple of days after he told me they had first slept together – but somehow the dynamic between us was changing a little and I began to think about the fact that there might come a time when we had to stop playing together. While I know lots of people who are happy with more casual relationships, polyamory and the like, I just didn't think that was me, or Thomas for that matter. At the same time a job came up nearer home, and I applied for and got it, much to both mine and my family's glee. Suddenly I wasn't going to be living near enough to Tom to pop over of a weekend, even if he was free enough to host. The times they were a-changin'.

Every time I submitted to him in that period between handing in my notice and making the big move it felt more intense – with a small voice whispering that it might be the last time he clamped my nipples, or the last time he used his belt on me, the last time he fucked my arse. Meanwhile we talked about Charlotte often – both in the bedroom, when he would whisper filthy comments that made me wet about what it would be like if she was in the room with us, and outside it. I talked to her directly a fair bit too, but apart from a flirty evening where we went out for drinks it was all fairly innocent.

Until the bank holiday weekend, the last weekend before I moved back to the city.

We'd made plans to get together for a barbecue at Thomas's house. The weather was gorgeous, and Charlotte and I had both brought stuff to stay over so we could have a drink without worrying about having to get home.

The afternoon was lazy. Charlotte and I lay in the garden, enjoying the warmth of the sun on our skin and trying for a bit of a tan, while Thomas threw a Frisbee for the dog, fired up the barbecue and pottered about, seemingly incapable of staying still. We ate a leisurely meal and then lingered at the table talking about nothing in particular, taking advantage of the good weather.

As the light changed and the shadows lengthened, the talk turned flirtier. Charlotte told me she loved my breasts in the vest top I'd been wearing to tan my shoulders. I leant over to wipe some stray potato salad from her mouth. Meanwhile Thomas sat, watching steadily, his gaze assessing us in a way that normally meant only one thing.

In typical fashion he took the initiative, although I wondered if in part that was because he'd had similar conversations with Charlotte to the ones he'd had with me. In further typical fashion, he was characteristically blunt. Really blunt. In an 'I wish I could make this sound more alluring than it was' sort of way.

'Shall we all go upstairs and fuck?'

Charlotte and I looked at each other and burst out laughing. She pulled my hand into hers and smiling at me said, 'I think I'd quite like that.'

I rolled my eyes. 'Well with an offer like that, who could say no?' But inside I was giddy.

Thomas sprang into action with all the energy of a natural planner – he'd definitely given this some thought. Stacking up the plates to take indoors, he told me to go upstairs and strip and wait for them on my hands and knees on the bed facing away from the door. While the idea of being the first one naked made me feel rather embarrassed, I knew that disobeying at this juncture would stall things before they started, as well as – let's face it – potentially store up trouble for myself later on in the process.

I nodded and went upstairs to his bedroom.

I'm not a patient person. Kneeling there, obediently waiting for the bedroom door to open, my stomach filled with butterflies and my nipples already erect at the prospect of what was to come, took all my self-control. There was no clock to look at, I wasn't wearing a watch, and it felt like ages. How long did it take to load a dishwasher anyway?

By the time I heard movement I was half convinced they had started downstairs without me and was pondering whether I could tiptoe downstairs quietly enough to not disturb them and see. Thankfully I didn't as then, finally, the door opened. It took all my self-control not to look round, but I knew I did so at my peril. Instead I stared intently at the pattern on the bedcover in front of me, while listening for any noise which might give a hint of what would happen.

The only thing I heard was . . . a quiet creaking?

As Charlotte walked to stand beside me, I realized why. She'd changed into a gorgeous leather corset, which she was wearing with knickers and stockings only. My throat felt dry. She was stunning and her elaborate outfit made me feel even more self-conscious in my nakedness.

Thomas walked round to the other side of the bed, pausing to stand opposite her, leaving me in the middle, not sure where to look first, or even if I should be looking anywhere other than down at the fixed point on the coverlet of the bed. Finally, when it felt like the silence would never end, Thomas broke it.

'Are you ready?'

I opened my mouth to reply, but before I could Charlotte did. 'Yes.'

'Good girl. Just remember what we discussed.'

Before I could even begin to unravel what that meant, Thomas was moving to the foot of the bed. Standing directly in front of me, he took my chin in his hand, pushing my face up to look into his eyes. 'You want to please me, don't you? Obey me?'

My usual feelings of wanting to please and yearning for a challenge to overcome were still there, but overshadowed by a fear in the pit of my stomach that I was about to be asked to do something more intense than I could imagine. My voice was quiet, betraying my confusion. 'Yes.'

He stroked my hair and for a second the affection of the movement soothed me. Until his words sank in. 'Good. Because right now I am going to sit down and leave you in Charlotte's capable hands. She's always wanted to try her hand at being dominant but lacked the confidence to do so. I told her she could play with you. Try some things out. You should obey her as you would obey me. I'm watching.'

And with that he moved to sit on the comfy chair in the corner of the room which was normally covered with clothes but had, I now noticed, been cleared off for the occasion.

As Charlotte moved towards me I felt a surge of fury

and confusion. What the fuck was he playing at? Did she really think I'd submit to her? And since when did she want to dominate anyone anyway? It would seem I didn't know Charlotte as well as I'd thought.

She crouched down a little to meet my eyes. 'You're going to hump my leg tonight, Sophie,' she told me.

Mentally I rolled my eyes. It would seem Charlotte didn't know me as well as she thought either. My tone was mocking. 'You think so? That's sweet. Wrong, but very sweet.'

There is a whole subculture of submissive women that focus on being contrary, disobedient, brattish. Women who enjoy acting out of line, so they can be pulled back into it, punished into submission. Now don't get me wrong, I'm as fond of being overpowered by someone stronger than me as the next woman, but generally where I can obey I will do. There are things I baulk at and will do grudgingly and with embarrassment, but for the most part my submission is more about doing something to please the person I am playing with. I'm not, generally, a brat.

But looking up at Charlotte, even dressed in that gorgeous corset which did such amazing things to her body, something clicked in my mind. I can be pretty stubborn at the best of times, but this was different, stronger than that. I was adamant. I was not going to submit to her just because Thomas said I should.

Does that make me a bad sub? A disobedient one? Probably, yes. But let's face it, it's not as if through the entire process I'd been the Stepford Sub and this was suddenly a break away from the norm. In my mind my submission is a gift, something to be earned, and while I gave it freely to Thomas, the idea of giving it to Charlotte, even at his behest, brought me up short.

I stared back at her steadily, not exactly glaring, but not looking in any way submissive. It was a look I knew I would never get away with in front of Thomas, but frankly I didn't give a toss.

Neither of us spoke. Out of the corner of my eye I could see Thomas smiling slightly. I was fearful he would intervene, and not entirely sure how I would respond if he pushed this whole 'submitting to her is submitting to him' line. But he seemed amused more than anything else and keen to see how things would play out.

Slowly, deliberately, Charlotte moved closer. And then she slapped my face. Hard. It stung and I felt myself going red – not just where she'd struck me but across my entire face and neck – in fury and embarrassment at the slight. For a split second I thought about slapping her back, but before the germ of the thought could flourish she'd grabbed a handful of my hair and yanked me towards her to kiss me.

I had spent a long time wondering what kissing Charlotte would be like, but I had never expected it to be like this. She tasted of mint and smelled of flowers, but while her lips were as soft as I had fantasized they would be, her hand in my hair and the way she kissed me made me whimper a little as she took control of the kiss, and of me. Her tongue pushed inside me, her teeth nipped at my mouth, her hand pulled my hair, bending me to her will until I was compliant underneath her.

She pulled away and the spell was broken. I knew I was gaping at her a little, my mouth swollen from her kisses, and her teeth. As she moved her hand back to my face it took all my self-control not to flinch, betraying my nerves. But I had nothing to fear; instead of slapping me again, she stroked my face gently.

'We'll see, shall we?'

In all honestly, at that moment I had no recollection at all of what she was talking about. Instead my mind was reeling at this gorgeous woman who I was beginning to think I might have underestimated.

As she stroked my hair her voice had taken on a different timbre too. It wasn't a dom voice – or I suppose technically a domme voice – in Thomas's style, but she was assured and unwavering. She had no doubts that whatever she was going to do would make me submit, and that made me nervous. What the fuck had the two of them been discussing over the same weeks Thomas was asking me whether thoughts of her breasts made me wet?

'We've been talking about you, Sophie. About how stubborn you can be. How disobedient.'

I bloody knew it.

'The thing is, Sophie, I don't intend to have you disobey me. I think you want to obey me, deep down. And I'm going to make sure that you do.'

I closed my eyes for a few seconds so she didn't see me rolling them.

'We talked about what to do when you don't obey.'

Eyes opened now, I kept looking ahead, trying to zone out a little. I wasn't expecting her to be able to push my emotional buttons quite this easily, and had no intention of rising to her bait.

'So tell me. What does Thomas do when you do things you're not supposed to?'

In spite of myself I began to feel myself blush. I knew what I was supposed to say and I was a little concerned now at the prospect of disobeying her. But I hated admitting this stuff aloud at the best of times. Saying it to her then, like that? The dual submission – not just to her but to the part of me that wanted this, needed this, gets turned on by the humiliation of it – stuck in my throat.

As I tried to gather my thoughts she slapped me again. In my peripheral vision I saw Thomas move forward to better watch my reaction.

'Answer me. What happens?'

I cleared my throat, wondering why this felt so humiliating, trying hard to soften my tone in a way that didn't betray my emotions.

'He punishes me.'

Her hand twisted in my hair, a tug of warning. 'I didn't hear you.' Fuck, Thomas had told her all his best moves. This woman was dangerous. Part of me loathed her and the other part of me was getting more aroused by the minute.

Louder: 'He punishes me.'

'Better. How does he punish you?'

My temper was rising – she knew how he punished me because he'd told her, no doubt gloating about the things he could get me to do, the things he could do to me. She knew, he knew and I knew and yet she was making me say it out loud because she knew it made me embarrassed. I was angry and I was wet and that I could feel myself getting wetter as I knelt on the bed in front of them only made me more angry.

I tried to hide my annoyance but I could hear the sharpness in my voice. 'It depends. Whip. Belt. Cane. Crop. Hand. Whatever he wants.'

As she moved away from me and the link between us was broken for a moment, I expelled the breath I hadn't even realized I was holding. For a second the relief was palpable, until she returned, holding something that made my stomach fall.

As she tapped me gently on the shoulder with the cane I began trembling uncontrollably. Surely he wasn't going to let her . . .

'I've always wondered what it feels like to cane someone.'

Shit.

After the first six hits Thomas took pity on me and moved closer to coach her. I'd have been grateful, but I was already weeping and frankly not sure he could do much to help. My mind was reeling at the agony she was inflicting, and I was trying to work out whether she'd either never been on the receiving end of the cane before or had been but hated it so much she wanted to share the misery.

The strikes kept going as Tom coached her on the best way to hit me, when to flick from the wrist, when to use the full arm. The angle to take. How to mix between hitting places you've hit before and hitting new places so you can watch the varying reactions to the different kinds of pain. When to hold back. When to push harder.

The pauses meant it was difficult to process the pain, as there was no rhythm to it, no way of riding the peaks and troughs. Instead I retreated into it, only half aware of their discussion about the welts on my arse and how long they would take to go down. I listened intently for the swish of the cane through the air, trying to prepare myself for the next wave of agony.

I don't know how long it went on but finally there was respite. Four hands ran over the marks, her fingernails tracing the lines of the hot welts, his fingers brutally squeezing the most punished part until I whimpered. Then, for the most fleeting moment, so gently that I wondered whether I was imagining it, a finger ran up my slit. I moaned in frustration as it moved away.

Her voice was filled with a quiet wonder. 'This is making her wet.'

She sighed in pleasure behind me and Thomas chuckled. 'It's making you wet too.' His voice was pleased. She laughed and I felt a surprising pang of jealousy. Thomas moved to me, running his finger briefly along the ridge between my top lip and my nose, before turning away. My frustration at this briefest of touches burned into an aroused fury a second later when her scent filled my nostrils. Listening to the sound of them kissing, touching, fucking even, inches away from me, knowing the wetness drying on my face was her juice, was erotic torture. But I didn't dare sneak a glance. I waited, docile, for them to turn their attentions back to me.

I can't tell you exactly when my mindset changed. It snuck up on me. One minute I was furious and embarrassed and a bit concerned at having submitted to Charlotte, and the next I was completely in the moment and none of that mattered any more.

After she'd finished with the cane, and Thomas had finished with her – for the moment at least – she moved back into my field of vision and picked up the accursed paddle. As my inner monologue wondered for the thousandth time why the fuck I'd thought buying it was a good idea, she stared at the lettering cut into it and smiled.

'So this is the famous slut paddle.'

I looked up to answer as Thomas replied. This keeping silent thing was not a natural state for me.

'This is the one. She hates it. Always concerned I'm going to mark her with it and she's going to end up caught out at the gym.'

Charlotte smiled and I felt a little cramp of fear in my stomach. Had I not noticed the slightly sadistic curve of her lips before? Or had I inspired this? It made me wet and fearful at the same time, even as I knelt there, my arse in the air, waiting for what happened next.

'So it does work then? You can end up effectively branding her with "slut"?'

Thomas laughed. 'Well, I can. Just about. It takes a lot of effort and some big swings though. In a lot of ways it's even more precise than the cane. It only works if you hit her in the right spot, really, really hard.'

As she moved behind me, for a split second I hated him. And then all thoughts except enduring this faded from my mind.

Well, you had to give her marks for trying. She hit me really hard, many times. I couldn't tell you how many, as all I was doing was trying to withstand the blows, to minimize my sobs and contain the worst of my shaking as the loud cracks rained down on my already burning arse. I don't know how effective I was at either if I'm honest.

There was no rhythm to her movements as, when she connected with a crack which she thought had made the mark, she stopped to check her handiwork. I would kneel there, hoping to hell that actually she *had* marked me, just because then at least she would stop. But then she would pick up the paddle and continue and the agony would start again. Suddenly any mental debate about whether I should or could or would submit to her was academic. Somehow, with that punishment, in that room, I was hers. It didn't occur to me to disobey her, although I wished she'd get the mark she wanted so she would stop hitting me.

After a while – a long while – she seemed to get bored trying. She dropped the paddle on the bed and, over my head, told Thomas she'd be back in a moment.

As she left the room he moved closer and crouched down level to my face. As he brushed tears from my cheeks with his thumbs his voice was soothing.

'How are you doing? Are you OK? Are you enjoying this?'

I nodded, pressing my lips together to stop them trembling, unable to even begin explaining in words exactly how I felt, knowing I might be able to after the event but that right now it was simply beyond me.

He smiled at me. 'Good. Because seeing you submit to her for me is so fucking hot. I love that you'll do anything for her because I tell you to.'

The usual running narrator of submission was there, protesting that actually I wouldn't do 'anything', but it was fogged out, pushed away by the sensations, the myriad of tides of pain and the ebbing warmth of the pleasure between my legs. As the door reopened he leaned forward and kissed me, briefly and brutally, and then moved away.

The action surprised me, as did the tenderness of his mouth on mine. But in that moment, that kiss was a reminder of his dominance and it warmed me. Reassured me. Which was particularly good as suddenly he and Charlotte were behind me, as she said: 'I didn't think it could happen, but I got bored of hitting her. Well, actually, I'm not bored, my arm got tired.'

Thomas laughed at the audible pout in her voice. I saw the humour, but didn't even smile as I wanted to know what was coming next.

'I had another idea.'

Shit. This would be what was coming next.

There was a tickling feeling on my arse. After all the punishment I had taken that evening, it should have felt like a welcome change, but actually it was just a different kind of pain. My legs wobbled as it traced across the lines of the cane, the red fire of the paddling. It wasn't hard, but it was focused, like she was tracing her finger along my flesh.

Except I soon realized that it wasn't her finger. Thomas's murmur of appreciation was the first giveaway.

'I like that. Give me a go.'

More pressure, this time on the other arse cheek. A giggle from Charlotte. I tried to turn my head subtly to catch even the briefest glimpse of what they were doing, but my movement caught Thomas's attention and a twist of my nipple made it clear he wasn't allowing any such thing.

He tutted, and then said, 'It would appear Sophie wants to see what we're doing. Should we show her?'

Charlotte giggled again. 'I think we should turn her over and then she can see.'

Between them they manoeuvred me on to my back on the bed, Charlotte making a little 'awwww' of sympathy at my gasp of pain as I first landed on my arse.

She leaned forward to brush some hair out of my eyes, and I was reminded for a second of the smiling girl drinking wine and blushing as we sat in the beer garden.

'I decided that rather than making my arm any more tired than it already was, I would write on you. The effect's the same and it's much simpler, don't you think?'

And then the girl from the beer garden was gone.

By the time they were finished my body was covered in insults, all in a rich, deep red lipstick. My arse marked me 'slut', obviously, but elsewhere I was 'whore', 'bitch', 'slave'. And once they had finished writing on me they mauled me with their hands, amusing themselves by trying to make the lipstick smudge – 'Well, all true sluts have smudged lipstick' – their touch making me writhe in pleasure, in spite of myself.

After a little while Charlotte tired of the game and urged me forward so she could paint my mouth with the sticky, blood-red lipstick. As Thomas stood beside her, I felt a pang at what a stunning couple they made – still dressed (well, she was still in her corset at least), pristine, sexy. I in comparison was a dishevelled mess – naked, covered in lipstick insults and marks from my punishment. The heavily painted red staining on my mouth just finished it off.

As they kissed in front of me, Charlotte urged me forward, gesturing at Thomas.

'On to your knees. I want you to show us how much of him you can take in your mouth. I'll check his cock for how high the mark of your slutty lipstick comes, and if it isn't far enough I'm sure I can force myself to punish you a little more.'

On an ordinary day my inner monologue would have been screaming, but I didn't give a toss. I moved from the bed eagerly, the pain of my arse ignored in my haste to sink to my knees in front of them both. I unzipped his trousers, pulled him out and put my mouth around him, enjoying the taste of him, feeling him grow as I angled my head to suck him deeper. I felt Charlotte move around me and suddenly I could hear the two of them kissing above me, as I kept sucking him. Charlotte's hand slid to my head and she stroked my hair. It was one of the most incongruously arousing things I have ever experienced. Well, at least until they started fucking and I crawled up between them to fasten my mouth round Charlotte's clit.

By the time Thomas had come once and Charlotte twice I was squirming with a desperate need to orgasm myself. All three of us were lying on the bed, Charlotte gently stroking my arm while I pressed a kiss to her stomach.

'Would you like to come, Sophie?'

I opened an eye suspiciously. I knew where this was going, and what was really awful was by this point I had no compunction about it. I knew I would hump her leg if I had to.

'Yes, please.'

Her smile was beautiful and her mouth curved when she leant down to kiss me softly. 'Come on, Sophie, you can do better than that. I've heard you beg before remember. I know how well you do it.'

I flushed as both Thomas and Charlotte turned to look at me. Staring past them a little, I managed to ask them both – I wasn't risking a breach of etiquette at this point in proceedings – in a stammering voice if they would please allow me to come.

Charlotte tutted. 'Are you begging, Sophie?'

I sighed. 'Yes, Charlotte, I'm begging you. Please let me come.'

Charlotte laughed at me. 'I will, if you kiss my arse.'

I'm fairly sure my eyes widened in comedy fashion. 'What?'

'Kiss my arse. And then, actually, I think I'd like to feel your tongue running up between my arse cheeks. If you do that, I'll let you come.'

I was agog. This was something I knew Thomas wasn't

into, would never ask me to do. I'd never worried about doing it, it just wasn't an option.

My body ached, I was so desperate to come. But her arse?

Suddenly, Thomas's voice was loud in my ear. 'I told you, she won't do it. Get her to hump your leg instead.'

I felt a twinge of fury, feeling like a piece of meat, something they could discuss between themselves. Then Charlotte moved closer, kissing me softly on the lips, looking intently at my face.

'Sophie, I could make you hump my leg. You know if I slapped you or picked up that cane again you'd be weeping and begging me to do whatever I wanted very quickly. Between us Thomas and I could hold you down, I could sit my arse on your face, I could force you. But I don't want to force you. I want you to submit to me willingly. I want you to crawl up here and worship my arse, to do something you've never done before and something I've never had anyone do to me before. And while you do it Tom will make you come. I don't want to punish you, but I do want your obedience. Yes, you've been obeying me because Thomas gave you to me –' I wasn't sure this was entirely true but didn't want to interrupt her flow '–but I want you to do this for me. Just me. Now.'

The room was silent and still for a few seconds. I didn't move, but I knew exactly what I was going to do, that I was going to obey her.

I crawled gently down her body and pressed a kiss to her lovely smooth arse. And then as Thomas pushed his fingers deeply inside me I began licking and kissing her in perhaps the most intimate way possible. It was a humiliation I had never considered, but in that room, in that moment, she had convinced me. I submitted for her, not Thomas, to please her, and did so eagerly. She moaned in pleasure, reaching back to stroke my hair, and then I came, gasping and whimpering into her arse as the release juddered through me.

Once my mind-blowing orgasm had dissipated a little, a smiling Charlotte explained the bet that she and Thomas had made. Tom was adamant that she would not be able to get me to rim her and had told her that if she did she would get to fuck me with her newly acquired strap on. If she didn't, then she would be severely punished, ending her turn as top. As we continued long into the night, a tangle of limbs and combinations and some of the sexiest experiences I've ever had, I was very thankful indeed at being inspired to submission.

I did still owe Charlotte some revenge for the whole leg-humping thing, though. On the other hand, she and Thomas both helped me move flat the following weekend, so she gets brownie points for that.

10

The move was both a long time coming and something
that happened ridiculously quickly. I'd been at my paper
for almost three years. The nature of regional journalism
is very much that wages start low and don't get too much
better unless you can get promoted. There's a straightforward process to go from trainee to senior reporter, and
the next obvious step if you want to stay in the same company is to go for a specialism or move into management,
the first rung of which is becoming a news editor.

I genuinely loved my paper, my patch and my newsroom. The people – both my colleagues and the people I
talked to through the course of writing my stories – were,
for the most part, interesting and good natured, and our
news area was big enough that there was always something good going on. But the fact was it wasn't just me
who loved the dynamic of the newsroom. There were no
specialisms available, and the news editor, deputy editor
and editor had around forty years' experience at the paper
between them and weren't going anywhere till it was time
for retirement.

There was no chance of promotion, and while thinking
about leaving made me sad, a couple of things made me
decide it was time – firstly, the fact that my salary, even as
a senior, made for a pretty frugal life once my student

loan, rent and bills were paid, and secondly, that I missed my family more and more. My parents came to visit whenever they could, filling my fridge and taking me out for lunches and clothes shopping when they did in a way that made me hug them even tighter and feel even more bereft when they went home. I popped home for a weekend every couple of months to see them and my brother, but suddenly it didn't feel enough. Every time I saw them my parents seemed a little older – their hair flecked with a little more silver, always an anecdote about a trip to the doctors with a new ailment for one or other of them. I wanted to be closer, to see them more regularly, although I wasn't planning a full return to the nest, as I was pretty sure that the novelty of me moving home would wear off sharpish once they had to live with me full time.

As there were no promotions available I did the next best thing for a journalist wanting to progress their career – I moved to a bigger patch and paper, where the money was slightly better and which, happily, was much closer to my parents. Of course, by the time I'd found somewhere to live the increase in pay had been eaten up, but my mum popped round a couple of times a week with portions of whatever new recipe she'd been trying 'for the freezer' or a cake, which helped me eke my money out (and her lemon cake made me friends in my new newsroom – there's only so much cake one woman can eat, after all).

Apart from the return into my life of epic baked goods and Sunday roasts en famille, the main change brought about by my altered living situation was the amount of time I spent with Thomas. Suddenly it was a few hours' drive to get to his, and my shifts, the costs of petrol and his burgeoning relationship with Charlotte meant we didn't have a lot of time to spend together setting the world to rights while watching DVD box sets in the way we had before. The change took quite some adjustment; it brought me up a little short. I'd enjoyed being with him, and the things we'd done together were fun and filthy milestones for me. But the fact was, I knew I wanted a proper, albeit improper, boyfriend, someone I could potentially live with, go on holiday with, marry, have kids with, all that good stuff. And while I was seeing Thomas every other weekend, having plenty of no-strings rude fun, there wasn't really the impetus to be open to potential new relationships or suitors – it all felt like too much faff, not least because I am the most rubbish person I know when it comes to the rules of dating.

My move felt like a good time to end things. Not our friendship – never that, we had too much in common, had shared too much, and he was and remains one of the kindest-hearted people I know – but the sexual side of our relationship. It made sense. I was moving away, things were getting serious with him and Charlotte, and in our typical no-muss, no-fuss way we decided we should just stop the beneficial side of our friends with benefits relationship.

For me it felt timely. While we'd talked about three-somes for a while, I'd always been a bit wary because, let's face it, sex is pretty much designed at its basest form to be a two-player game, and as such I feared threesomes were ripe for making someone feel left out or overlooked. While the risks were, in my mind at least, reduced because I didn't have the feelings of sexual jealousy that I might have had if it were my boyfriend who was doing filthy yet hot things to another woman right in front of me, the intensity of the threesome was still a bit discombobulating and while I'd enjoyed it, somehow it cemented in my mind the feeling that I was ready to move on from rude fun with someone I trusted to a fully fledged relationship. In addition, while I had by no means felt overlooked, even to my occasionally oblivious eyes the connection between Thomas and Charlotte was strong – it definitely felt the right time for me to take a step back.

Of course, just because it made sense didn't mean that it didn't ache a bit for a while. Moving home is fine and dandy, but you forget in your years away that everyone else has also moved along. What with that, taking a deliberate step away from relying on Tom as my support network and social circle, a new flat and a new job, it's fair to say it took me a while to find my feet.

It's ironic now, but when I first met James, I really didn't like him, although if I'm honest, at that stage I really didn't like anyone. Despite the fact I'd ostensibly moved 'home', I found myself confused by how much I missed Thomas and I was in a bit of an odd funk. We chatted as much as ever, and he was the supportive friend he'd always been. He was chatty, open about his own life – clearly happy with Charlotte, who had begun spending weekends with him in the way I had previously. But it hurt. I was annoyed with him, confused as to whether I should be annoyed with him, annoyed with myself for not knowing if it was right to be annoyed with him, and having constant flashbacks to the things we had done together. It left me feeling both aroused and furious, simultaneously. My brain was always working, trying to understand it. I was exhausted.

I was also mostly a hermit, disinterested in seeing people, going out or making small talk that suggested I was interested in anything other than my misery. Unfortunately, when your job is that of a journalist there are times you get pushed out of the office to do those things, whether you want to or not − and trust me, at that point I really didn't. Despite the new job, bigger patch and increased responsibility, apathy was impacting my work life for the first time, which of course just made me feel worse. However, even in the depths of the doldrums, my new force-of-nature news editor was not going to let me stew too long. Having reminded me several times about an interview I had scheduled for a forthcoming article, in the end she shoved my coat, bag and umbrella into my hands and corralled me towards the door. I was too apathetic to demur, which, I guess, means I only have myself to blame.

He kept me waiting, the man I was to interview. I sat for more than half an hour, seething, in the reception of his posh office building. It was all chrome and glass and minimalist flower arrangements, which looked like bunches of twigs picked up from the side of the road but undoubtedly cost more than I made in a week. By the time he finally did deign to appear I was already glaring a bit. Except it wasn't him I was glaring at. He'd sent someone down to get me and take me up to his office. Not unusual behaviour, admittedly, but by that time it was just another thing to add to the list of reasons he was, seemingly without effort, pissing me off. If the apologetic glances sent my way by the preppy-looking assistant who accompanied me up in the lift were anything to go by, it wasn't an unusual occurrence.

James was, and indeed is, a stockbroker, and against my better judgement I had been sent out to interview him for a feature on the new fluffy ethical financier sorts apparently so prevalent in the post-credit crunch world. I expected an alfalfa-sprout-eating, sandal-wearing hippy stockbroker – maybe in a suit made of hemp or something. What I got was the kind of person who I'd eye up in a bar in a slightly wistful way, secure in the knowledge that he'd be too busy dating pert-bottomed women called Pippa to look twice at me, my glass of red and my bag of crisps. He certainly didn't look like the sort that would sully his fingers with cheese-and-onion dust. In fact, as I risked a quick glance at his chest, I'd have bet money there were chiselled pecs under there, belying the fact he wasn't a snack food sort in the least.

His handshake was firm and while he apologized for keeping me waiting his tone didn't sound sorry. To be fair, by the time the interview had finished I was wishing he'd left me down in reception. If this was meant to be a colour piece, a fairly non-controversial feature, clearly no one had sent him the memo letting him know that. Getting a straight answer out of him about anything was difficult; he clarified and re-clarified his points until basically he had sucked anything in the way of controversy or even interest out of them, and the more I shifted my line of questioning to try and get him to open up, the more closed he got. It was frustrating as hell.

In the end, after more than an hour, I gave up. I had enough to file my copy but I knew that I hadn't got a killer quote, something to lift the piece. This just made me grumpier, and when we were done I slapped my notebook shut and threw it into the depths of my handbag with a little more viciousness than really necessary. That was the point he asked me out to dinner.

I couldn't help it, I laughed. 'Sorry?' And then I laughed again at his look of confusion that my first instinct hadn't been just to agree, possibly with associated swooning.

'I asked if you wanted to go out for dinner. Or maybe drinks, I understand journalists are partial to a jar or two.'

My irritation with him rose, even while I gaped at him. 'Why do you want to go for a drink with me? And why would I want to go out for a drink with you? You couldn't bring yourself to answer a single question straightfor-wardly. How on earth do you get through casual date small talk?'

He tutted. 'Who said it would be a date?'

I flushed scarlet, and felt a stab of fury – at him for being so blunt and me for being daft enough to think he'd have been asking me out. I really was crap at this dating thing. I turned on my heels and stalked towards the door, but his hand on my arm held me back. It was gentle but firm enough to stop me making my grand-gesture exit.

His tone was softer. 'It'd be fun. Come on, arguing

just now was fun. Trying to outwit each other. It was like jousting.'

I rolled my eyes. 'I think you've misunderstood the concept of jousting. Also, I think dinner with you would be exhausting. Thanks for the interview but –'

My fingers were clasped round the door handle when he interrupted me. 'What are you scared of, Soph?'

I couldn't stop myself. 'It's Sophie actually. And I'm not scared.'

He raised an eyebrow, stepping back to fold his arms across his chest. I think he thought it was endearing, but it made me want to punch him for being so unutterably smug. 'Really?'

And that is how we ended up going out for drinks. In hindsight the signs were there early.

Suffice to say, I regretted agreeing to go out with James pretty much as soon as I'd said yes. But the only thing worse than sounding like such a ditherer was sounding like a gutless ditherer, so I let him take my number. As he programmed it into his BlackBerry he pronounced, half in reassurance, half in warning, that if he couldn't get hold of me to sort out a time he would just ring me at work. We both knew I'd answer my mobile rather than risk stoking office gossip about my personal life. We both knew I'd meet him and that I'd be doing so through gritted teeth. And when I got back to the office and played back the tape of our interview my jaw clenched further. He was smart but he knew it and that arrogance made me want to kick things.

But it wasn't just his innate smugness that made me wary of spending a few hours staring at him over overpriced drinks and nibbles. It wasn't even just that I was still licking my wounds after what had happened with Thomas, still trying to understand how my sexual compulsions could overtake my brain so utterly.

Basically I was knackered. My time with Thomas had made me realize that no matter how amazing the sex, there needed to be some kind of emotional attachment behind it too, but I was a bit worried that finding my romantic ideal would be like looking for a needle in a haystack. I knew I was fussy, but frankly I wasn't planning on settling for anyone who didn't tick a fair few of my boxes, not least being loving, thoughtful, clever, funny, holding down a job he cared about (it was the only way I could ensure he'd put up with mine, which I loved but which had terrible hours), liking children and animals, and not minding the smell of Marmite-y breath. Oh, and he had to have a penchant for hurting, controlling and humiliating me in as many imaginative, degrading ways as he could come up with, while not being an actual honest-to-goodness psychopath. As wish lists go I might as well have added 'the moon on a stick' for the full set.

I'd come to the conclusion that my relationship had to have a D/s element to it, but I had no idea of what to do to find the right person and worried quietly to myself that perhaps I wouldn't be able to have it all. That what I was looking for wasn't really there.

And then I got finagled into the date with the stockbroker.

*

We met on a Tuesday night. It was my suggestion, in part because I begrudged taking up a precious and rare full weekend off to be with him, and in part because I'd already decided that having a ready-made excuse of an early shift the next morning was a good plan. We met in a pub near his office, despite his sweet yet surprising suggestion that he save me time and meet nearer mine – I was keen to keep to his side of the city lest I bump into anyone I knew. Why stir up annoying personal questions for something that was only ever going to be one date?

The thing was, as we chatted over a couple of drinks in the bar, as he asked solicitously about my work and how I'd got into journalism and why I enjoyed it so much, I began to feel slight pangs at the prospect of it being one date. He was surprisingly good company. Funny. Clever. Up-to-date with the news in a way that showed he wasn't one of those annoying people who 'just finds current affairs so depressing' and so doesn't bother. We argued a bit about politics, and when I accused him of suggesting plans for healthcare reform so right-wing they made Attila the Hun look fluffy, he threw back his head and laughed. As I watched him chuckle I felt a pang of lust in the pit of my stomach, followed immediately by an attempt to push it down with realism. This wouldn't work even if he liked me enough to suggest a second date. He clearly wasn't going to be the D/s sort – he was too urbane, very proper and polite, standing when I entered a room, helping me out of my coat and holding my chair. I bet his undeniably suave smile (not that I cared it was suave, I really didn't, I just happened to notice, as you do) would turn to surprise if I asked him how he felt about face slapping. I took a gulp of my own drink, grinning a little at the ridiculousness of my thoughts as I did so, and dove back into a conversation about the children's TV shows we'd grown up with, deciding that instead of over-thinking it all I should just have a fun night out and stop borrowing trouble.

After a couple of drinks we decided, in an unspoken mutual acceptance that things were going OK, to move on to dinner. We walked through the city, looking for a gap in the traffic so we could cross the road. When there was a break he was happy with he made a dash for it, grabbing my hand as he went and pulling me across with him. The warmth of his hand in mine made me tingle for a second, and I felt myself begin to blush, suddenly feeling like a teenager with her first crush. We reached the kerb on the other side of the road and I went to pull away, but his fingers entwined firmly in mine. I tried to stamp down the little voice inside me that was giddily pointing out *he was holding my hand*, reminding myself it didn't mean anything and is probably what he would have done escorting an elderly relative across the road. It didn't stop me grinning though. I struggled to keep up with his longer legs as he strode to the restaurant, clearly keen on not staying outside in the cold any longer than necessary. I rolled my eyes and upped my pace, trying not shiver. Suddenly he stopped, and I walked right into him. I looked around us, confused.

'Is everything OK? What's up?' I asked, as he began unbuttoning his coat.

'Everything's fine, Sophie, except you're shivering.'

'We're standing in the cold. That's not helping.' I was honestly trying not to sound too sarcastic, but it might have bled through.

He began wrapping his overcoat around my shoulders. I think he felt my back stiffen, my instinct to shrug it off, as his hands clenched around my shoulders, part massage part warning. 'Keep it, come on. The longer you stand out here the more cold you're letting me get.'

I bowed my head to hide my smile, and took his hand and began to pull him into a trot. I breathed in the gorgeous, fresh lemon smell of cologne on his jacket. I couldn't help myself, it made me grin more.

Dinner was good. He'd taken me to an understated but clearly good-quality restaurant, all secluded tables and attentive but virtually invisible service. The conversation flowed well and there was a lot of laughter. Lots of banter too, which is important because words matter as far as I'm concerned. I like people who are articulate, clever and can think on their feet. He was able to do all these things, with a side order of argumentativeness which kept me on my toes, my brain engaged. I hadn't felt so interested in talking to someone for a long time, and suddenly remembered how much fun it was getting to know someone. He even made terrible puns. Of course I groaned at them and mocked him for their lameness, but inside I was grinning. Never underestimate the power of a pun, no matter how terrible, to amuse and impress a journalist. From his end, he seemed to enjoy the spark between us too. His face was animated and his gestures were wide as we debated, with varying degrees of seriousness, a range of subjects. Despite a couple of jokes about my strength of character and one 'good grief woman, someone needs to keep you in line' when I said something that made him particularly exasperated, he seemed to not be phased by my intelligence or my argumentative streak. I liked that. I liked him. Also, I realized as I watched him swallow from his glass and found myself staring at his mouth for the umpteenth time, I was beginning to feel real pangs of lust.

By the time it got to half eleven I was regretting suggesting we meet midweek. My 6am start was already looking like it would only happen with the help of coffee and a chocolate croissant, and it was with real regret that I suggested we get the bill. He paid, waving away my debit card like he was shooing a fly, something I was suddenly grateful for when I caught an upside-down glimpse of how much exactly this evening had cost him. We walked to the taxi rank and waited for a car to pull up. I hopped from foot to foot to keep warm while we waited; the evening was now downright cold even with his overcoat, which he'd given me custody of once more. He was standing in front of me, suddenly looking less assured than he had at the beginning of the night. Maybe it was because his tie was loosened and his jacket more crumpled, but he suddenly looked more approachable and prone to the same nerves as the rest of us. He cleared his throat.

'I've had a really good night tonight, actually.'

I laughed. 'Actually? You sound surprised.'

He started to stammer the beginning of a response to

clarify but, bearing in mind how I'd really come on the date out of forbearance, I felt mean making him feel awkward about it. 'It's OK,' I grinned. 'I'm surprised too. You're much better company than I thought you would be when we first met.'

The look on his face was a picture, a look of confusion as he tried to work out whether to focus on the compliment or the insult in my words. As he opened his mouth to speak I stopped him, leaning forward to kiss him. For a second I had free rein, but then his surprise at my sudden move dissipated and his tongue was vying with mine. He tasted of red wine and red meat, a fact that made me smile against his mouth for a second before the insistence of his tongue drew me back into the kiss. His kiss was assured, strong, his lips firm on mine, his tongue assaulting my mouth. His hands enclosed my wrists, drawing me closer by pulling them behind my back, urging me into him. I felt a taxi pull into the empty rank beside us and began to pull away, but his hands held me tight, his mouth still on mine as I moaned into his mouth, a sound of arousal and a little regret. As he finally let me pull away we looked at each other dumbstruck for a second, our breathing heavy, and then before he had a chance to speak I hopped in the cab, throwing a brief 'see ya' over my shoulder as I slammed the door. I told the driver where I wanted to go and as he pulled off I smiled and waved at James, whose mouth was agape, presumably because normally his dates didn't finish with the woman he was with making such an obvious escape. I giggled at his face and stuck my tongue out at him, watching the grin split his face as he disappeared from view. As I turned back into my seat I caught the cab driver's eyes in his rear view mirror.

'Good night then, was it?'

My lips, swollen with kisses, curved into a smile in spite of myself. 'Actually, it really was.'

By the time I got home he'd already texted me.

> You're lucky I only waited a
> couple of minutes for a second
> cab or I'd have put you over
> my knee the next time
> I saw you.

I felt twinge of excitement at 'next time'. Maybe I wasn't the only one keen for the kissing to resume.

> Promises, promises : P

I paused, my fingers over the buttons of my phone, wondering whether to reply to the spanking threat directly. Three glasses of wine and still on a kissing high, I threw caution to the wind.

> Anyway, I doubt you'd spank
> hard enough to hurt: P.

By the time I'd got out of the cab and into my flat he'd replied again.

> 'Why, have you been
> spanked a lot?'

I decided it was probably safest not to reply. James was lovely but if a slightly pissed woman launching herself at him for a kiss left him agog, then hearing some of the vagaries of my sex life might leave him traumatized. It's one thing knowing he's too vanilla for anything to really happen; it's another to deliberately scupper it before anything starts. I went to bed, but not before my phone had pinged at a follow-up text:

Also, you stole my coat.

Bum. I suppose I'd *have* to see him again now . . .

Never before have I met a man so keen to flirt by text. Don't get me wrong, he was clearly busy. While I had very little idea what stockbrokers actually did, I assumed it was high pressure and long hours for good financial reward. But in between all the work, the early mornings, the corporate entertaining, a random business trip to Geneva and, of course, the cycling (so *that's* why he looked so buff) he still had plenty of time to send me texts or emails, about anything and everything. If he read something he thought I would be interested in he would mail me a link to it. He texted me a picture of an error on a restaurant menu because he knew it would enrage the grammar fascist part of me. He even sent a comment through about the story I'd written about him, which made me blush because I'd filed the copy before our first dinner and, while it was perfectly polite, it felt to me very much like it had a subtext of *this man is a knob*. Thankfully he didn't notice. Or if he did he was too charmed by me to say anything. Who knows? Maybe in a world of yes-women he found me quaint.

I basked in his attention, all the while trying desperately to remind myself that it didn't mean anything and that people like him did not end up with people like me, even if I *had* wanted to date him. Which I wasn't sure I did. There was bound to be some down side to it, if I were given enough time to figure it out. The worrying thing was that every extra message just made me like him more. I went through phases of trying to restrain the urge to reply for a while, trying to hide how keen I was, but I found it hugely challenging. I found myself rereading his messages over and over, unable to stop myself tapping out at least a brief few lines of response. He was articulate, funny and referenced the *West Wing*, which is a good barometer of character as far as I'm concerned. We slowly found out more about each other, our day-to-day lives and the things we had in common. There was flirting, and he made a few comments that made me feel butterflies in my stomach – or would have if I didn't think the kiss I'd given him at the taxi rank had freaked him out a little. It was his initial reaction to that kiss that made me decide he really couldn't cope with the kind of sex I now knew was a deal breaker for me. Even knowing that, even knowing all the things that made us incompatible – our bank balances, social standing and political views, which were all at opposite ends of the spectrum – I found myself wistfully thinking about him. I liked him, but tried to convince myself he couldn't be that amazing at all.

Self-preservation? Possibly. But also realism. I was not ready for a broken heart.

As the days passed I found myself thinking of the glint in his eye before he said something funny, the way his lips curved when he smiled and pondering exactly what it would be like to sleep with him. Danger, Will Robinson. Meeting him again was crazy. Foolish. Likely to end in embarrassment at best and hurt at worst. I should deliver his coat to his office, in a parcel so no one could see why I had it. I wasn't going to ever see him again. I wasn't going to mail him any more. I wasn't going to agree to meet him for dinner in a gorgeous restaurant in central London.

And I certainly wasn't going to be going home from said dinner without any knickers, having taken them off and given them to him in a crazy show of bravado shortly before dessert.

Best laid plans and all that.

I know the knickers thing is mind-boggling; if it helps, it broke my brain too. And I really didn't anticipate it. In fact I'd deliberately worn comfy non-date undies, so adamant was I that, despite my occasional daydreams of time spent together hanging out at home, reading the paper, ending up ankle deep in discarded Sunday supplements in rooms straight from an Ikea catalogue, absolutely nothing was going to happen. It was absolutely not going to lead to anything. I was giving him his coat back, we'd have a perfectly nice dinner, and then I'd go home and – since I wasn't holding his coat effectively to ransom any more – he'd never contact me again. And for most of the evening it didn't seem like it would be an issue.

I arrived late – a crisis at work from a late-developing story conspiring with train trauma – to find him sitting at the bar. He stood formally to greet me and seeing him again made my heart beat faster. His eyes shone with good humour and, despite my fears about the awkwardness of the drunken kiss and my abrupt escape, I instantly felt comfortable with him once more. Which is probably just as well, bearing in mind everything that happened afterwards.

He was understanding about my tardiness, brushing aside my stammered apologies as we were shown to our table and seated. Over the next few hours we ate a leisurely meal, dragging it out in a way that, if it had been anything other than a grim January Monday, would have seen our waiting staff dropping hints that we get the bill or adjourn back to the bar.

We talked about films, the media, argued about whether a recent run of derogatory headlines relating to the Home Secretary were unnecessary (him) or newsworthy (me, unsurprisingly). It was fun, mentally challenging and filled with laughter. From the outside it would have looked like a proper date. Certainly someone passing our table might have noticed my face reddening at times, flushed as if I'd had a little too much wine. But they had no way of knowing that I was only drinking sparkling water and instead was squirming because James was mocking me for the tone of my feature – so much for the saccharine sweet tone going over his head – and for stealing his coat.

He was solicitous throughout dinner, the same James I had gotten to know through our textual chats, but he was also an undeniable, tangible force in the room, drawing attention from men and women alike. I could understand it – hell, with him sat in front of me, it was all I could do to string a sentence together at times, but it made me grumpy too, and underlined more than ever that he really was not my sort.

The mantra 'not my sort' was running through my head on a loop by the time coffee had been served, which meant I wasn't as sharp as perhaps I could have been when he leaned back in his chair, dabbed at his mouth with his napkin, set it down neatly on the table and told me I should give him a present before I left him that evening, to make up for keeping his coat for so long. The atmosphere had shifted imperceptibly; his smile was still as charming and as warm, but now there was something else lurking beneath the surface. I pressed my hands together to hide the slight tremble in them and feigned insouciance as I asked what exactly he had in mind, praying to the overdraft gods that whatever it was wouldn't leave me having to pull overtime to make the rent.

That's when he said, 'Your knickers.' *Good, well that's not going to cost me anyth . . . — Wait. What?*

It took every ounce of effort to not flinch slightly. Pride? Probably. A stubborn need to prove I wouldn't be fazed by any challenge? Definitely. He waited silently for my response. I shifted in my seat.

With what I thought was a remarkably calm voice and straight face under the circumstances I asked him if he had considered going to a specialist shop and buying women's undies of his own there. He let out a bark of laughter, his teeth white in the candlelight and shook his head.

'You know I don't want them for that. I want *your* knickers. Right now.'

I was confused. This was James – befuddled-at-a-kiss, posh, urbane James. What was he saying? He waited, clearly enjoying the confusion as it flashed across my face, but not doing anything to ease it.

Suddenly it clicked. Ha. After I kissed him and then leapt in the cab he felt all embarrassed at being on the back foot. So now he was playing a joke on me, trying to put *me* on the back foot. I'd never let him know how close he'd been to getting me. But two could play at this game.

I took a slow sip of water and leaned forward in my chair, politely and sweetly inquiring as to how this would work. As I'd met him from work and I find skirts impractical at the best of times, I was wearing trousers. Would I be permitted to go to the bathroom to remove my knickers and then give them to him later? He looked scandalized – of course I would, he wouldn't want to cause a scene in public.

He watched me intently as we discussed it, his smile getting wider until he was practically laughing at me outright. Growing tired of playing along, I couldn't stop myself from asking exactly what he found so funny.

He gestured at me. 'You're delightful. Your chin is up and your voice is casual. But your body gives you away.'

In spite of myself I felt my chin rising even further as I replied, trying for a calmness of tone that felt just a fingertip out of reach – although I hoped he didn't know me well enough to be able to pick up on that too.

'I don't know what you mean.'

He touched me, skin against skin, and it felt like an electric shock surging through my body. His finger brushed the top of my hand as he spoke, stroking me in a way that felt oddly hypnotic, making my pulse race and my breaths get shallower as I tried to focus on what he was saying. In the tiny part of my brain that wasn't thinking about how surreal it was to be discussing the practicalities of giving my knickers to a man I'd met twice before and still wasn't sure I even liked, I wondered what pleasure he could wring from my body, when with one finger he was already driving me to a kind of distraction.

'You're focusing hard on controlling your voice, your words. But your cheeks are flushed, and look at your hand –' at that he tapped gently on the top of it '– suddenly clutching at the edge of the table for support.' I blinked and looked down to see my fingers gripping the dark wood. I felt like my hand belonged to someone else, seeing myself as he saw me, knowing he was right, and blushing even harder. So much for remaining in control. Bugger. I unfurled my fingers and left my hand resting gently on the table, aiming for a casualness we both knew I wasn't feeling. I swallowed hard, fighting to regain a sense of equilibrium.

'I really don't know what you mean.'

He smiled again, almost indulgently, the way you would at an entertaining and yet naive child. 'I think you do. Perhaps you don't. But you're bright, you'll figure it out in the end.' And then he patted my hand one last time.

'Shall we get the bill?' I leaned down to pick up my hand-bag, and he looked at me, long and hard. His voice was quiet, firm, and spoke to a part of me that had been pretty quiet since the move.

'Go to the bathroom.'

My legs felt like they belonged to someone else, and I was halfway across the room before I could comprehend what I was doing. I'd clearly gone mad. *Fuck him*, I thought to myself as I stood in the bathroom, shoving my knick-ers into my bag. If he wanted to play this game I bet I could shock him more than he shocked me. As I walked back on to the restaurant floor I wasn't entirely sure I was right though.

I came back from the toilet to find he had paid the bill and retrieved my coat, and was standing by the door look-ing out into the night. I walked the full length of the restaurant to join him, the seam of my trousers pressing against my slit with every step, creating a delicious friction that exacerbated my increasing arousal in the light of this slightly surreal turn.

As he helped me into my coat, he pressed a seemingly solicitous hand to the small of my back under my jacket to usher me out of the restaurant. Only I knew that he was actually sliding a finger under my waistband to see whether I'd obeyed his order. His murmur of pleasure when he realized made me blush. Damnit.

He walked me to the cab rank, where we were to go our separate ways. Shortly before we got to the taxi at the front of the queue he grabbed my wrist, pulling me around. Pressing my back into the wall with his body, he anchored one hand in my hair and kissed me deeply, pillaging my mouth. His other hand was still around my wrist, pulling my hand down to feel his erection under his jacket. I felt shy, embarrassed – long beyond the age of snogging and copping a feel in public in this way – but I couldn't resist running my hand along the front of his trousers, feeling him grow.

He ended the kiss and we moved apart, both of us breathing heavily. I was dumbstruck; any attempt to play it cool was a distant memory. He was looking at me expectantly, but for the life of me I couldn't work out what he wanted me to say. I wasn't actually sure I could form words. Eventually he smiled and held out his hand.

'I believe you have something for me.'

I closed my eyes for a second to try and mask my embarrassment at having momentarily forgotten all about his stupid joke, having become so caught up in the kisses.

'My knickers? You really want them? Really?'

His smile made my stomach flip. 'I do. Really. I think you owe me.'

I turned slightly, hiding my bag from public view to pull out my neatly folded pants. Of course I'd folded them, balling them up just seemed so uncouth somehow. I passed my knickers to him, focusing completely on ensuring my hand didn't shake, dreading he was going to unfurl them, sniff them, goodness knows what. He smiled, thanked me and put them in his pocket. I let out the trembling breath I hadn't realized I was holding, and as I did so he brushed one last kiss across my now-swollen lips and leant to whisper in my ear.

'We're going to see each other soon. You're going to come and collect these, from my place, and we're going to continue that kiss –' he stared at my mouth '– and go further.'

I'd have argued, at the very least mocked him for his ego, but as I got into the taxi, knowing how aroused I was, knowing if he'd suggested it I'd have been going home with him even then, I just couldn't begin to form the lie. I was confused, aroused, torn between what my heart, my head and – frankly – my cunt were saying. And then my phone pinged.

Are you free tomorrow night?

I wasn't, I was supposed to be covering a book launch. However, I knew I'd be calling in favours – and no doubt signing up for weekend shifts for weeks to come – to ensure I was available for whatever he had in mind. Lust wins.

11

I have a tendency to overthink. It's something that developed when I was a child – I was always the precocious kid who would be told one simple thing which would then spin round in their brain until it was transformed into something completely different. My mum often repeats the story of the day, aged around ten, when we had a lesson about global warming at school and by the time I had ruminated on it for the afternoon I had come to the conclusion that we needed urgently to make a boat so we, the dog, our neighbours and Mrs Johnson, my class teacher, could all be safe when the tidal wave came. I actually drew the ten-year-old equivalent of blueprints and gave them to my mum so she could go to B&Q to start preparing, although my wonderful mum – used to these surreal conversations – showed me a picture of a cross channel ferry and told me Dad had already built it and had it waiting at the harbour for any eventuality.

Sadly these flights of fancy have not abated with age. In fact, if anything, they've got worse, or better if I'm trying to spin it in a 'thinking through all angles', overachieving sort of way. It never feels like that at 3am though, when everyone else in the world is asleep, every creak of the house sounds like something falling over, and something simple suddenly becomes more complicated.

I'd worked it all through in my mind, over and over, like an erotic 'Choose Your Own Adventure' book, complete with endings with varying degrees of satisfaction. My favourite was the one where James was secretly a dominant, but felt awkward bringing it up, and was thus sending me lots of subtle hints that he was into the same kind of thing I was, ranging from grabbing my hand to demanding my knickers – that *had* to be a sign, surely? Whether he meant for it to be or not we had fallen into the dominant and submissive roles, right? Unless I'd misread the signs, thrown myself into my fantasy world and thus assumed it matched his, and he was sitting at home wondering what on earth to do with a pair of M&S high leg pants and how to disentangle himself from the clearly loopy woman who'd pushed them into his palm. God, what WOULD he do with the pants? Would he give them back to me? Would he wash them first? Or did he have someone else to wash them? Oh god, which was worse? By the time I'd extrapolated a scenario whereby he posted my pants back to me, at the office, to be opened by our editorial assistant because he hadn't marked the envelope 'Private and Confidential', I was almost frantic, blushing by proxy at the hideousness of it.

All I could do was to meet him, go to his house and see what happened – all the while trying to keep my head, not get my hopes up, and without doing anything so hideous I'd need to hide under the duvet for months to get over it. Simple.

Of course, nothing is ever simple.

I got busy calling in favours. I bought our crime reporter

an epic lunch and turned his head with tales (OK, optimistic lies) of glittering celebrities, goodie bags and – of course – a complimentary bar, to get him to go to the book launch for me. I had a lunchtime eyebrow wax and bought some new undies - I figured I had to pull something hotter out of the bag than the pair I'd given James if things were going to go the way I hoped. It felt a bit presumptuous and rather girlie, but I couldn't stop myself indulging. For the first time in a long time I felt like this was a date – not just hanging out with a friend with additional naughty fun, but a date, even, maybe, the start of an actual honest-to-goodness relationship. It was an odd feeling, discombobulating but lovely. Hell, I even pondered buying a new dress, since everything else non-trouser related in my wardrobe had been worn at weddings or christenings over the last few years and was probably the wrong side of garden party chic. In the end, I decided against it. I felt out of my comfort zone enough before throwing in worrying about whether curling my legs under myself on a chair was accidentally flashing more than I intended. I was sorted. Ready. I had the kind of butterflies that meant the afternoon was going to be part anticipation, part torture. And the waiting was kind of fun. I returned from lunch with a spring in my step, wishing away my afternoon.

Of course, while I'd been away all hell and broken loose.

As a relative newcomer to the newsroom I wasn't getting a great many lead stories yet. I understood why – a mixture of finding my feet on the patch and waiting for the news editors to feel confident giving me something meaty that wouldn't land them a load of extra work in rewriting, paired with the fact that all the other reporters were keen to protect their own contacts and ongoing stories. I didn't feel grumpy about it as I knew that I had to pay my dues a little while people got to know me, so instead I quietly took all the leads I was given, researching and then writing them up as well as I could, starting the process of building my own contact book once more, so I could bring in my own stories.

Little did I realize the little work I'd had a chance to do on that score was about to pay inconvenient dividends.

As I shuffled back to my desk Ian, the news editor, caught my eye and waved me over. My eyes flicked to the clock as I moved towards him, checking I hadn't earned myself a bollocking by taking too long for lunch. I was OK. I waited for him to finish his call. He hung up.

'Hey. Glad you're back. We need you to head out again.'

What? Balls. Although actually, this wasn't a bad thing, I could slope off home afterwards if I got what I needed early. Ever the optimist.

'The staff at St Luke's are revolting.'

I blinked, confused. 'What?'

'St Luke's primary. There's some kind of issue with a kid being excluded. The local authority's involved, so we have to be careful how we tread, but someone's called in saying there's a letter going round, put out by the parents, accusing several teachers of being overzealous in disciplining kids in their classes. Accusations of racism. Apparently the staff are furious and several teachers are threatening legal action. There could be a walk out.'

My mind was already whirring with possibilities as he spoke. 'Do we know who called?'

'No, they wanted to stay anonymous, didn't want to be quoted.'

'OK, could either be a parent, or a teacher wanting to push the council's hand.'

Ian smiled. 'I'll let you sweat that stuff – it's why we pay you the mediocre bucks. But the councillor you interviewed last week on library cuts is a governor there. I thought you might be able to get him to talk, even off the record.'

I nodded. 'I'll call him before I go, but if I head out now I can go see the headmistress face to face too, and still be around for any obvious parental rabble rousing at home time.'

He nodded. 'All I need is for you to get a feel for what's happening. Stand it up first, then we can decide how big it is. Call me when you know roughly what it'll make.'

I headed out, stopping briefly by my desk to grab the number of my contact. My lazy afternoon was a distant hope, although the adrenaline was also starting to course through me at the prospect of trying to figure out what was going on, especially with the clock ticking.

In hindsight, I should have texted James early to warn him that I might be running late. But until I knew how much work I was signed up for it didn't seem worth causing extra faff. By the time I'd spoken to the headmistress – unhelpful and understandably grumpy – and some of the mothers waiting at the school gate, it was clear this was going to make something, and I'd need to go back to the office to write it up. Sitting outside the councillor's house in my car at half five, I sent James a text. Suffice to say I wasn't going to get to his for 7pm.

> Really sorry, work's mad. Can
> we push back meeting? x

I didn't get his reply until an hour later, when I was finally out, with a notebook full of background to shore up the colour of the quotes from the school gates. I frowned when I read it.

> Fine. Let me know another
> night you're free if you do
> want to meet.

Balls. I reread the message I'd sent him, suddenly realizing that what I'd taken to mean me turning up an hour (OK, realistically, two) later had to his eyes meant I was cancelling completely. I started typing a reply but then realized it was likely to sound more strained. I threw my phone back in my bag – best to sort it later once I'd finished for the night.

Of course, trying to get across the city at half six by car is a joke. By the time I'd got back to the office and done what I needed to do I was thinking it was probably just as well he'd cancelled me, or I'd accidentally cancelled him, or whatever had actually just happened. I felt a pang at not having gotten to meet, though, made worse by the fact he hardly seemed that concerned about it; the tone of his text was frosty in comparison to the easygoing friendly messages of earlier. I don't want to be *that* girl, deconstructing texts on the basis of kisses, but I couldn't help but notice some of them had disappeared over the course of the day.

When I got home I tried calling him, but it went through to voicemail. I left a quick message and hopped in the bath before going to bed, exhausted, but not in the way I'd envisaged I'd be when the day started.

The next day I emailed him to see if he was about later in the week to meet up. His response was non-committal and left me wondering if he'd actually ever been interested in meeting properly at all. I chalked it up to experience, moved along and chucked the matching bra and knicker set into my underwear drawer, hopeful there would be another point where I'd get to use it. Just, apparently, not for him. I was disappointed, but decided I wasn't really that interested in his sexy smile, quick wit and overcoat-sharing brand of chivalry anyway.

Chivalry was overrated. I kept saying it to myself over and over during the following week, but even I knew I was kidding myself. The following Monday I cracked and sent him a link to a story from a political blog that I knew would make him incandescent with rage.

He replied within a few minutes of me sending it. My mental image of him tapping out his lengthy rant furiously on his BlackBerry made me smile.

I replied, calmly, reasonably and completely disagreeing with everything he said, as was inevitable whenever we discussed politics. Suddenly we were back and forth chatting again. Every time my phone pinged I'd get butterflies in my stomach, hopeful it was him, and a lot of times it was.

Finally, at the end of an email where the discussion had deteriorated to the point where I was accusing him of despotic tendencies while he dismissed my ramblings as those of a 'bloody hippy', came a sentence that made my heart pound.

> Look, I know this is possibly a
> bad idea, but do you fancy
> coming round for dinner?

He was right, it was a terrible idea, although I wasn't sure I felt reassured that he felt that way too. Throwing caution to the wind, though, I immediately accepted. We could be idiots together, and at least I'd see how this played out.

I have a terrible sense of direction. Awful. If there is one thing about myself that I dislike above all others it is the fact I am incapable of finding my way anywhere. It makes me feel out of control, powerless, and not in a good way. I've been known to get lost in people's houses.

James lived over the other side of the city to me, in an area so achingly upmarket I'd only driven through it a couple of times, for work. I decided that driving was a sensible course of action as it meant I could leave as early or as late as I wanted without having to rely on public transport. Of course, my crappy navigation skills made for a stressful drive over, even before I discovered his apartment block was so exclusive it apparently didn't have a sign showing its name. Plus most of my mind was focused on exactly what would happen when I got there. I trusted him in the sense that I knew enough about him that my nutter radar wasn't sounding, but I couldn't for the life of me marry up the James who seemed so confused by the drunk girl jumping him with the one who demanded I hand over my knickers. Or the one who thought having me come round for dinner was a terrible idea. Which was the real him? What on earth was I letting myself in for? And why was I even bothering, when we were in such different worlds? My serious case of the butterflies had only been exacerbated when I got a text from him a few hours earlier:

I am having concentration issues today. Keep thinking about exactly
  what to do with you. X

What did that mean? Was he talking about the rude things he'd hinted at before our school-scuppered date, or wondering whether to break open post-dinner Scrabble? I had no clue; my social capability was completely skewed. He'd broken my brain with a few kisses and emails. I had no hope.

It pretty much ended the productivity of my afternoon too as, with the best will in the world, writing up council planning application news is never going to hold the attention when your mind's pondering smut. I found myself unable to stop thinking about what he might be thinking about. There was certainly a D/s-ish element to the things in my head, but was that him? Or was that me, in a post-Thomas funk, seeing rudeness where there was none? Was I going to head over and make a complete arse of myself? The fact I'd resigned myself to this happening and yet still found I was unable to face cancelling depressed me immensely. I really *was* a masochist.

An attempt at reasserting some semblance of control didn't end especially well. When I sent him a text asking if I could bring anything with me, I was thinking a bottle of wine or dessert. But his response was unequivocal and made me flush as I sat at my desk.

Condoms. Lots of condoms. x

Oh my. So he was thinking about us having sex then. That was a promising sign. Suffice to say my story on council planning didn't get anywhere near the level of professional attention it should have done that afternoon. I did, however, undoubtedly look the cheeriest I ever have while writing it.

Finally I arrived at what I was fairly sure must be his road, parked my car in what I hoped was his basement and walked over to what I was hoping was his door. I rang the doorbell and as he came down to greet me, barefoot and smiling, I found myself smiling back in spite of my nerves. We walked up the stairs to his flat, although my distractedness was such that I managed to walk halfway up before he turned to look at me and said: 'Sophie? You need to close my front door.'

Oooops. I blushed, went back down the stairs and closed it, before walking back up trying to look as if nothing had happened. Smooth. I know, I impress even myself with my ability to hold it together in challenging social situations.

We got into the flat and he gestured towards the living room. I walked in and turned around, taking the opportunity to scope out the shelves and clutter for more clues about the kind of man he was. I know this makes me sound like a stalker; I maintain it's my journalistic tendencies, although some people might argue that's the same thing. Then he cleared his throat.

'Close the door please, Sophie.'

I was halfway across the room to obey before I realized I'd moved instinctively. I shut the door gently and turned round to find him right behind me, invading my personal space. His hands became entwined in my hair as he bent his head towards mine for a kiss. I closed my eyes, enjoying the moment, how he towered over me and held me in place as his tongue invaded my mouth and his hands ran over my body, cupping my arse to pull me closer to him. He was the tallest man I had kissed, and – not being short myself – it was a novelty to feel dwarfed by his size. I felt he could either protect or overpower me easily depending on his intent. He broke the kiss and stroked my bare arms, which had, embarrassingly come out in goosebumps. Taking my hand he led me out of the room. No overpowering going on here then. I felt a pang of disappointment, at least until I smelled the unmistakable scent of garlic and rosemary coming from his kitchen. OK, I could work with this.

I love home cooking. Seriously. A lovely home-cooked dinner means more to me than the swishest restaurant. Living alone means I tend to not bother for the most part, living on stir fry, soup and cereal. Every so often I'll go the other way and make something elaborate, although what usually happens is I get halfway through the process and am bored by the chopping, stuffing and basting and then revert back to soup for another three months.

So being around anyone who can cook is always a welcome novelty. As I sat on a stool in his kitchen with a glass of wine, James pottered around, chopping vegetables to go with some steak he'd apparently seasoned earlier. We chatted about work and TV, he told me about a long weekend he was planning with his sister to celebrate their parents' golden wedding anniversary, and generally it was comfortable and relaxed and felt a million miles away from the ferocity of his kisses a few moments before. The change of gear left me completely on the back foot even though, being me, I was doing everything I could to show that I wasn't in any way bothered at all, even if it was taking all my effort to stop myself from putting a finger to my lips to feel exactly how puffy my mouth was.

As it was, dinner was lovely, the company was good, as was the conversation. But through it all at least three quarters of my conscious thought was about sex, and never has a man eating a steak been so arousing. Even watching him chew and swallow made my throat dry. I'd clearly gone bonkers and should have gone home for my own safety. At one point I had to make a deliberate effort to stop my hand shaking around my glass, my equilibrium was so off kilter. By the time we had stacked the plates in the sink and it looked to my hopeful eyes like we might resume the kissing, I was already like a cat on hot bricks.

The analogy was actually rather apt. James had two very cute Siamese kittens who padded around his flat like feline ninjas. I'd been surprised when I saw them: 'How can you have time to look after these guys?' I exclaimed as I leaned down to see them better.

He looked a little bit sheepish, which made me smile. 'I have a woman who comes in to check on them.'

I chuckled. 'Of course you do.'

Initially the kittens were wary of me, but by the time I'd been sat still for a while the braver of the two came up to sit on my lap. Having not had a pet of my own since I moved away from my parents, I'd missed this simple pleasure, and before I knew it I'd been fussing him for a long while, chuckling at him cleaning my fingers with his sandpapery tongue. In what was probably slightly bad form, I wasn't hugely aware of where James was until suddenly he was stroking the back of my neck, echoing the way I was fussing his cat. I shivered slightly underneath him, enjoying it, my body responding to – finally! – his touch. Then I froze, unsure how to react, not wanting to scare him into stopping. Aware that, vanilla or not, I was aching to sleep with this man, to finally get to explore him, to try and sate the need and tension that had been building since pretty much the moment we met.

I sat stroking the cat, staring intently at his fur, listening to him purr as James stood behind me, stroking me. As the silence lengthened, finally he moved in front of me, and plucked the cat from my lap, stroking him tenderly and rubbing his cheek against his face before putting him on the floor and taking my hand.

'I think it's time for us to leave them to it for the night.'

My throat was suddenly dry and the butterflies that had been in my stomach for the last few weeks started fluttering harder than ever. How was it possible to feel such relief and such nerves at the same time? Finally this was going to happen, whatever *this* was. He led me to his bedroom, closing the door firmly behind him to deter feline interlopers.

We propelled ourselves over to the bed, and suddenly we were sprawled across it, turning over and over, each of us vying to be on top. I undid his shirt, my hands stroking the sculpted chest beneath, enjoying, finally, getting to dictate the pace. I reached down, undid his belt and began to undo his trousers, all without removing my mouth from his. There are sensual, erotic seductions, but this was almost feral, neither of us able to wait any longer. He broke away from my mouth for a moment and bucked his hips so he could pull his trousers down and put on a condom, while I pulled off my knickers, and then I impaled myself on him. That first moment there was silence, no movement, just his eyes widening, in shock – at the feeling, the abruptness, at me being such an impatient hussy, who can say? – while I adjusted to him inside me, enjoying the feeling, after so long spent thinking about it. For long seconds we stayed there, our breathing the only thing causing movement between us, but suddenly he became impatient; his hands clawing at my hips began pulling me up and down, starting the movement, demanding wordlessly that I rode him. How's a girl to argue? I began to move my hips, leaning down to kiss him as I went.

I don't know how long we kept moving back and forth, hands moving across each other, our fingers exploring every inch, mouths duelling, hips meshing together, but suddenly his hand, which was squeezing my arse, had let go. In the split second that it took for my brain to register the loss he slapped the fleshy curve of my arse cheek. I whimpered and then blushed, wondering if he could tell how much it turned me on.

He did it again. It was light, playful, but it made my blood hum. His hands moved, stroking my breasts, running his fingers along the soft skin above the curve of my bra, before reaching in and pulling me out. He played with my nipples, gently pinching them, twisting them a little, not enough for me to feel a pang of pain, but certainly enough to feel a wave of pleasure.

I smiled down at him, enjoying the moment, the fact that I could look at him intently, drink in his gaze. For a moment my hips stilled, as I became so caught up in looking at this enigmatic man that I literally forgot what I was doing. But then I saw a tinge of impatience flare in his eyes and suddenly I was moving, rolling across the bed on to my back propelled by his hips. He grabbed my wrists in one of his hands, and began moving at his own speed. As he moved, faster and faster, I moved up to meet him, my hips urging him deeper. I pulled my hands out of his grasp and began running my fingers along his back, enjoying his tiny shiver as one of my fingernails traced gently along his spine. But then his fingers were between our bodies, finding my clit, pushing me further until finally I was unable to push back the inevitable. I came, and as I did he followed me, both of us tensing and then relaxing, replete in each other.

He nuzzled my neck, pressing a kiss to the edge of my collarbone. I shivered, still sensitive from the force of my orgasm. He grinned and nibbled where he'd just kissed, and I poked him in the chest with a finger. 'Oi!'

His laugh vibrated against my skin. 'Sorry, I'll be good.'

I laughed too. 'I very much doubt that.'

'Good point.'

We lay for a while, curled together, the shadows lengthening in the room as night drew in. It didn't feel like an awkward silence, and I didn't feel a burning need to talk, but my brain was whirring, trying to fit what had happened and James's general loveliness within a wider context, of his motivations, of any potential relationship (*was* it a relationship?), of my hopes for a D/s flavour to any romance I might end up in. Is it fair to stay with someone when you're not sure you're fundamentally compatible in a way you know is important to you? And is it crazy to be trying to make these decisions when you don't even really know what the other party actually wants? Also, is it normal to be thinking of someone who has just fucked you till your toes curled as a 'party'? As the confusion blossomed I realized that James had dozed off next to me. It made me smile, and my heart clench a little; he looked so young and trouble-free while asleep, but it also helped give me a mental shake. This stuff might matter, but it didn't matter yet. Baby steps. I tried to switch off my chattering brain, and enjoy the languor of that post-orgasm bliss. I might even have dozed off myself for a bit.

When I woke the room was properly dark. James was still beside me, although a tiny light in the darkness showed he was checking his BlackBerry.

'Hey.'

He looked up at me. 'Hey yourself. Good sleep?'

I nodded and began to stretch. 'Mmmmm. Yes thanks. How about you?'

He had the grace to look a little discomfited. 'So I did fall asleep first? How stereotypical of me.'

I laughed. 'It's OK.' I leaned forward to kiss him. 'I shall take it as a sign I wore you out.'

He pressed a chaste kiss to my mouth and murmured, 'Minx.' And then he was groping along the bedside table to put the BlackBerry down safely before bringing his arm back to begin stroking my back. He deepened the kiss and we began again. I smiled against his mouth. I could definitely get used to this.

I didn't stay over in the end. He offered, and I was sorely tempted, but I'd not brought an overnight bag because I didn't want to be presumptuous.

'Surely me telling you to bring condoms was a give-away that presumption wasn't unreasonable?' he asked grumpily as I started getting my things together, but the idea of doing the walk of shame back into the office in yesterday's clothes didn't appeal. He walked me down to my car at 2am, and after thoroughly kissing me goodnight, again, told me I should text him when I got home. I demurred, pointing out he should probably get some sleep before he started work at eight (ooops) but he high-handedly demanded that I text him.

I sighed. 'Fine. But when you're feeling knackered later don't blame me.'

He leaned into my open window as I pulled my seat belt on. 'I absolutely will blame you and your tempting ways,' he said, leaning in for one last kiss. I gestured for him to move back, fairly sure that reversing over his foot was going to put a downer on the evening.

'You started it.'

He was smiling in my rear view mirror as I drove away, but he looked thoughtful and way less carefree than he had when he was asleep.

The next time we met was for lunch. I was on lates for the week, and as such it was completely pointless trying to make any kinds of plans to do anything in the evening because by the time I'd got out of work most normal folk – especially working the early morning starts James had – were thinking about heading to bed. Part of me was tempted to suggest just coming round *for* bed, but frankly, while we'd clearly both enjoyed what had happened after my long-awaited dinner at his, he hadn't suggested a repeat yet, and I wasn't going to give away too much myself – although it's fair to say if *he* had suggested it I'd have been round there like a shot, presumptuous overnight bag and all.

Lunch was fun though. He picked a lovely pub by the river and – taking advantage of some unseasonably good weather – we braved sitting outside, even while most of the tourists in the pub on a weekday afternoon stayed indoors, gravitating towards an open fire. We chatted about work. I told him about a recent phone row between Ian and an affronted reader, an argument so epic that everyone had stopped for a few minutes to shamelessly earwig Ian's side of things at the increasingly surreal accusations being thrown his way, before applauding when after two minutes of repeating 'if you continue swearing at me in this manner I will have to hang up the phone and end this conversation' he finally did just that, before turning, bemused, to tell us his adversary had been elderly Mrs Vickers, a parish councillor who had been complaining about a less than effusive review of the village's am dram production of *An Inspector Calls*.

James told me more about the plans to celebrate his parents' anniversary, which he was organizing around a work trip to Geneva. He and his sister were booking a cottage in Cornwall for a long weekend for everyone to amass to congratulate the happy couple, before a big dinner at a seafood restaurant. Talking about his family made him much more animated than talking about his job did, and it was lovely to get a feel for the man whose nephew's attempts to speak caused him such mirth.

'My sister is a brilliant mum, and Joseph is a lovely kid,' he said. 'But he's at that stage where he'll make a kind of burbling noise and I'll nod and then Emily will solemnly tell me that actually he's just asked me to pass him his yoghurt spoon. I try and keep a straight face, but it's the human equivalent of "what's that Lassie? Little Timmy's stuck down a well?"'

I laughed. 'I bet he's good value though when it comes to running round the garden.'

James swallowed a gulp of his drink and nodded. 'Too right. I'll be making sure we've got a football to run around after while we're down there. Who needs words anyway? Words are overrated.'

I know I'm terrible, but I blushed quite a lot, suddenly mindful of another opportunity when they were entirely superfluous. I stared down at my plate for a moment, willing the flush to dissipate, and suddenly his hand was in mine and, as I looked up, he was smiling at me.

I wasn't sure if it was reassuring or annoying that he seemed to read me so well.

We finished up, and I finally managed to nab a waiter and pay a bill before James could, which left me feeling triumphant, although also amused that he thought it was such an unusual thing. He tried, unsuccessfully, to flag back the waiter, who clearly had no time for such nonsense, then ran a hand through his hair.

'Thank you for lunch, it's a wonderful gesture, but normally on a lunch date I'd pay the bill.'

I stuck my tongue out at him. 'Who said this was a date?'

There was a split second where his face flashed, first embarrassed, and then confused, before finally breaking into a smile of recognition of the words he'd said to me the first time we'd met. 'Ouch. Touché, Ms Morgan.' Then a self-conscious chuckle. 'In hindsight I fear I came across as a bit of an arse the first time we met.'

I nodded. 'A little bit. But you've made up for it since. And you can make up for it some more by letting me pay for lunch.'

He shook his head in exasperation. 'Normally women don't have a problem with me paying.'

I ignored the unexpected sting at the idea there was a plethora of women in his lunch list and instead started putting my scarf on. 'Maybe you just hang out with the wrong kind of woman.'

He gave me a measured look, which eventually broke into a grin. 'Maybe I do.'

By the time I'd got to the office I had decided it was time to be slightly more forthright. Our lingering kiss before we went our separate ways at the restaurant seemed to indicate that James was still interested in something more than friendship. However, he seemed to have taken a slight step back since we'd first slept together. I was fairly sure he wasn't a player of any kind – to put it crudely, he'd already had his chance to get in my pants and was still in contact – so that didn't worry me. But as broaching it in person felt rather tough, I figured discussing the sex virtually was less embarrassing – at least then I didn't have to look him in the eye. I booted up Messenger.

SOPHIE SAYS: Just wanted to say thanks for a lovely lunch. Was good to see you, we should do it again when you're back from Geneva.

Give me a break, I'm building up to it. It's not like I can just launch into the sex chat. I'd scare him. A reply dropped in a minute later.

JAMES SAYS: Surely since you paid I should be thanking you? It was great to see you too. Definitely do it again soon.

JAMES SAYS: PS Thank you.

JAMES SAYS: PPS You looked amazing in that top.

I grinned. OK, this kind of flirty banter I could cope with. It was fun even.

SOPHIE SAYS: You have to get over the paying thing. It doesn't mean you have to put out.

His reply was quick, brief and made me grin like a loon.

JAMES SAYS: But what if I WANT to put out?

SOPHIE SAYS: The easiest way would be for you to, yannow, actually make a move. Seize the moment!

JAMES SAYS: I thought nice guys didn't do that . . .

I grimaced, suddenly reminded that for all the ways we were compatible and I really liked him, on one level James and I were fundamentally different. Don't get me wrong, I have neither the time nor the inclination to be messed around by bastards, but if he wasn't aware that you could be something in between then he really wasn't my sort.

Balls. I replied, but some of the fun had been sucked out of the banter.

> SOPHIE SAYS: I think it's possible to be a nice guy without being a boring one. As long as you're fairly sure the move would be welcomed, I think you're OK.
>
> SOPHIE SAYS: PS For the avoidance of doubt, it would be.
>
> JAMES SAYS: Ah, but you haven't seen my best moves yet. They might scare you off . . .

This sounded promising, although I rolled my eyes at the idea that he could scare me.

> SOPHIE SAYS: I'm sure I can cope with whatever you come up with.
>
> JAMES SAYS: Oh really? The knicker thing gave you pause though, didn't it?

I was genuinely nonplussed, and not a little grumpy. I didn't pause at all, cheeky git. I'm not sure how much of my outrage showed in my response.

> SOPHIE SAYS: I don't think I paused at all!
>
> SOPHIE SAYS: Also, you owe me a pair of knickers.

It took a few minutes for a response to come through and when it did the short sentence sounded much less playful than anything that had come before.

JAMES SAYS: You were fine caught up in the moment, but when you cancelled dinner I worried in all seriousness it was because I'd pushed you too far.

I was bemused, and a bit annoyed that he didn't trust me to be honest. Hell, my honesty – my occasional bluntness - was probably the thing that got me into most trouble in life.

SOPHIE SAYS: No, I really had to work. It wasn't an excuse, it was work. If I'd decided I didn't want to see you, I'd have just said I didn't want to see you.

He didn't reply for a good few minutes, long enough for me to finish a piece I was writing, pick it up off the printer and return with a cup of tea. I felt like I needed to say more, but didn't really have a clue what could make it better, if indeed anything could.

SOPHIE SAYS: The knicker thing was fine. Hot even. Certainly nothing I couldn't handle.

Then a thought occurred to me.

SOPHIE SAYS: Anyway, if I'd felt embarrassed, or awkward or concerned or any of those things, why would I have happily come round to dinner later?

My phone vibrated on the edge of my desk.

JAMES SAYS: Good steak and kitten fussing?

I grinned. Before I could formulate a reply, he messaged again

JAMES SAYS: The knicker thing was 'hot' eh? Hot as in arousing? Or hot as in 'your face was pink to your ears'?

I flushed just thinking about it.

SOPHIE SAYS: Can't it be both?

JAMES SAYS: I think it can be, but lots of people would disagree.

SOPHIE SAYS: I think I might be in your camp on that front.

JAMES SAYS: Interestingly, I think you might be in my camp on several fronts. Off into a meeting now. More later. X

Talk about leaving me on a cliffhanger. I knew what I hoped that meant, was feeling a slight blossoming in my chest that somehow the signs I'd been subconsciously picking up on were right, and James was dominant sexually. But I was too cynical to do anything other than compile a list of things that he could have meant that didn't involve rocking my world in all the filthy and nonfilthy ways that I hoped he could. Plan for the worst and hope for the best and all that.

He definitely kept me waiting, though.

Finally, around 9pm that night, as I was just packing up for the evening, I got the familiar instant message ping on my phone.

JAMES SAYS: . . . So apart from the knickers thing was there anything
specific from our dinner out that you found hot?

I grinned a little, hopeful about what he was trying to get
at, but still disinclined to help until he showed his hand a
bit more. I know, I sound like I was game playing, and I
promise I wasn't, but until I knew exactly how far he felt
he was I wasn't risking scaring him off.

SOPHIE SAYS: This sounds like fishing for compliments . . . Did you have
anything specific to ask about?

I imagined his look of outrage at being accused of fishing
for compliments. It amused me quite a lot.

JAMES SAYS: How about when I spanked you?

At this point I was properly grinning. OK, I think I was
safe in assuming what he was into. Although I couldn't
resist making the look of outrage worse.

SOPHIE SAYS: I did like that, although you didn't hurt me really.

Wilful? Me? OK, maybe a bit. It was fun though.

JAMES SAYS: Who says I was properly trying to hurt you?

OK, that made my throat go dry. I honestly didn't know
how to respond. Before I could drag my thoughts together
to come up with something, my phone vibrated in my
hands.

JAMES SAYS: Would you like me to hurt you more?

I knew the answer. I was fairly sure he knew the answer. But typing those three little letters felt like a massive step into the unknown. I wasn't sure I dared. I hedged instead.

SOPHIE SAYS: I thought you said nice guys didn't do that sort of thing?

JAMES SAYS: I thought you said boring guys didn't do that sort of thing but nice guys could?

Hmmm. Hoist by own petard.

SOPHIE SAYS: Yes.

JAMES SAYS: Yes to what? Nice guys can or you want me to hurt you?

The butterflies in my stomach were fluttering like I'd never felt them before. This was either going to be amazing or it was going to be a hideous misunderstanding, where I made a complete arse of myself. I screwed up my courage.

SOPHIE SAYS: Both.

I stared at the phone, unsure what I wanted the next message to say, half exhilarated, half terrified at where this could go if things were as I hoped. I should have let the moment pass, just in case it was banter, but I couldn't. Curious minds needed to know.

SOPHIE SAYS: Do you WANT to make me cry?

I didn't realize it until my phone vibrated, but I was holding my breath waiting for his response. I'm not sure that I even knew what I wanted the answer to my question to be.

JAMES SAYS: If you're asking if I'm a sadist, I don't think so, not really. Not usually. Causing pain doesn't get me off, but challenging a submissive who gets off on pain does, if that makes sense. I love the idea of pushing her to her limits, breaking through that barrier to open sobbing.

SOPHIE SAYS: I understand.

I think I do at least. This use of the term 'submissive' fills me with hope. I have no idea what on earth else to say though.

JAMES SAYS: I think this is the least wordy I've ever known you . . .

I rolled my eyes. I knew he was right, but talking about this with him felt awkward in a way talking to Thomas about it never had, and while I knew it was because I was less concerned with Thomas judging me because I didn't intend to date him, frankly that didn't help.

SOPHIE SAYS: I feel uncharacteristically tongue tied.

JAMES SAYS: I suppose it's bad form to admit I like knowing I discombobulate you?

I grinned, feeling more myself.

SOPHIE SAYS: Yes, it is bad form. But you do get brownie points for use
of the word discombobulate.

We spent the entire evening tapping messages back and forth. It sounds daft – I could have nipped round to his straight from work to have the conversations we had, but I think both of us felt that talking in person would be too awkward to start with, make it harder to admit those whispered desires that others could so easily judge. I finally realized though that, while I had figured it was pretty difficult explaining to a potential boyfriend that I might like him to dominate me in lots of filthy and mutually pleasurable ways, the other way round was even tougher – as James explained his fears of being seen as a misogynist, an abuser or worse.

Talking about it with him was fascinating. I'd talked to Thomas about his motivations in dominating someone, but getting to know this whole other facet of James, slotting it in with the hard-working, clever, family-oriented man I had already gotten to know was intriguing. I had so many questions, and he answered them all. From how long he'd known he was interested in such things – hilariously, he'd been entranced by reruns of the perils of cartoon character Penelope Pitstop from a young age, enjoying seeing her captured and tied up even while I'd been pondering the difficulties of Maid Marion – to how he came up with ideas on what to do with his submissives:

JAMES SAYS: Obviously a lot of the time sex, even D/s sex, is spontaneous. Sex can even start as being fairly vanilla but then a quick slap or a certain look can change the dynamic, even if there is little else beyond that. But for me the best D/s sex comes from a decent amount of planning. Sometimes I'm indulging a fantasy and sometimes I'm just experimenting, but I'll usually have some sort of goal that I want to achieve. If a sub is particularly bratty and is doing what she can to push my buttons, get attention and be 'punished' then I will make sure that she doesn't get her own way. Chances are I'll tie her up and put her in a corner, ignoring her until she realizes that I cannot be manipulated into giving her what she wants.

JAMES SAYS: Alternatively a sub might find it difficult to be vocal during a D/s scene because she is embarrassed or just in that space that makes it difficult to communicate. In that case I will make sure that I create a situation where she is punished for not speaking when I want her to and rewarded for responding quickly.

JAMES SAYS: I like to have a plan and I'll stick to it if I can but I also need to be flexible sometimes depending on the situation. If I know that something is proving to be a real challenge for my sub I need to make the decision as to whether she will benefit from being pushed through it or if I need to back off. It's very rare for me to push a sub through something that it later turns out they are not ready for but I sometimes look back and think that perhaps I backed off too quickly – not that I ever let them off easily. I think I know if my sub wants to be challenged and wants me to make her do these things.

He had more experience than me, with a few long-term, albeit vanilla, relationships and some D/s-tinged flings under his belt. He too was trying to strike the balance between someone to play with and someone to be with. And he answered all my many questions reasonably and rationally, even the ones that made my breath hitch as I read them.

JAMES SAYS: I got into it pretty much as soon as sex became more regular for me. One day I was in bed with a girl who mentioned spanking. It was something I'd thought about before, but I didn't really jump at the chance like you might expect. I became Mr Rational and had a conversation with her about how the idea of that and other, similar things turned me on but I wouldn't do it unless she was sure. She said that she was and so, when we had sex and she was on top I gave her a light spanking. She said it felt good but that I could do it harder, so I did. By the time we both came her arse was red and my hand stung. Initially I found it awkward – my parents really did raise me not to lift a hand to anyone – but her reaction was very positive and I soon realized that the difference between this and any form of abuse lay in consent. She gave me permission to spank her, tie her up, etc. The level to which I could hurt her and the things I could do to her were up to her, not me. If she ever said stop (or used her safety word, I always use them) then everything stopped immediately. I enjoy the power, and the control and the game of it. I find the psychology fascinating – what's the best way to get you to do what I want you to do? I could keep you guessing, confuse you, have you on the back foot at every turn, only able to react to the next thing I bring in. Or I could have given you a week's notice of exactly what I'm going to do and let you think it over and over in your mind, teasing and tormenting yourself, testing yourself before I even have to. Both work in different contexts to get you to do what I want you to do.

His insight made me uppity. I couldn't help myself.

SOPHIE SAYS: Who says I want to do what you want me to do?

His response took my breath away.

JAMES SAYS: I thought I read early signs, but then after the night where you cancelled and then your reaction when I held your wrists while we fucked I wasn't sure so I didn't want to push it. But now I'm pretty sure. Of course you want to do what I want you to do. It'll make me happy, and you want to please me.

I knew I sounded confrontational, but I didn't care.

SOPHIE SAYS: Oh really?

JAMES SAYS: Now, now. But yes, really. I'm loathe to pigeonhole anyone, not least because labelling something isn't always helpful. But in my experience I've met submissives with, for want of a better word, a bratty exterior, who misbehave to get a reaction, who enjoy that feeling of being overpowered or controlled in spite of their rebellion. While you've got a smart mouth and a sarcastic streak, I don't think it's that with you. Think of the restaurant. I didn't force you to give me your knickers. I laid down a challenge, which you could either take up or not. You took it up, to prove to me you could do it. You wanted to win, ironically because of course giving me your knickers was, in another way, completely my victory. You like being pushed to do things you find difficult because you enjoy overcoming them. It's the challenge of it, the game for you.

My phone felt heavy in my hands. He was right, although I wouldn't have articulated it that way. The fact that he'd known that, been able to understand my mindset that way, simultaneously made me excited and scared. It was erotic, bewitching and offered possibilities I could barely think of, but I also had a feeling he'd be the most challenging man I'd ever known.

215

To be fair to him, he reassured me of the most serious of my concerns. No, while he called them 'punishments', he wasn't really punishing me for some kind of misbehaviour, he was punishing me because he enjoyed the power, and knew I enjoyed the pain – it sounds daft but that reassured me. Not least because the idea of a relationship where turning up ten minutes late resulted in painful recourse just didn't do it for me; that just felt the wrong side of play somehow.

He also promised he'd go easy on me. I thought we probably had very differing ideas on what counted as easy but I was intrigued, and more than happy to give it a try.

He went to Geneva for four days. By the end of it we had driven each other crazy with questions, flirty thoughts, late-night emails. Deciding this was a game we were at least going to give a try, we'd sketched out the rules of engagement in their broadest terms. As James said in one late-night text message, 'It's not like we need to put together a bloody contract', but we'd discussed safe words, limits, hard ones and soft ones, and we'd decided that I was going to come to his on the first evening he was back.

The tone of our chats had, reassuringly for me, not changed too substantially. There was no sense of superiority in our day-to-day talk, no po-facedness, and he remained as interested in my opinions and my expertise as he'd ever been. It sounds a no brainer, and it definitely was in hindsight, but at the time I was relieved that, despite the dance of dominance and submission we'd somehow begun, the wider dynamic of our friendship, our relationship, whatever it was, remained unchanged.

The only difference came in the form of a pedantic game we began playing after I called him on a typo in an email he sent me (I know, but forgive me, it's the grammar fascist in me). He responded by pointing out an error of mine – which, for the record, was predictive text-related and thus utterly different – and then a good-natured bickering started, which turned into a thing. Every time I made an error, or called him on an error which later turned out to be correct, he would add five marks to a tally which he would somehow act upon when we were in the same country. Every time he made an error which I flagged up five would be removed from the list. Our emails and text messages suddenly became literal wars of words, both of us fighting to retract errors before the other had the chance to call them. It was silly, funny, and the kind of daft competitive banter that reassured me that James was someone I could cope with – when I finally got round to his to begin whatever this was we were beginning, he wasn't going to be dragging me down to a secluded basement to hurt me. He was, for the most part, a kind, charming, funny sort who disliked misuse of apostrophes almost as much as I did.

12

Well, he didn't drag me down to the basement when I met him upon his return. Actually, he barely let me in the door at all. I was very nervous. Excited, so excited, about where this could go and what it would be like, but also a little perturbed. I was going round to see my friend (my boy-friend? my inner voice questioned), having not seen him for almost a week, but then, at the same time, I was also going to have some presumably intense sex with a new dominant at the same time. I was excited, but a little scared. Not fearful of him, but fearful of not being able to with-stand what he had in store for me – and the awareness of that made me feel even more nervous, because he had seen that part of me before I'd had a chance to tell him about it.

He looked well when he opened the door. He was wearing a soft white buttoned shirt and casual trousers, and was barefoot again. He smiled and led me inside by the arm, closing the door softly with a click behind me.

I went to walk up the stairs in front of him, but before I could he grabbed my wrist and pulled me back to him, enveloping me in a half hug as he pushed his mouth down on to mine. We kissed. I sighed into his mouth, enjoying the taste of him, the dance of our tongues, the closeness of being together after what felt like so long, after so much anticipation. I stood, looking at him, trying to work out if things felt any different, now I knew his own interests meshed so well with mine.

Even as I thought to myself that things felt OK, not too awkward at all, he leaned forward, moving his mouth towards me. I leaned up, hoping for another kiss, but his hands on my shoulders held me back a little, so he could move closer to my ear.

He was as well-spoken as ever; his voice still made my pulse quicken, but as he hissed into my ear my heart began beating faster for a completely different reason.

His words tickled my ear. 'We both know you've spent all week thinking rude thoughts. And I'm looking forward to exploring some of them. But before we do that I want you to do something for me. I'm going to let you taste me before dinner. Get down on your knees. Now.'

He moved back slightly so he could watch my reaction. Everything was silent. Still. We looked at each other for long seconds. He raised an eyebrow in a way that felt like he was both mocking and challenging me. It made the argumentative part of me chafe and long to butt heads with him, even while I found it – him – sexy. Since our chat had turned filthy this had been an inevitability. I wanted to submit to him, had been dreaming of it, wondering how it would feel, what submission with a more emotional connection would be like. In my heart I knew what I was feeling, knew what I was going to do, even while my head told me it was crazy, risky, daft. But as he stared down at me, so secure in the knowledge that I was going to sink to my knees, part of me felt furious. I hadn't even taken my fucking coat off yet.

I wanted to tell him to knob off, and was fairly sure that my mutinous glare was probably saying just that. But as I looked into his eyes I knew the only way I would find out if he was what I hoped he was would be by obeying him now. Right now. It was time to put up or shut up.

I put up. Or perhaps 'put out' is more apt.

I sighed slightly and sank to my knees, thrilled and yet irritated by the smirk of satisfaction on his face as he watched me settle myself at his feet.

He stroked my hair. 'Good girl.'

Being called a girl is one of the things that makes me bristle more than any other. But while part of me bridled at the patronizing nature of the endearment, another part revelled in his praise, keen to show him exactly how good I could be. I leaned forward, opened his fly and gently pulled his cock out. I took my time, running my tongue up and down his length, before sucking it fully into my mouth. As I did so, though, he grabbed the back of my head and began pushing himself into me, leaving me gasping around him. We were battling for control of the rhythm. I struggled to take him, and he took his pleasure at his own pace. As I gasped around his cock he pulled out, a moment of relief.

As my breathing slowed he rubbed his cock against me, anointing my face with our mixed juices. Writing it down, it seems like such a little thing, but my first instinct was pure fury. Feeling him rub the stickiness over my face made me flush with anger. I clenched my hands at my sides, fought to control the loud voice in my head scream-ing out to rebel, to pull away. No one had ever treated me that way before and it felt so degrading that it took all my effort not to react, and instead to let him continue. Despite the part of me that enjoyed it, the greater part of me was furious. But I didn't want that part to win – I was as angry with myself for reacting so violently to the very first thing he'd done as I was with him for doing something so demeaning.

The strength of my reaction threw me for a minute. Fighting to control myself, I closed my eyes against the view to block it out, and to mask my response to it. I took deep breaths and did everything I could to continue my submission in spite of myself. With my eyes shut the slap was a surprise. It didn't hurt exactly, although it felt like enough of a blow that I opened my eyes to see what he had done – just in time to get a close-up view of him hitting me with his cock. I moaned in humiliation, as he continued his assault, his hand in my hair holding me in place as he used me, alternately slapping me and rubbing himself across my face. I was disgusted, debased, and yet – to my own amazement – oh so wet. I shifted slightly on my knees.

He slapped me once more, before grabbing a clump of my hair and forcing himself back into my mouth. I opened as wide as possible to accommodate him, moving my tongue along him as fast as he fucked my face. Then – so suddenly that I almost choked when the first spurt hit the back of my throat – he came in my mouth. As I swallowed and began licking him clean he pulled away from me, putting his cock back in his boxers and doing up his trousers.

I knelt there at his feet, unsure what was to happen now, my nipples hard in my bra, and the taste of his spunk in my throat. He stroked my hair for a second before reaching down to take my arm and solicitously help me to my feet.

'Let me take your coat. And now let's just go and cook some dinner and relax for a little while.'

Feeling not unlike Alice having fallen down a sexy and yet mind-boggling rabbit hole, I took my coat off and followed him into the kitchen. I had been in his house for about ten minutes. I couldn't help noticing the marked difference from the last time I'd visited.

We ate. Talked. Drank a glass of wine each, although no more because both of us were mindful of what was coming later and the necessity for clear heads. Clear-ish heads, anyway. I found the change of gear somewhat mind-boggling, but was just about holding up my end of the conversation, even while I was mentally counting down the minutes until he would lead me to his bedroom so we could play. Finally the moment came.

The cats, it seemed, wanted to play too. As they followed us inside he picked them up one at a time and indulgently fussed them before gently, but firmly, leading them to the bedroom door, whispering to them and stroking behind their ears as he put them down in the hallway. It was so sweet to watch, and made the change in tone when he closed the door and turned to me even more incongruous. He told me to strip and sat down to watch as I began to take my clothes off.

Every woman, no matter how perfect, has parts of her

body she's unhappy with, and trust me when I say I have a fair few imperfections. Generally, however, I try not to worry. I eat healthily, go to the gym at least three times a week, and am fairly optimistic that in the throes of passion most blokes are concerned about many, many things but *not* with whether your stomach's looking a bit flabby.

That said, being told to strip naked in front of someone you fancy who is (a) staying resolutely clothed and (b) thus not doing anything other than watching you intently as your remove your clothes is a very disconcerting thing. With an economy of movements and very little grace, I took my top off, pulled my trousers down – pulling my socks off at the same time, since they really are inherently unsexy – and then stayed still for a moment, screwing up my courage for the next step.

I looked at him looking at me, saw the smile playing at the corner of his mouth, and decided it was time to play him at his own game. I could do this. I could fake a confidence I didn't feel. Hell, I had to do it for work sometimes, admittedly for non-naked reasons, and no one ever cottoned on. So smiling slightly, and hoping that I wasn't blushing as red as much as I feared I was, I pulled my hands behind my back and undid my bra, pulling it forward and off. Not stopping, I then went straight for my knickers, stacking both items on top of everything else on his bed. Then I turned back to him, resisting the urge to cross my arms across my chest with every fibre of my being.

We stayed like that for a few minutes. Me, with the breeze of the open window playing across my naked body, James sitting, watching me. The early evening sunshine lit up the room and the sounds of car doors opening and closing and some kids playing football outside made it feel surreal. But still I stood there.

Finally he moved.

He walked across the room and put his arm around me to cup my arse. I curled into him, needing this, needing him. He leant down to kiss me and everything else melted away except feeling his hands on my body and his lips on mine. Then he pulled back, brushing a strand of my hair over my shoulder, and smiled at me.

'Mmmmm. Before we do anything else you need to take your punishment.'

I felt a surge of rebellion and fury. For god's sake, what was his compulsion with keeping me on the back foot, did it have to be *all* the time? Balls. I looked at him warily, mindful as well that, thanks to the vagaries of predictive text and an ill-informed bet on who the next England manager was going to be, I was now at a hundred points on our little scorecard. I didn't even know what it was a hundred of, but it made me very nervous indeed. I was at least hoping for a night's sleep first.

'Do we have to do it now?' I asked hopefully.

'Nah, if you want to wait I'll just fit in with when you decide you can be arsed.' I glared at him and he shook his head, even while he stroked my face.

'You're just making it worse for yourself. Do you want to see where this goes or not Sophie? Seize the day, remember?'

He was smiling, joking a little I think, but I still felt stung. And I knew that the choice I made was important.

The problem is, I already knew I was going to do what he wanted *again* and it was still annoying me. How could it chafe this way to submit to someone I actually like, find attractive, would like to date? He was watching me intently. I sighed.

'Fine, OK, what do I have to do?'

His smile made my stomach flip. He looked so happy, and that made me happy. At least until he spoke again. He led me across the room to a rug in front of his fireplace. 'I'd like you to bend over. You can put your hands on your ankles or your knees, whichever is more comfortable. But once you're in position you stay there. You're going to count to a hundred for me and thank me for every strike. Is that clear?'

My voice was muffled by my long hair falling into my face as I moved my hands to my knees, my mind whirring as to what he was going to use if he was intending to hit me a full hundred times. For the first time ever I felt genuinely scared at having pain inflicted on me in this way. How on earth would I be able to withstand so much?

He tapped me on the arse in warning, stirring me out of my rising panic. 'Sorry. Yes, I . . . Yes, I understand.'

I tensed myself for the first strike, but he had come round to face me, was leaning in, searching for my eyes under the curtain of my hair. We stared at each other for long seconds. His voice, when he finally spoke, was calming, oddly soothing. 'I'm going to use the crop on you, Sophie. You'll be able to withstand it, I promise, but if for any reason you want to stop, just use your safe word. You remember it, right?'

I nodded, feeling now wasn't the time to point out my

subconscious was already screaming it. He smiled at me, and in that moment he was James and I was Sophie and it was all OK. Then he began.

The first ten didn't hurt at all. I counted them off, thanking him for each one, generally not really bothered about the taps on my arse, thinking instead with anticipation about what would happen once we'd got this daft punishment out of the way, relieved it wasn't hurting as much as I had feared.

Then suddenly something clicked – the angle he was using changed imperceptibly, or he found his rhythm, or something, and suddenly it hurt so much it took my breath away. I kept counting, stayed upright – just – although at one point he caught me with such force at the point where my arse met my thigh that I stumbled slightly and had to use my hands to right myself. I did so quickly, apologizing desperately lest he decide to add more for me moving from position. Fortunately he didn't.

With every stroke I thanked him, although by the time we reached fifty my teeth were gritted and my voice didn't sound very thankful at all. It hurt so much more than I had expected it to, and sheer bloody-mindedness was the only thing keeping me upright and counting. His rhythm was relentless, focusing purely on my left arse cheek, and as he kept hitting the same spot the pain began to build until I was finding it harder and harder to force any thanks from my dry throat.

At sixty he stopped for a moment. He grabbed a handful of hair and pulled my face up so he could look into my eyes.

226

'Are you crying? You sound like you're crying.'

The part of me that is all stubborn pride and no self-preservation answered before the rest of me could even think. 'I'm not.'

He looked closely, his eyes searching mine to assess how close he was to breaking me – something which actually made me feel safer and more calm, despite the pain I was processing. He nodded slightly at what he saw in my face. 'Do you need to stop?'

My chin raised and I heard my voice as if from far away, sounding more assured than I felt. 'No. I'm fine.' What an idiot.

As he let go of my hair and moved behind me all I could think of was my mum's continual warning that stubbornness would one day be my downfall – although I don't think this was exactly what she had in mind. He started on my arse again and – thankfully – thoughts of Mum disappeared as I began desperately trying to process the pain once more.

By the time we got to eighty it was all I could do to stand. I remained in position – a victory for pigheadedness – but with every stroke my inner monologue was screaming 'Twenty to go, nineteen to go, eighteen to go.' My legs were wobbling and I was in agony. When we got to a hundred the relief rushed through me. So much for it not hurting that much.

James allowed me to stand upright and moved in front of me, kissing my forehead gently as I trembled in front of him, the pain and adrenaline thrumming through me.

'Good girl. Well done. You were very brave.'

I bit back a grimace at the hated endearment and he ran

a finger between my legs. I moaned in pleasure, leaning into him and enjoying him exploring me with his fingers. He chuckled at how wet I was, how my legs started to shake as he pushed me – ridiculously easily – to the brink of orgasm. Then he pulled away. I managed to bite back a whimper – I had no intention of doing anything that would see him picking up the crop again – but I'm sure my eyes betrayed my frustration as he sat down on the edge of the bed, undid his trousers and beckoned me down to kneel in front of him.

I looked at him hopefully, unconsciously waiting for his nod of approval, then finally opened my mouth to take him. I licked him greedily, loving the feeling of his hands in my hair, feeling him clench and unclench his fingers as I began to worship him with my mouth. I lost myself completely in the task. Even the pain of my left arse cheek receded as I sucked.

But then he pulled me away by my hair, took my arms and lifted me up from my knees and back towards the rug. My brain actually short-circuited for a minute. I could see the direction he was trying to manoeuvre me in, and all I could think of was the crop and the pain. But I couldn't form words, much less sentences, and instead I heard myself making a desperate mewing noise in the back of my throat. It was both a plea and a refusal. For a few seconds as he spoke to me I couldn't understand what he was saying, such was the depth of my panic at being made to return to the punishment. But then he kissed my forehead again and stroked me with the same tenderness he'd shown his cats earlier, and somehow I knew he was trying to alleviate my fears, even through the rushing noise in my head. Finally I understood him.

'I'm not going to punish you again. I want you to stand over there so I can fuck you.'

Oh.

I let him help me to my feet and returned to the position I had been in a few minutes before. He rolled on a condom and began to fuck me, grabbing my hips to ensure he could fuck me as hard as possible, hitting my stinging arse with every thrust. It felt amazing. I was still on an adrenaline high from the punishment; I wasn't thinking about anything, I was just responding to him, reacting as he mastered me. He reached round and began frigging my clit and I came around him.

By the time I returned to earth he had moved us both to the bed and I was lying (on my side, as putting any pressure on my arse was going to be uncomfortable for at least the next week) alongside him. I looked up, suddenly a bit embarrassed at exactly how out-of-the-moment I had gone, to see him smiling down at me. He stroked my hair and pressed another kiss to my forehead.

'You were wonderful this evening. Good girl.'

I smiled, closing my eyes for a second to savour the gentleness of his lips. I can honestly say I wasn't bothered about the patronizing tone now. Instead all I felt was achievement, a kind of pride at having pleased him, the thought of a job well done.

Little did I realize this was just the beginning.

13

I pride myself on not getting caught up in the clichéd etiquette of dating. Most of my friends are the same. There's none of that 'these are the rules on when to call or not call' bollocks; we're all straightforward, sensible people. If you like someone, what's the point in bullshitting?

So you'll never see me worrying about when I'm going to see someone again. If I want to see someone I'll ask. If they want to see me too then ace. If not, well, that's crap and my confidence will take a knock, but I'll get over it.

Except it wasn't that way with James.

I'm honestly not hung up on gender stereotypes and try not to turn into that blithering cliché – *should I text, or is that too keen? If I text how many kisses should I put on the end? Hold on, he hasn't put a kiss on the end, but he did before, what does that mean?* But if I thought the etiquette of dating was bad, that's nothing compared to what happens when you throw in a D/s power element. Is suggesting we meet again pushy? Unsubmissive? Should I be waiting for him to arrange something? If he doesn't, do I just keep waiting? At what point should I give up and assume that actually he's not interested? Is the fact I'm the most impatient person I know likely to cause me a problem?

Meeting James coincided with the kind of time at work

that made for a Sophie of all work and no play. Various people were on holiday and the big launch of a new publication was in the works, and that translated into the kind of hours that made sleeping under my desk seem like a tempting prospect. It also meant I was a bit, well, disengaged. I talked to James by email every day and found him as interesting as ever but over a period of a week or two things went from being steamy to, well, a bit tepid. I'd be bouncing work moans back and forth or linking him to stuff coming in on our newswire, but the smutty stuff? Somewhere along the way it dissipated in a way that left me thinking, 'Damn, obviously he's not as interested in me that way as I am in him.' So in characteristic fashion I decided the thing to do was to not address it, pretend everything was fine and leave it be. Until, erm, I couldn't any more and it burst forth like a slightly frightening torrent. Great.

It was a Thursday afternoon. The Thursday afternoon before The Big Project™ launched and the point in the process where all the problems seemed insurmountable, except you know they'll be resolved because they have to be and you'll just keep going until your eyes fall out of the back of your head and you can't think of another decent headline pun.

I was on Messenger in part because I was discussing final colour choices for headers for the different sections of the magazine with our chief designer. But I'd been chatting to James in another window as he sat wrestling with some dry financial gubbins.

The conversation had started incongruously enough but a passing comment that normally I'd have been sensible enough to leave alone started me off.

JAMES SAYS: We'll have to see what happens when we next meet.

SOPHIE SAYS: Indeed. Although when will that be? Because we've yet to set anything up . . . :P

Ah, yes, a little jaunty tongue hides the neediness oozing from every syllable of that sentence. Oh dear. Must make it better.

SOPHIE SAYS: Not that I'm moaning.

SOPHIE SAYS: Just saying.

SOPHIE SAYS: And if you don't want to meet again – cause it has been a while now – then that's fine too. Really.

Shit, do I now sound like I'm not interested in him?

SOPHIE SAYS: I mean obviously I'd *like* to meet again.

Why is Vera Lynn running through my head now? How have I dug myself such a big bloody hole? How do I get out of it?

SOPHIE SAYS: But if you don't then that's fine, I'd just rather know.

Wow. You'd think it was difficult to sound both standoffish and needy at the same time, but I appeared to have managed it. Brilliant.

As I pondered whether disconnecting and blaming technical difficulties (and possibly partial lobotomy) was the best way of stopping this conversation without making it worse, I heard the ping of a response. I was fairly convinced it wouldn't be about whether green or purple best portrayed 'lifestyle' but could hardly bring myself to look at the screen to see.

JAMES SAYS: Of course I'd like to meet. What made you think I wouldn't?

JAMES SAYS: I just figured, bearing in mind how stressed you sound every time I speak to you lately, that looming over you like some überdom was perhaps not the most supportive course of action.

JAMES SAYS: I take it this is a subtle hint that you might be free and inclined to play some time soon then?

Oh. Suddenly even the shittiest day at work wasn't bothering me at all and I caught myself grinning at the screen in a way that may well have terrified my co-workers, since it was the first time I'd cracked a smile in working hours for about a fortnight.

And that's how I ended up spending a full twenty-four hours under James's control. At his suggestion I booked a day off work for the day after the big, big project went to press – on time and with my sanity still intact. It was a great idea, as the morning after something comes out all you do is sit at your desk drinking coffee and praying the phone won't ring, as if it does it's usually someone telling you something's gone wrong, which you now can do nothing about anyway. So spending a day alone with him, not knowing exactly what would happen, and burning off some excess energy was an idea that sounded relaxing and brilliant. At least it did until I realized exactly what I'd let myself in for, and that 'relaxing' was never in a million years going to be an adjective to describe it.

I arrived at 7.30pm after a schlep through the rush-hour traffic, and any curiosity about how this would all start was ended rather abruptly. I followed him into his flat and bent down to pet the cats hello. As I stood up, I swapped my overnight bag to my other hand. As his eyes took it in, he moved towards me and plucked it from my grasp.

'You won't be needing that,' he told me as he led me into the living room, chucking it on the floor. He plonked himself down on the sofa and I stood in front of him, feeling awkward, not entirely sure what to do as he was sprawled across it in a way that left no space for me. At least I was unsure until he spoke, and then it all made sense.

'Strip for me. Now.'

I looked at him, relaxed and smiling like someone in a sofa commercial, secure in the knowledge that I was going to do what he asked. As ever, the beginning of the scene remained the most difficult part for me and the picture of arrogance he made lying there, waiting for me to move, knowing that I would, made me grit my teeth as I slipped out of my shoes and began undoing my shirt.

'Hold on a second, stop.'

My hands stopped on my third button at his order.

I looked over at him, wishing he'd make up his mind – did he want me to undress or not?

'Yes?' My voice sounded a bit shrill to my own ears. I knew it was from embarrassment, but I worried that he might interpret it as attitude and so I lowered my tone. 'Yes?'

His eyes sparkled as he spoke to me, inspiring a surge of affection even while it caused butterflies in the pit of my stomach. Those butterflies started going mad at what he said next.

'For the next twenty-four hours you are mine. Mine only. Everything you do is for me. Your wishes, your needs, even your dignity, count for nothing. You will do everything I ask you to do, to the best of your ability, in the way that you know will bring me the most pleasure. Is that clear?'

I had to swallow hard before I could speak. The immediate ramifications of this had already started running through my mind, and a blush was beginning to stain my cheeks. 'Yes.'

'Well then, don't you think you should slow down and take your clothes off in a way that you know will please me?'

I didn't trust myself to speak, so nodded.

'Good girl. Well then, strip for me. Not functionally, sensually. Show me your body. Show me my property.'

While intellectually I knew he was pushing me to see a reaction, it took a lot of effort not to push back, particularly at the idea of being his 'property'. I knew that was effectively the deal we had done, and that – actually – there was a great part of me keen to surrender to him in that way for a little while to see where he took us.

My teeth were gritted and my fingers clumsy as I began playing with my partially open top, flashing a glimpse of my bra as I ran my hands down my body, over my hips and skirt before I slowly began to undress once more.

The five minutes that followed felt like an eternity. If it wasn't for the fact that I spent a great part of the time too embarrassed to look at James and instead staring over his shoulder, looking at the wall behind him which happened to have a clock on it, I'd have sworn it went on for nearer an hour.

I'm comfortable in my own skin, but I'm both aware my body is far from perfect and not the kind of person who likes being the centre of attention at the best of times. Being made to strip in that way made me feel ridiculous, embarrassed, objectified. Every instinct was telling me to get it over with quickly, even while I knew I had to take my time, tease and tantalize as well as I could.

By the time I was down to my knickers an embarrassed flush had bloomed across my chest as well as my face, and I was hiding behind my hair as much as possible. I don't think I had ever felt as vulnerable and the feeling was prickly, unpleasant. My throat felt clogged and I was inexplicably close to tears.

I finally pulled down my knickers and stood in front of him, naked, physically and emotionally. After long seconds he moved towards me.

'Your posture really is atrocious, you know.'

His face was unreadable as he leant around me, his

hands reaching around my back to push my shoulder blades, making my breasts stand out, the nipples rubbing against the rough wool of his jumper.

'I know it's because you feel embarrassed about the size of your breasts,' – at that he ran a finger along the line of fire across my chest – 'but there really is no excuse for it and hunching over doesn't make them look smaller. You shouldn't be hiding them anyway.'

I felt shy, which was ridiculous. 'Sorry.'

He tutted, tweaking a nipple in rebuke.

'I see we're also going to have to work on ensuring you use the correct modes of address as well.' What?

'For the next twenty-four hours you're going to address me as Sir.' I looked askance at him. While calling him that wasn't a hard limit, it was something we'd discussed previously and which I'd said I thought was ridiculous. His smile and twinkling eyes suggested he remembered the conversation well. 'Just for the next twenty-four hours.'

I looked at him and could deny him nothing. 'Fine.'

He tweaked my nipple again, harder.

'Sorry. Fine. Sir.'

He smiled and the queasy feeling in my stomach disappeared, replaced with a pride that was as shocking as it was warming. Knowing I'd pleased him made the awkwardness seem somehow worthwhile, although the sooner he ended up naked too, the happier I knew I'd be.

He smoothed my hair away from my face as I stood still, waiting for what came next. But he kissed my shoulder and then moved behind me.

I could hear sounds of rummaging, a cupboard door opening, and then a jangling sound that made me want to turn around even though I knew I shouldn't. I stood, shoulders back, waiting nervously for whatever was to happen next.

He was back in front of me, not carrying anything that would send me running for the hills. In fact, not carrying anything at all, so far as I could see.

'Do you trust me?'

'Yes.' My answer was quick, firm and sure. I honestly did.

The last thing I saw was his smile as he pulled a blindfold he'd had scrunched in one of his hands over my eyes.

'Good.'

I had never been blindfolded during sex before, or, come to think of it, for anything other than a few games of blind man's buff at birthday parties as a child. I was surprised at how vulnerable I felt.

Despite having deliberately avoided his gaze during my strip tease just minutes earlier, being in a position where I couldn't see anything at all didn't make me feel less embarrassed or shy, it just made me feel more exposed. And, of course, it meant I had even less idea about what would happen next.

I waited.

The jangling was back and he was behind me, grabbing my wrists, cuffing them in something that felt cold and unyielding. Then my ankles were tied together with something tighter, something fabric, that gave me a tiny bit of shuffle room but not much else.

I felt him straighten up behind me. His voice whispering directly into my ear made me jump.

'I think we're going to work on your posture now, sweet. I know you feel embarrassed showing yourself to me, but right now that's all I want from you. I'm going to get a glass of wine and sit down and just admire you for a little bit while I decide what I'm going to do to you next.'

His teeth nipped my ear and he chuckled as I shivered. 'So many possibilities. So many ideas. I just don't know where to start. Get down on your knees.'

Dropping to your knees when your ankles are tied together and your hands are behind you, making you more off balance, takes a little while and left me feeling rather ungainly.

I'd lost track of where he was in the room, couldn't even be sure he hadn't popped to the kitchen for his wine, and yet I still felt like his eyes were on me. Finally I got to my knees, pulled my shoulders back to push my breasts out, and sat and waited.

And waited.

Every movement and change of air in the room made me start. Was that him? Was that one of the cats? And if so, how the hell was I going to shoo them away?

Suddenly his hand was in my hair and his voice was back in my ear, making me jump.

'Spread your legs for me. I want to see you.'

I shuffled on the carpet, opening my knees a little.

His tut – now in front of me – made me start, and I felt his foot push at my knee, making me spread myself wider in wanton fashion.

'That's better. I want to see how aroused treating you like this makes you, even in spite of yourself, even though I've not touched you yet. You're flushed – but I'm not sure it's embarrassment any more, although god knows it should be. Instead you're turned on. Your nipples look like they're aching for my touch, or my teeth. As for the rest of you, you're glistening.'

Suddenly I was very glad for the blindfold as I knew, despite – or perhaps because of – my discomfort, he was right. I could feel the heavy wetness between my legs.

He pushed me yet wider with his foot and I wondered fleetingly why I didn't feel the fury I would normally. The bonds, the blindfold, something had changed the dynamic and it felt unreal. Hyper-real. Something.

'Your juice is on my shoe. Dirty girl. I should make you lick it off. If you make a mess you should clean it up. It's only fair, right?'

OK, the fury was back. I didn't argue, but my tone was more mutinous than I'd have liked as I replied. 'Whatever you wish, sir.'

He laughed. 'Good answer. And I do like the idea of your tongue on my shoes, licking off the evidence of your arousal. But right now I'm liking looking up between your legs best of all.'

Even behind the blindfold I closed my eyes. I heard him take a drink – of his wine, I assumed.

He told me how he'd been wondering what it would be like to push me. How all the messages back and forth, the relatively sedate dinner, the initial play date, had all been leading to this. How I didn't know what was going to hit me, had no idea what I'd let myself in for, that I was his now. And while I knew he was in the moment, and that I could trust him, fear cramped my stomach just a little. I couldn't move, I couldn't see. Suddenly I wished the blindfold was off, that I could look into his eyes for a moment and see the reassurance there. As it was, I felt myself get a little panicky and yet more aroused at the feeling of powerlessness.

I knelt in silence, my lips pressed together to stop them trembling, waiting to see what would happen next. I felt his eyes on me – I think – and every movement in the room made me shrink slightly, waiting for a touch, something.

I heard him take another drink and my throat felt suddenly dry. I swallowed.

'Are you thirsty?' he asked, from the direction of the sofa. 'Would you like something to drink?'

I nodded and then thought better of it. 'Yes, please.' He didn't respond, and after a few seconds I realized why. Damnit. 'Sir.'

I felt him leaning towards me. 'Good girl. I'm tempted to fill a bowl with some water and see if I can tempt you to drink from it like an animal.' Suddenly I thought I could manage without a drink for now, and something in my demeanour must have betrayed how unhappy I was with this suggestion as he laughed at my reaction. 'But I'll be kind this time.'

He pushed a glass to my lips. I put my mouth round it tentatively, wondering suspiciously for a moment what it was, before he tilted it and I had to swallow or have it pour down my front.

It was soda water with ice and some lemon, and it tasted amazing. As he tilted the glass further I had to drink faster to avoid wearing it. I felt a surge of anger at the fact he was demonstrating his power over me with even the simplest of things.

He moved back to the sofa, and I heard the crunch of him eating something. My position, the fact that I had become some kind of blind floorshow while he had a snack, made me furious. Thank goodness I had the blindfold on to hide it.

'Are you all right there, sweet? Is there something you want to say?'

I wasn't hiding it well then. I knew he was trying to get a rise out of me, and you'd think that knowing that would have made it easier to keep a feeling of Zen-like calm. It's wasn't.

'No, thank you. I'm fine.'

He stroked my hair.

'If you're sure. I'd hate for you to feel you couldn't speak freely.'

I knew that speaking freely would get me into lots of trouble so I shook my head and pressed my lips together to avoid the urge.

'Are you hungry? Is that the problem? Would you like me to feed you?'

Mindful of his threat to have me drinking from a bowl, I had no intention of eating food in a similar way; that was definitely a debasement too far. I opened my mouth to say no, and his fingers were at my lips, pushing something in. A cube of some kind of cheese. I chewed it slowly, enjoying it. As I swallowed, his fingers were back, this time with an olive. Oily, sweet. As I swallowed, his fingers were back at my mouth, empty this time. Without thinking I sucked them into my mouth and licked them clean. So much for not being demeaned or treated like some kind of animal. Suddenly I felt like one of his cats.

He pulled his fingers away and he was pushing at my mouth again, although this time it was his cock he was pressing to my lips. I opened my mouth to welcome him, eager, enjoying sucking him, until he grabbed me by the hair, holding me in place as he began fucking my mouth. I wriggled my arms for a second, the panic of beginning to feel choked making me forget that I couldn't move my hands round to do anything. I was snuffling round him, desperately trying to breathe, twisting my head to try and pull back, just a little. I felt him thicken in my mouth at my struggles, making it worse, and I tried to signal somehow that this was too much, that he needed to give me a second. Except I couldn't gesture, couldn't speak, and while the blindfold was wet with my tears I wasn't entirely sure he was aware of that. Or actually that he cared.

When he came in my mouth I swallowed him as well as I could, although as he pulled out I gasped to catch my breath and I felt something – either his spunk or my drool – dripping down my chin. Classy.

He tugged on my hair, and I half crawled, half shuffled across the floor as best I could in my bonds towards the sofa so he could stroke my hair as he sat down. I calmed a little, my heartbeat slowing, although I still felt well and truly on the back foot.

I don't know how long we sat there, but it was long enough for our breathing to slow. His hand on my hair was almost hypnotic and I was soothed as we sat quietly. Until he spoke again.

'We still have to work on your posture. And your modes of address. Don't we?'

Bugger. Where's this coming from? How many times had I not called him sir in the last hour? And how bad had the slouching been? I pushed my shoulders back, closing the stable door after the horse has bolted? Possibly. But it couldn't hurt could it?

He tweaked my nipple, bringing me out of my panic. 'Don't we?'

'Yes.'

'Yes?'

Gah.

'Yes, sir.'

He pulled me to my feet and freed my arms. I stretched a little, feeling happier and slightly more in control – for half a second, until he refastened them in front of me.

'Bend over.'

My heart was pounding already as this posture was James's preferred punishment stance.

Shit.

His voice was in my ear, It was harsh in a way that probably would have been less intimidating if I could see him, but that made me feel a jolt of genuine fear.

'I won't tell you again. Bend over.'

I trembled as I moved into position, but I didn't think of disobeying. Was this progress or stupidity? I wasn't entirely sure. He started hitting me, not with the crop but with something else. Something longer, with more give and which hurt so much that the air rushed out of my lungs with every strike in time with the swooshing noise of it cutting the air and connecting with my arse.

He hit one cheek, and then the other. There was no rhythm to it, nothing to count, no indication of how long it would last. I have no idea how many times he hit me, just that it hurt. It hurt so damn much. Each strike hurt, and the feeling of the residual strikes was like a burning agony, layer upon layer of pain as he kept going. It made Charlotte's punishment seem feather-light in comparison, and not knowing how long it would last made it feel impossible to bear.

Finally he stopped. His hand squeezed my arse and made me suck air in through my teeth.

'Do you think you'll remember now?'

My reply was garbled, desperate, quick. 'Yes. Yes. Definitely.'

Quick and stupid. I realized the error as he moved away again.

'Sorry. Sir. Yes, sir.'

He began again. The strikes were faster than I could process. Faster than I could endure. Each one cut across my arse leaving a line of agony. I was sure I was bleeding, I couldn't imagine withstanding this amount of pain without it drawing blood.

I wanted to stop. But I didn't want to disappoint him.

I didn't want to use a safe word. I could withstand it. Not just out of stubborn bloody-minded pride, but because this was the most challenging thing we had ever done and I didn't intend to fail it. But it hurt so much and I had no idea how long it would last and I just couldn't cope. After the stresses and strains of the last few weeks at work, the humiliation and embarrassment of stripping earlier, the sensory deprivation that meant I couldn't even look to him for reassurance, it was all too much.

I started to cry, snotty, guttural sobbing. I couldn't stop myself. The noise sounded alien, shocking, even to my own ears. I sounded broken, desperate, wounded. He hit me a couple more times, and then I heard the clatter of whatever it was he was hitting me with landing on the floor. It had stopped. But I couldn't. I cried as he undid my wrists and ankles, pulled the blindfold from my eyes, grabbed a blanket from somewhere I didn't see. I cried as he led me to the sofa where he sat, patting his lap and encouraging me to curl up next to him and put my head on his thigh. I cried as he gently draped the blanket over my nakedness, making sure not to touch my arse as he did so. I cried until my throat was raw, until my sobs dissipated into snuffles and an occasional hiccup. I cried until I felt like I couldn't cry any more. They were tears of catharsis, releasing a tension that I didn't even know I was carrying. I felt broken down and rebuilt. They weren't tears of upset, but I couldn't stop them. So I cried, and through it all he just stroked my hair and waited.

And then I fell asleep.

*

246

I woke up in a puddle of my own drool. On his thigh. Classy. He must have thought I was a complete nut job, all things considered. In a split second everything that had come before flashed through my mind and I was horrified. I couldn't remember the last time I had made such a complete twat of myself and I felt stupid, and embarrassed and tearful and sick. I wanted to fling on my clothes and run away and not ever look at him again, but doing that would have involved moving and that would have involved speaking and having him look at me. So I lay very still in the flickering light of the TV, which appeared to have been switched on at some point while I slept, trying to figure out what time it was and what on earth to do next.

'Are you awake?'

His voice was solicitous, neither laughing nor seemingly concerned about the fact he'd invited a nutter into his home, and that this nutter had then jiggled about in unalluring fashion and nearly choked to death on his cock, before having a kind of panic attack and then passing out on his leg in a tidal wave of dribble.

The urge to feign sleep was strong but I figured he must have had his suspicions since he'd asked about ten seconds after I woke up. This probably meant I had been snoring on top of everything else. God, I could never see this man again.

My voice was quiet. 'No.'

He laughed and the vibrations of it make me jiggle slightly on his leg.

He stroked my hair and I felt warmed by the connection.

'"No, sir." Surely?'

Fuck. I went to sit up, desperate to set things straight before he started up again with whatever the hell that was. In my haste I managed to bash my arse with my foot and it hurt so much I whimpered. I began apologizing, saying 'sir' every other word, desperate, giddy, horrified, looking into his face with pleading eyes for reassurance.

He stopped me with a single finger to my mouth. He was smiling, kind.

'Shhhhhhh. It's OK. It's OK. We're done for now. And you did very well. Really well.'

He kissed me and adjusted the blanket so it covered us both better.

I think that was the moment when I started to fall in love with him.

14

From that point James and I settled into the typical first flushes of an almost-relationship. By unspoken agreement we didn't define it, perhaps because subconsciously we felt that to do so might make the magic dissipate like early-morning mist, but we had a lot of fun. We spoke every day, either by phone or email, texting at odd little moments when that didn't feel enough. We saw lots of films, walked by the river, spent hours talking over wine and cheese in a subterranean wine bar and generally did the sort of things that would be at home in the depiction of a burgeoning relationship in a chick flick. Except for the bit at the end where we'd go back to one or other of our homes and fuck and suck and bite and play until we were both exhausted and I was bruised and whimpering.

Don't get me wrong, we weren't joined at the hip. I visited Ella and Thomas, nipped home for my dad's birthday weekend, and had a couple of shifts that involved Saturdays or Sundays at my desk. But while I was busily telling my subconscious this didn't count as a new relationship yet, I thought of James throughout the day like a love-struck teenager, to the point where my first instinct when it came to talking about my day or sharing something great that had happened was to ring or text him. For six weeks we were almost permanently connected, always just a few moments from speaking. And then I had to go away for work.

Hot on the heels of The-Big-Project-that-by-some-miracle-had-not-turned-into-a-catastrophe, I was asked to go and spend a week visiting another part of the company I work for, based in a different part of the country, to help them launch something similar. In typical journalistic fashion it meant long days and late nights, all of which meant I didn't get to speak with James anywhere near as much as I had in the past few weeks. I missed him – not just for the smut, although my days were so packed that I found his absence made me especially wistful when I lay in bed at night and my mind finally had time to wander. But life was so busy that I didn't get to speak to him much, and I certainly didn't get a chance to write down my explicit fantasy of what we'd do the first night we were reunited that I'd promised to email to him while I was away. Frankly, hunched over my laptop at a hot desk ten hours a day meant by the time I got back to the hotel room – invariably after a few glasses of red and some war stories and gossip with colleagues about friends of friends from the incestuous world of journalism – I just wasn't in the mindset to write anything sexy. And by the final night of my stay I figured it was enough that I'd be seeing him shortly and we could get reacquainted in person, particularly since, having asked about it a couple of times on the phone and by text, he hadn't mentioned it since.

He rang not long after I'd got in from the pub. Freshly showered, I was curled up in bed with *Newsnight* on low when his name flashed up on my phone. I answered with a smile in my voice, which dimmed slightly when I heard his tone. While he answered my questions about how his day had gone, told me his cats' latest escapades, and asked politely about my launch, he was brusque in a way that left me feeling vaguely uneasy.

I soon found out why.

Normally our silences were easy but as the static on the line echoed in my ear and I waited for him to say something, I couldn't think of anything to fill the void. It was obvious from the fact he'd rung that he wanted to talk about something specific, but waiting for him to begin was excruciating. In the long seconds I waited I had a sick feeling in the pit of my stomach, knowing how important a part of my life he had become in such a short period of time, and wondering how I would cope with the grief at the loss of this undefined relationship, if that was what he was gearing up to. Although how could he end it? We hadn't even properly decided what it was yet, damn it.

Finally he spoke. 'Do you have anything you want to tell me?'

My mind froze up for a second and suddenly I felt guilt-ridden. I know, it's ridiculous. I'd done nothing wrong that I could think of, but I still felt worried. What did he think I had to tell him? What had I done? I was one of the most boring people I knew – the closest thing to a secret I had was the D/s aspect of my life, and he knew all about that. My heart was racing but I had no idea what I was supposed to say and the knowledge of my ignorance made me feel completely powerless – and not in the way that would normally make my pulse race.

'Well?' I didn't think his voice in my ear could get even more irritable, but it most definitely had.

I took a deep breath and went to speak but, honestly, I had nothing. I let the breath out and tried to at least sound calm. 'Like what? Is everything OK?'

Seconds ticked by. 'Do you think everything's OK, Sophie?'

Shit. What did he mean by everything? Everything in the world? Everything in our non-relationshipy relationship? Everything we'd talked about today? I needed clues, something so I didn't feel this bloody tentative. 'I think so. Why? Do you not? Has something happened?'

His response was quick. 'No, Sophie, nothing's happened, which is rather my point.'

I like to think that on a normal day, when my head wasn't fuzzy with a couple of glasses of wine and rising concern over him using my name twice in quick succession – one thing I'd learned with James was that this was a sign of impending trouble – I'd have got it then. Of course on this occasion I didn't, which was my eventual downfall.

'What do you mean?'

'What do you think I mean, Sophie?' Three Sophies. This was bad. And I still had no clue.

I tried to tamp down the sound of my frustration, as I knew that would just makes things worse, but it was touch and go. I bit the words out – this kind of powerlessness makes me want to kick things. 'I don't know, that's why I'm asking.'

He sighed, and I felt a pang at annoying him, in spite of

the fact he was fast annoying me to the point I wished I'd just not picked up the phone when he rang and told him later I was asleep. 'What was the one thing you were supposed to do this week, Sophie?'

Oh. Bugger. He hadn't forgotten. Of course not.

'The email, of course, the email. I'm sorry I haven't got round to it, it's just work's been so mad, the net connection at the hotel's rubbish, I've not been feeling especially sexy and, well, I'm just so tired every night . . .' I tailed off. My voice sounded whiny even to me.

His voice was so quiet that I had to put a finger to my other ear to block out the world to hear it. 'I asked you to do one thing Sophie. Have you done it?'

Suddenly I had a lump in my throat and an odd ache in my heart and I wished with every fibre of my being that I had a different answer for him. And this wasn't playing, wasn't fun. It was about me feeling bad for having let him down, for – perhaps – having inadvertently hurt him by not doing something to prove I'd been thinking of him while I'd been away, and for not obeying him in the way I should have. It was odd. On one level it felt like an irrational feeling, but it was definitely a deeply felt one.

My voice was quiet. 'No. I haven't. I'm sorry.'

There was no noise on the line but static, and as I listened to it the feeling of guilt at letting him down weighed on me.

'I put something into the side pocket of your overnight bag. Go and get it.'

I don't know what I was expecting when I opened the brown paper bag, but my trepidation dissipated when

I pulled out four pairs of chopsticks not unlike those you'd get at your local Chinese takeaway.

'So what have you got?'

I couldn't hide the bemusement in my voice. 'Chopsticks. Enough for a party, actually.'

He chuckled and for a moment he was my James and even though he was pissed off I felt a little less worried. And then he was back to business. 'You'll need three pairs, and the rubber bands.'

Rubber bands? I dug them out of the bottom of the bag. Hmmm.

'Wind a rubber band round each end of each of the three pairs. Tightly.' I began doing so, unsure exactly about where this was going to go, but trying to make amends. 'And when you've done that, strip naked.'

Oh.

His voice in my ear was reasonable. There was no anger, not even his earlier pique. He sounded resolute yet calm. What was about to happen was inevitable. It might or might not give him pleasure, but that was academic, it had to be done, as a lesson. I knew this before he said it, as I heard him explain how, in a moment I was going to punish myself.

To be honest I wasn't entirely sure how that would work, bearing in mind I am such a wuss when it comes to inflicting pain on myself. I don't pluck my own eyebrows because it hurts too much. Still, on the plus side, how hard could it be? Anything that I inflicted on myself was going to be significantly lighter-handed than James would have done, had he been there in person. Right? Of course,

I underestimated him. As he explained to me how I was to trap each of my nipples between these impromptu chopstick clamps, I realized that it wasn't as simple as I thought. And then he told me to put the first one on.

For a split second before the bands holding the chopsticks together snapped back into place I thought it would be all right. More proof, if any were needed, that I am in fact an idiot. It hurt. A lot. I pushed air through my nose, trying to process the pain by breathing deeply, riding it, waiting desperately for it to change to a dull ache as my nipple became numb rather than the excruciating fire I currently felt. By the time it did, my breathing was ragged and I was trying not to cry.

Finally I trusted myself to speak. 'It's on.'

'Really? That's interesting. I didn't realize you were telepathic. Are you a fucking mind reader then, Sophie?'

'What?' I actually couldn't focus on what he was saying, the pain in my nipple was so acute.

'Did you ask me which way round I wanted you to place the clamp?'

Bugger it. 'No, no I didn't.'

'Silly, silly girl. Which way round did you put it?'

I could see where this was going and I was filled with both trepidation and fury. I answered, my tone mutinous, made so by the knowledge that whichever way it was, it wasn't going to be right. 'It's horizontal across my breast.'

He tutted loudly in a way that made me grateful we weren't in the same room, as I knew I wouldn't be able to stop myself glaring at him, and that would have just got me into more trouble. 'Oh dear. If only you'd asked me first. I want it running diagonally towards your shoulder. Twist it round. Now.'

The small voice in the back of my mind that always does a running commentary throughout my submission was asking me why on earth I was acquiescing to this agony, when James was so far away and couldn't even see me. But the larger part of me wanted to please him, to make amends, to be brave, to make him proud. And I was going to do exactly that, as soon as I stopped my hands shaking.

I had to pull the chopsticks apart for a second before I could twist the clamp around. Releasing my nipple caused a surge of agony. I couldn't stop my whimper even as it snapped back into place.

He murmured in approval. 'Good girl. Now put the second one on.'

'Which way round do you want it?' I couldn't stop myself from snapping.

Thankfully he laughed, ignoring my tone. 'Good question. Symmetrical to the first. Do it right and you won't have to move it.'

I picked up the second set of chopsticks and pulled them apart, steeling myself for the pain.

I had been lying on the bed, naked and unmoving, for about ten minutes when he spoke again. Having put the second pair of chopsticks on, and then the third, it was all I could do to lie quietly, holding the phone, listening to him breathing gently a few hundred miles away. My breathing was, in comparison, ragged. I hadn't cried out again; I was focused on dealing with the pain, watching distantly as the chopstick clamps rose and fell with each breath.

Putting the chopsticks on my second nipple caused more trepidation than the first set, because I knew how much it was going to hurt. My nipples were taut, red, hurting with a pulsating pain which came in throbbing waves. As for my clit, the poor recipient of the third and final set of chopsticks, it was engorged, sore and aching, held tightly in place between my spread legs.

I lay there, trying my hardest not to move, not to do anything that would exacerbate the pain thrumming through my body. Enduring it, knowing in a weird way, that might only make sense to James and me, that I owed him this, trying to withstand it, determined not to let him down again. And then I nearly dropped the phone when he said, 'Right. Now I think it's time for us to start your punishment Sophie, don't you?'

Start? Oh hell.

His voice in my ear was charming, reasonable. He didn't sound angry, just matter of fact, when he said that he'd known I wouldn't get round to writing my assignment, that for someone whose professional life depended so much on deadlines I was a procrastinator, leaving things till the last minute or letting them slide completely. He told me how he'd slipped the chopsticks in the side pocket of my bag the last night we'd seen each other, hoping he wouldn't need to use them. How he'd asked me about how the writing was going in the hope I'd have done some, and become increasingly disappointed with me when it became apparent that not only was I not bothering but that I was flippantly dismissing his questions about when it would be done. How it showed a lack of respect.

I lay there, my body aching, listening to him intently, filled with remorse at disappointing him, waiting for my chance to apologize. Except then he asked me how wet I was. I didn't know what to say. Even with the agony pinched around my clit – I was thankful the pain in my nipples had eased to a dull ache as the minutes lengthened – I knew I was wet. But this was punishment after all. Should I admit that to him? Or would that make it worse? While my pain-addled brain wrestled with the conundrum – was it worse to lie or worse to admit the truth? – he chuckled.

'Don't worry, sweet, I know you are. You can't help it, in spite of yourself, can you?'

I made a noise of disagreement in the back of my throat, and then, frankly, thought better of it.

'Slip a finger between your legs. Cover your clit with your juice. Can you do that?'

I moved tentatively, frightened of knocking one of the sets of chopsticks at my breasts. I pushed a finger inside my slickness and began rubbing my clit, moving it slightly within its chopstick prison in a way which hurt. In spite of myself I began to enjoy the delicious sensation merging with the pain. But as my breathing changed, betraying me, James firmly told me to stop. I restrained a whimper of frustration – I thought it was safest under the circumstances, and I was definitely right as it turned out.

'What am I punishing you for?'

'For not sending you the email I promised. I'm so sorry.'

'You will be, I promise you that. But that's not all. What else?'

Shit. What else? What else had I done? I honestly couldn't think of anything more but if I said that and was wrong . . .

As I tried desperately to think of what he could be referring to, he tutted in my ear. 'You don't even remember it, do you?' My heart started to pound. 'Not only did you not do what I asked – the one small thing in amongst everything else you've been doing this last week – but I asked you on three separate occasions whether you were doing it and three times you told me you were. On one notable occasion you sent me a text where you blew a raspberry –' his voice was incredulous at the idea I would dare do such a thing, '– at me for implying that you wouldn't do what I had asked you to.'

Oh god. I started to apologize again but he cut me off. 'I don't want you to speak until I tell you to. Frankly, I don't trust any of the words that come tripping off your tongue. Which leads me to your punishment.'

Leads him to? If I had the breath I would probably have asked him what the fuck everything up to this point was. With hindsight it's better that I didn't.

'Take the clamp off your clit. Now.'

I was relieved at his order, thankful that whatever I was to endure at least it wouldn't involve the throbbing agony of my clit too. My hands moved eagerly and although my gasp as I pulled the clamp clear was loud, I remained silent as the blood returned to my poor tortured clit. I squirmed on the bed at the increased pain.

The change in my breathing didn't go unnoticed. 'Good girl.' I felt warmed by his praise, even in the middle of his punishment, and it meant I was lulled into a false sense of security. 'Now take that clamp and put it around your tongue.'

The security vanished like mist and I couldn't stay silent. 'What?'

'You heard me. Your sarcastic tongue has got you into this mess, and it's going to get its part of your punishment. Stick your tongue out and put the chopsticks around it. As far back as you can. Now. Clamp it for me.'

My hands were shaking. I was furious. Embarrassed. Guilty. Shy. Wondering why the fuck I was letting him do this, but knowing that I would, that this would be my penance. Not knowing how much it would hurt made me feel queasy with fear, but I knew I owed it to him, and just hoped I could do it. Yes, I'd look stupid, but no one would be able to see. And James wouldn't be able to hear me. It'd be fine. I could do this. I could.

I did it.

The first thing I was aware of as the impromptu clamp closed around my tongue was the taste of my juice. A split second later the sensation caught up and I felt a surge of pain. I whimpered, and I honestly wouldn't have been able to say which feeling was more upsetting – well, actually I wouldn't have been able to say anything. I tried to roll the chopsticks along my tongue a little, so they would settle comfortably between my teeth, like a bit for a wayward horse.

'Is it on?'

Stupidly I nodded before murmuring my assent.

'I bet you can taste yourself, can't you?'

I know he expected an answer but my second murmur was quieter and – if it's possible for a murmur to sound that way – filled with shame.

He laughed. 'Come on now, Sophie. You know the rules. Answer me properly.'

I was furious. I clamped my lips round the chopsticks as well as I could when my tongue was sticking out into the night air.

'You can speak with a clamp like that on, Sophie, and you will speak. I've got all night and all you're doing is causing more problems for yourself.'

I stayed silent.

'Right. Slap yourself between the legs. Three times. Hard enough that I can hear it. If I can't I'll just make you do it again until I do.'

I didn't think to disobey him, but I was feeling rising panic, fearful at how with every passing moment what he was having me do was getting worse.

My hand was clenching and unclenching above my head while I screwed up enough courage to inflict the first blow. I slapped myself, harder than I meant to, catching my clit. I accidentally bit my tongue trying to stifle a moan. The second blow was fine – if vicious self-torture can ever be described as fine – but the third was agony, as I managed to knock the clamp around my left nipple as

I moved my hand down. I couldn't stop myself crying out and I heard a tut in my ear for my trouble. The sound of his tuts was seriously beginning to piss me off even as I struggled to obey him.

'You're rude tonight, Sophie, as well as disobedient. You know you should thank me for every blow I inflict on you.'

I couldn't speak. I wouldn't speak. And then he said something to fill me with a terror I couldn't quell.

'We can keep on at this all night. You're now going to slap yourself six times. And if you don't count them off and thank me for each blow then I am going to double it, and double that, and we are going to keep going until you give me what I want. So it's entirely up to you. I'm happy to lie here all evening listening to your snuffling desperation; it's quite entertaining actually. But one way or another you are going to take your punishment. And you are going to speak to me.'

In that moment I hated him. This wasn't about submitting to feel challenged, or be aroused or even to arouse him. He wasn't pushing me out of my comfort zone or humiliating me for our mutual pleasure. But he was humiliating me, demeaning me, in a way he never had before. I properly hated him, but the loathing was tinged with prickly embarrassment and a genuine feeling of guilt. I opened my mouth to try and speak, tried to form words around my immobile tongue, tried to swallow back some of the drool pooling at the corners of my mouth. It was like standing on the edge of the precipice. I knew what he wanted. Knew the choice was mine. Knew that I didn't want to do it, that my every instinct was shouting for me not to, that I should hang up. But I wanted to make amends. I wanted to please him. I wanted to be able to reach the bar he had raised rather than fail him, fail myself. The choice was mine. In a way I hated that it was, as it made the submission, the humiliation, more acute, more distressing. The choice was mine, and I was choosing to take this punishment, to be demeaned in this way, and what's more he knew I was going to, even as he knew how much I was hating every second of it.

I slapped myself. Hard enough that I gasped at the impact. And then, stiltedly, my voice thick with tears, I managed to say: 'One. Thank you.'

Actually, I didn't. I said something that sounded ridiculous. Lisping and unintelligible except for the fact it was the right number of syllables. Probably. I felt a surge of shame and humiliation, and, trying to ignore it, I slapped myself again. Hearing myself speak a second time was actually worse than the first, although I can't exactly explain why. I still sounded like an idiot and as I heard myself, how ridiculous I sounded, I started to cry, becoming even less intelligible. I kept slapping and counting and thanking (although I'm not sure how thankful I actually came across) and by the time I got to six I was sobbing, hoping this unlikely indignity would soon be over.

Punishments are funny things. A lot of the D/s dynamic is about pain – inflicting it, withstanding it. Being spanked or caned for some spurious play reason is fun, makes me wet, but this was different. I felt so sorry for having disappointed him, sad that he had seen it as inevitable to the extent he had pre-packed punishment implements, and suddenly, lying on a hotel bed far from home, with aching nipples and a sore tongue, being made to do demeaning and horrifying things, I felt awful and alone. And yes, I appreciate that's what a punishment should do. I just wasn't expecting six chopsticks and half a dozen rubber bands to do the job so well.

After a little while I was able to slow my tears, and tentatively tried to brush them away without knocking any chopsticks. My sobs switched to the occasional snuffle and finally he spoke.

'Do you understand why I've punished you this way?'

I swallowed round the chopsticks the best I could before lisping my 'yes', shutting my eyes at the ridiculous sound I made.

'I have punished you like this because you've been a silly little girl and this is how silly little girls get punished.' If I was being my normal smart-arsed self I'd have said something then, or at the very least rolled my eyes at his use of the word 'girl'. As it was, I lay there in shamed silence, trying not to dribble, my swollen tongue aching desperately in my mouth.

'You are a silly little girl aren't you?'

Oh no, I thought, *please don't do this*. Being called a good girl, at a push, is something I felt worrying pangs of joy at by then, but this . . . I felt myself clamping my lips around the chopsticks and my protruding tongue in silent rebellion.

'Slap yourself again.'

Even as I was forming thoughts of outrage my hand was moving to do his bidding. I thanked him.

'Tell me.'

I sighed. Opened my mouth. Closed it. Tried again. Suddenly the chopsticks seemed to be in the way of my teeth when I tried to speak, in a way they weren't a few seconds before.

The shame was audible even if the actual words weren't, thanks to my immobilized tongue. 'I'm a silly little girl.'

'Silly little girls blow raspberries don't they?'

I was whimpering acquiescence to everything he was saying, agreeing desperately to anything that would make this end because it hurt so much and felt so humiliating.

'Can you blow a raspberry now?'

I was gabbling, my words incomprehensible for anything but a lisping tone of desperation. 'No, no I can't.'

'Try,' he hissed.

Come on, Sophie, this'll soon be over. This has to be the worst it can get. With tears streaming down my face, I tried. Desperately, repeatedly, I blew air out of my mouth, huffing pathetically, my lips unpursed, unpursable, desperate for it to end, for my aching jaws to close.

And then of course it got worse.

'Put a hand between your legs. What do you feel?'

I flushed. I knew what I was going to feel as, in spite of everything, I was achingly wet. The increasingly wet sound of the palm of my hand as I slapped myself had given it away by degrees, even without the glistening proof on my fingers.

'Too shy to say? Press your fingers to that outstretched tongue of yours. Taste yourself. Tell me.'

I moved my hand to my aching mouth and transferred

the taste of my body's betrayal of my mind to my throbbing tongue. With gritted teeth I told him what he already knew. 'I'm wet.'

'What?'

In this second I loathed James even as I wanted to obey him. I wanted to best him with my submission. In my mind this was a competition and I could only win by not wussing out now. Delusional? Possibly. I blame it on the lack of blood to my tongue. Through gritted teeth, I bit out the words: 'I'm wet.'

'Good girl.'

My loathing dissipated and I felt a burst of pride, before a slight twinge of panic at how conditioned I was becoming.

'Now make yourself come. Once I've heard you bring yourself off I'll let you remove all the clamps.'

I honestly don't know if it would have made it better or worse if I'd come easily at his treatment of me then. For what it's worth, the pain in my tongue and the difficulties I had swallowing away the drool, paired with a deep-felt feeling of humiliation and remorse meant I was distracted and unable to come easily. By the time I begged him for my orgasm, my voice high-pitched and desperate and unintelligible, my body sore and aching, I felt like he had stripped me of everything. I was totally his, for better or worse, and I wouldn't ever make an error like that again.

As I came back to earth, tentatively removing the clamps from my breasts and tongue and feeling the surging agony as blood began pulsing through them again, I felt exhausted, utterly spent and oddly upset. I wanted to speak to him, but I didn't know what to say. I felt so ashamed – both at having disappointed him and having just done so many humiliating things at his bidding, at my own hand – that I couldn't shrug the feeling off and converse normally. I felt more tongue-tied than I had with the sodding clamp on.

He was incongruously and yet reassuringly solicitous, asking me if I was OK, whether I needed to find some ice to help with my sore tongue. Ridiculously, his kindness made my eyes fill with tears again.

My voice sounded crackly as I tried to speak, my mouth dry after having been forcibly held open for so long. 'I'll be fine, thank you.' I knew I would be, but I also knew this lesson would stay in my mind for a long time, and that I would never look at chopsticks in quite the same way again.

'Good girl.'

I swallowed quietly and with a plaintiveness I couldn't quite shake said, 'I am sorry, you know.'

His voice was warm, comforting. 'I know. And if you want I can give you another assignment to make it up to me.'

Even before he'd finished the sentence I was agreeing with him, asking for my chance to make amends. He directed me back to my bag, this time to the front outside pocket – I was fast realizing I should have paid more attention to what exactly was in my luggage – where there was a small drawstring bag which he told me to pull open. I took out a small vibrator, a butt plug and a sachet of lube.

As I looked at the collection of items on the edge of

my bed my heart started pounding again, not sure after everything that had come before that I could endure anything more that night. He told me he wanted me to plug my own arse, and push the vibrator high into myself and write a new assignment, but instead of telling him what I fantasized about us doing when we were reunited he wanted me to explain how I felt during every humiliating moment of the punishment I had just endured, all while desperate to come. I was not to orgasm until I'd finished and emailed the piece to him to read. It needed to be at least 2,000 words long – unless I came before I'd finished, in which case it needed to be an extra 1,000 words for each 'accident'. And if he didn't have it at some point in the few short hours before I was due to finish up and return home to see him, he would punish me again, in person, maybe with the tongue clamp as he knew now how much I hated it and was actually amused at the idea of seeing me try to speak round it while he caned me.

My mouth was dry as I stared with trepidation at the butt plug, which was significantly thicker than anything else I'd had in my arse. My voice wavered. 'It's almost 1am.'

I imagined his smile. 'I know. I should go to bed, I need to get up early for work. I suggest you get started.'

I shoved myself full and, aching all over, sat myself at the little desk in the anonymous hotel room. I wrote for hours, desperate to explain myself, to apologize, to please him. The responsibility weighed heavily on me, and finally, by the time I finished writing something that I was pleased with, I ended up with just a few hours' sleep before my final day on site.

I felt a fair amount of trepidation on the journey home. I had been adamant, from the beginning, that I wasn't into having a relationship where any day-to-day girlfriend/boyfriend stuff was tinged by D/s, where if I did something to upset him in regular life he could bring about retribution through pain or humiliation. I didn't *think* that was what the previous night had been, but I felt unsure; it was definitely closer to the line than I had hoped. He hadn't replied to or even acknowledged my email. I couldn't help worrying that perhaps I had crossed a line. Or he had. I just couldn't see how things could go back to their relatively easy-going norm.

And then I got off my train, wheeled my errant bag across the concourse while trying to keep hold of the handbag slipping off my shoulder, and shoved a ticket at the man at the barrier. I tried to figure out how I would get home and whether I should ring James when I did. Then suddenly, he was in front of me, smiling. He folded me into a hug and then kissed me thoroughly, until both of us were looking wistful and in need of a private corner. He took my hand in one of his and the handle of my wheelie case in the other and started leading me out of the station. Suddenly my oppressive nervousness about coming home had dissipated and all I felt was joy to have him there, to be with him. Well, that and the usual amount of lust . . .

15

The lust between us was definitely ongoing. I'd experienced the honeymoon phase of several relationships, and with Thomas there had been a real sense of enjoying ticking a selection of different experiences off the list, but with James the sexual tension was something different. It was always there. In part, I had no doubt, that was because I found him unutterably attractive, but somehow the D/s element of our relationship tinged everything else; everything was potent with possibilities. It was fun, and – even more so than any ordinary sexual pairing – gave me a feeling of a shared secret; that we had these special moments between us that no one else could know about or impinge on.

At any moment the atmosphere between us could shift a little, and then suddenly things would change. We'd be curled on the sofa, watching TV, when he would lean over and tickle me. I'd poke him in the ribs to stop him, and then suddenly he would have my wrists held in his hand. We'd lie there, continuing to watch the show, his hand firmly holding both of mine, tightening imperceptibly when I shifted to move them and silently, playfully tested him to see if he would let me go. Then suddenly he would get up and disappear from the room, returning with rope to twist around my wrists, tying them firmly but not uncomfortably in front of me for the duration of our time on the sofa. It was an odd dynamic, blurring the lines between sexuality and those quiet moments of a relationship where you're just enjoying hanging out, being together doing random things, but I found it intoxicating. We would lie there, in companionable quietness, reading the papers or whatever, with a small nod to the less conventional element of our relationship. These little moments made the air heavy with anticipation; with my hands bound, I might lean forward slightly awkwardly to pick up my tea, which thrilled James – he loved seeing me working round the difficulties he put in my path, even while he came up with ever more fiendish ways to challenge me further – or his hand might slide into my top or stroke my shoulder as I sat there in my restraints. The blurring of the line between the two contexts – sex and 'normal' life – made for an intriguing blend, though: at any moment things could change, and even simple things, like me lying on the floor in front of the TV while he sat on the sofa, suddenly became weighted with a strange kind of double meaning. Watching *Question Time* had never been so fun.

As the weeks passed we got more into the rhythm of life together. We weren't together all the time – both of our jobs were very busy and involved a lot of out-of-hours meetings and socializing – but we met at least one night in the week and at some point on the weekends when I wasn't working. Things were easy going, fun; the D/s element of what we were doing ebbed and flowed a little bit, but in a good, reassuring way. Some nights we'd curl up in bed and chat, or he'd rub my back if I'd spent a long time the car and was feeling achy. The duality of it felt really right. Of course that means that when suddenly the ground beneath your feet shifts again, things feel even more intense . . .

Barring the tongue-clamping debacle, I'd say I'm usually pretty good with deadlines. As a journalist it's drummed into you. You don't miss a deadline. Ever. No ifs, no buts, no maybes. A deadline is a deadline is a deadline. That's it. No matter what pressure you're under or how close to the wire you get, the adrenaline kicks in and you make sure you make it. Because there's no sliding scale. You either hit or you don't. And if you don't then it's game over, whether you've missed the boat by a millimetre or a mile.

But that's when I'm trying to finish a page lead, or put some breaking copy on one of our websites. Sometimes, with the best will in the world, other deadlines seem almost unreachable.

I was crying. Tears had run down my face in rivulets and splashed on to my naked breasts, tiny drips which did nothing to cool the flush across my chest, which signalled both arousal and embarrassment. In a small corner of my mind I was worried there might be a little snot too, but since my hands were cuffed behind me there was no surreptitious way to brush it away even if was there. Suddenly, as he moved, any similarities between me and the woman from the *Blair Witch Project* seemed the least of my worries. James's hand tangled viciously in my hair, pulling my head so I was forced to look him in the eye, see his dominance reflected back at my submission.

It was breathtaking, terrifying, and did nothing to help me regain the shattered vestiges of my equilibrium.

My breath was coming fast in little sobs that I was trying my best to swallow. I bit my lip, staring past his ear into the middle distance, trying to pull myself together, trying to process the conflicting sensations and emotions flickering through me. Pain. Fear. Excitement.

James's voice, so close to me that his breath kissed my face, actually made me jump.

'Do you understand?'

I went to nod, realized that his hand was clamped so tightly into my hair that it would hurt, and instead forced the words through parched and trembling lips.

'Yes, sir.'

Calling him 'sir' was something that came much more easily by then, to the extent I'd even caught myself mentally referring to him that way. He'd made me call him 'Master' a couple of times, although that chafed. That night I would have called him Grand Vizier Smorgasbord of the Planet Zarg if I thought it would help. But it wouldn't. This was a new level of dominance, requiring a new level of submission, and while the pooling of my juice under me proved that I was enjoying stepping up to the plate, I was more on the back foot than ever before. This was affecting me more than the tongue clamping, or the increasingly intense evenings we'd had together since my return from that trip, in between the fun stuff, the trips to the cinema and the pub and cooking together. It was liberating, terrifying, challenging.

His voice was charming. 'Good. Well, since we've not

been counting up to this point, I think we'll assume that I've given you twenty smacks so far. Does that sound reasonable?'

I agreed quickly, eagerly, having no idea how many times he'd hit me but thinking this sounded like a suitably high number. There shouldn't be too much more to endure; I didn't think he'd ever punished me so extensively before so –

'If we count on to a hundred, I think that'll be fair.'

At his words I started trembling again, harder than I had at any point so far. *What the fuck was it with him and the round number one hundred?*

It had started with, I thought, a relatively playful spanking. He had me strip and sit on the high-backed chair, spreading my legs wide in the cool seat so he could secure an ankle to each chair leg, leaving me open wide to his gaze – and his hand. He had a definite gleam in his eye when he produced the handcuffs, pulled my hands behind the chair and secured me into place. But it wasn't until he disappeared off to the kitchen and came back with a wooden spoon and two clothes pegs that the alarm bells started ringing fully, and by then there wasn't a huge amount I could do other than struggle ineffectually against the chair.

He played with my breasts to start with, running his hands over and around them. His touch was soothing, lulling me into a feeling of security. He lightly pinched my nipples, watching them harden, my body basking in his attention. Then he put his mouth around my nipple, lapping at it and suckling deep until I closed my eyes in bliss at the sensation.

I should have known better. Almost as soon as I relaxed into his ministrations, he changed, grazing my nipple with his teeth, getting harsher, biting, until I cried out. My moans of pain didn't stop him though, and both my breasts were wet with his saliva and red with marks from biting and vicious suckling by the time he put the pegs on. My breasts were sore by then and since the pegs were household-style robust wooden clothes pegs, they hurt as the springs snapped back into place, making for a whole new layer of agony. I clenched and unclenched my hands in the cuffs, trying to become acclimatized to the pain, blushing at how intently he stared at my breasts, bouncing with the movement of the deep breaths I was pushing through my nose as I tried to withstand the sensations.

I was so intent on dealing with the tight hot pain in my nipples, which was fast becoming the centre of my world, that I forgot about the spoon until he slapped one of my breasts with it. He'd slapped my breasts with his hands before but this, particularly after the biting and suckling, really hurt. The layers of pain were running one on top of another, like conflicting currents, like waves rushing in my head. In that moment my entire world was focused only on that noise – and the pain in my nipples.

Up until the point he smacked me hard between the legs with the wooden spoon.

I screamed. I couldn't stop myself. The silence after my voice pierced the room felt as loud as actual noise. Everything was still, my eyes were filled with tears and it was all silent for a moment bar the sound of my rasping breathing. He didn't ask me if I was all right. He just looked at me very intently, staring into my eyes, while I – undoubtedly – glared back at him, my mind furious at not only him for inflicting this agony but at the part of myself that actually, despite it all, craved it. After a few seconds he must have seen what he needed to see, as the air changed and he moved.

As he shifted closer, I closed my eyes, unable to bear watching the second strike. Of course all that meant was that I wasn't ready for it. The sound of the impact seemed to echo around the room and the pain felt like nothing I'd ever felt before. In the back of my mind a panicked voice was whimpering, 'I can't take this,' but before I could do anything to stop it (or stop him, even – I was closer to doing that than I had ever been before) the third crack connected and I was gasping through the pain and my tears again. Every fibre of my being was focused on the man in front of me and trying to ride the waves of pain he was inflicting.

I don't know if it's just me, but normally after a few strokes of whatever implement I am on the receiving end of my body can start to adjust to the pain, embrace it. It still hurts, of course it does, but something alters in my head and the pain starts to bring with it a delicious pleasure. But as James kept up the relentless spanking rhythm of the wooden spoon, it only hurt, and then hurt more. I shifted against my bound ankles, desperate to close my legs against the onslaught but unable to do so. All I could do was endure, cling on and hope it would get better, that it wouldn't be the thing I couldn't cope with, that I would have to call a halt to, disappointing him and myself. I really wasn't sure I could get through it, even endure it, never mind enjoying it. But he had a different opinion.

That's when he set me my deadline.

He tucked a strand of hair back behind my ear as he explained what would happen next. And it made the world shift for a second as I tried to understand what he was saying, what he was expecting.

'The thing is, even while you're crying and whimpering and shaking this is making you wet.'

I opened my mouth to argue, but before I could speak he pressed the curved end of the spoon against my lips. I tasted myself on the wood, blushed and closed my eyes, to hide the truth of my body's betrayal. As he moved the spoon away I pressed my trembling lips together and swallowed the denial, deciding discretion was the better part of valour and I should probably just shut up.

'I think if I spanked you for long enough you could come.'

My eyes flashed open and I looked at him smiling down at me, a picture of smugness. The more we'd played the better he'd got to know my limits. This was sometimes amazing, as when he pushed me into the unknown it felt like I was flying. However, at other points – points like this, when he was looking arrogant as he merrily pushed me into the abyss – I could have quite happily told him to go and fuck himself. Except, as ever, the small voice in my head already yearning for the next time this would happen kept me quiet. For a while.

'So I'm going to give you a deadline. A certain number of strokes by which time you have to come. If you don't,

I am going to do things to you that will make this feel like a walk in the park. And if you don't come, well, it won't matter to me. Because I will, either by having you suck me off or by just giving you a damn good fucking' – at that he ran a hand between my legs, which made me buck underneath him as much as I could within the constraints of my bonds – 'and then I will punish you in ways you can't even begin to imagine. You will be begging me and you won't know whether you're begging me to stop or continue. But I will use you however I want, for however long I want until you want to just crawl away and recover. And since neither of us has to be back at work until after the weekend now, that could be a very long time. Do you understand?'

I felt fear in the pit of my stomach, excitement, and – ridiculously – the kind of burst of adrenaline that I always get when given something to work to. Yes, I am a journalistic cliché. I was already aching to come and competitive enough that I was going to try and get through this no matter what. I could do this. The pain couldn't go on too long. My voice was quiet but, I like to think, fairly assured. 'Yes, sir.'

'Good. Well, since we've not been counting up to this point, I think we'll assume that I've given you twenty smacks so far. Does that sound reasonable? If we count on to a hundred. I think that'll be fair.'

The rhythm was what got me. Even with the pain – and believe me, it was a kind of agony I had never felt before – the insidious rhythm of his strikes began to work its warmth through me. He made me count off the strokes and thank him for them and his pace was so fast that I was gasping out my thanks as fast as I could speak, as fast as I could process the pain. At stroke sixty-three the sensations shifted. He hit me, as hard as he had up to that point, but the sound of the wood connecting was wet. The sound of my arousal was obvious. And with every hit it got more so, until I closed my eyes in embarrassment. My tears of pain were still streaming from beneath my closed lids, and yet the increasing wet patch I was squirming in, that was coating the back of my thighs and my arse, proved that, despite my brain telling me otherwise, on a cellular level this was working for me.

At stroke sixty-nine I opened my eyes, and saw him pulling away from the stroke I was still gasping at. There was a strand of wetness leading from between my legs to the spoon as he moved away and the visible evidence of how much this pain was turning me on shocked me for a second, freezing my brain. When he hit me again I couldn't think of the number. Were we on sixty-nine and this was seventy? Or was this sixty-nine? Shit. I guessed, 'sixty-nine.' He shook his head in displeasure and told me we'd go back to sixty to make up for my error. I had to bite my lip to stop myself beginning to sob at the thought of nine extra strokes.

By the time we got to eighty-five he had shifted his angle so every strike had maximum impact on my clit. It was the most intense treatment it had ever received and my body was already building up to an orgasm which I feared the strength of. As we moved inexorably closer to one hundred my breathing was ragged, my still-pegged nipples jiggling as I gasped, and my thighs trembled as I built to my climax.

On the hundredth strike I orgasmed. I would have been

rolling my eyes at the fact I had metamorphosed into some ridiculous cliché of slutty kinky conditioning, but, having endured all I'd endured, after every ounce of feeling had been wrung from my body, I didn't give a toss. I wanted to come so much it consumed me. It was all I could taste, all I could smell, and I felt like I needed it more than I needed to breathe.

My orgasm was vicious and painful and made me thrash against my bonds in a way that left me with marks round my wrists and ankles that I had to hide with long sleeves and trousers for a few days. The keening noises coming from the back of my throat didn't sound like me and as I came, pulsating around the spoon, James had to grab the back of the chair as I was about to tip both it and myself over with the force of my movements.

As I came back down to earth as if coming out of a trance, still shivering with aftershocks from the intensity of what had come before, he was undoing his trousers and moving over to me. He pushed viciously inside me, putting his weight on to my still-pulsating, puffy, bruised and aching core. I couldn't hold back a scream. He started to fuck me, a cruel reminder of the rhythm of the spoon just minutes before, the sensations so painful and intense that I was bucking from underneath him, doing everything I could to push him off, which, because of the handcuffs and rope securing my ankles, was very little.

He shifted deeper inside me and then stopped moving for a moment. He anchored his hands in my hair, and kissed me deeply, then bit hard on my bottom lip until I was sure I could taste blood. His fingers twisted on the pegs on my nipples, adjusting and tightening them until it felt like my entire body was on fire. I was sobbing, tears streaming down my face, and as he resumed fucking me he whispered, 'You came on stroke 109 because we went back when you miscounted. You missed your deadline.'

Through a haze of pain and intense pleasure I realized exactly what this meant. And I trembled, knowing that over the next minutes, hours, days – however long he wanted – I was going to be pushed further than I ever had been before.

No ifs, no buts, no maybes. You never miss a deadline.

The days that followed were the most challenging of my life. He used me. Abused me. Humiliated me. He made me cry. He made me ache. Pushed me. He never broke me but at times it felt like he was trying to. He fucked me, when he wanted, how he wanted, and when I was so exhausted I could not summon up the energy to do any-thing more than lie there, a fuckhole for his pleasure, he slapped my face and pulled my hair to make me move my weary body. By the time he finished I was marked all over, like an abstract canvas documenting our time together: the bite marks on my breasts, the angry redness of my tormented nipples; the bruises on the tops of my arms; my arse cheeks criss-crossed with red welts that made me squirm, made me wet thinking of what had happened, for weeks afterwards; his spunk drying in my hair and on my breasts. By the end, the tracks of my tears had washed away my carefully applied make up and my hair was a mess. I was a mess. He had demolished my defences.

It was freeing, cathartic and yet, at points, terrifying. He pushed me to the very edge of what felt acceptable to me. As the hours and days passed all I cared about was him – pleasing him, satisfying him, not doing anything to give him reason to punish me. He was my world and for the first time I truly understood the kind of submission which consumes you as, for the first time ever, the voice in the back of my head, calling out my shame, asking me why I was doing this, was silenced. I felt connected to him in a way that I never had to another person – he understood me completely, even when I didn't understand myself. As I sobbed, begging him to stop caning me, pleading that I couldn't take any more, and he continued anyway, I hated him. But he pulled my face to his, his hands hard on my chin and, while I stared at him with loathing in my eyes, he asked me if I remembered my safe word. Through gritted teeth I said yes, and while I battled with stubborn pride and a competitive spirit that meant I then lapsed into silence, he made me beg him to resume before he started again. He caned me until it hurt so much I couldn't breathe, until I was sure I must be bleeding, and then, when he felt I couldn't take any more, he ran a leisurely finger down my slit. I came, from this gentlest of touches, and when I came back to earth, sated and yet confused at how the caning could have inspired such a vicious orgasm, I saw him smiling down at me, leaning to kiss me softly before he told me I would have to be punished for coming without permission.

When he finally finished he tethered me to the foot of the bed like an animal, my wrists tied behind my back, and left me to sleep the sleep of the exhausted, curled in an ungainly way as I unconsciously tried to find a part of my body to lie on comfortably.

It may sound odd that such cruelty and humiliation inspired the thought, but by the end of our weekend I knew I loved this twisted, clever, tender man who got upset at people being cruel to animals but took joy in doing horrible things to me. He had understood the parts of me I could barely articulate, and coaxed them into achieving and enduring amazing and cathartic things. The intensity of it took my breath away – it was like no one had ever known me as well as he did; no one could understand my nature, my personality, better than him.

16

So what happens after the most intense sexual experience of your life, the thing that leaves you aching and mentally and physically affected for days afterwards?

Well, it would seem, the answer was nothing.

When we said goodbye he was quiet but no more so than he would normally have been at the prospect of us going back to our respective homes, the weekend over and work beginning again. At least that's what I thought at the time, when I stretched up to kiss him, enjoying the warmth of his embrace as he hugged me goodbye and we went our separate ways.

I texted him when I got home, the way I always did. I didn't get a reply but figured that as it was late he'd crashed out in readiness for his early start the next day. But the next morning I didn't hear anything; in fact, I didn't hear anything at all that day. It was odd – James and I had spent months in contact multiple times a day and his silence meant I couldn't help but worry that something was wrong. I sent him a second text, asking him if all was OK. Nothing. Then I tried dropping him an email – a link to a news story I thought might interest him – I didn't want to seem clingy, although I sent it to both his home and work addresses, but I wanted a response.

Nothing.

For three days I was pretty much beside myself. Texts and an aiming-for-casual-and-bright-but-really-not voice-mail went unanswered. I went about my daily business, going to work, heading out for birthday drinks with a friend, but through it all in the back of my mind all I was thinking about was James. Was he all right? Why hadn't he got in touch? On the morning of the fourth day I couldn't stand it any more. I rang his office. I didn't give my name, which perhaps makes me sound like a mad stalker woman. The receptionist was very helpful: yes he was definitely in, she'd seen him this morning, he was at his desk already, but on another call. Did I want to leave a message or did I have his address to email him?

I told her I had his address and very politely hung up.

I was furious. I was upset. I was confused. It was so unlike him, but I couldn't really think of the best way to deal with it at that moment – I knew that any attempt to talk to him while he was at work was a complete waste of time so I spent most of the day thinking about the best way to raise my concerns without seeming like some furious harridan. There was also the D/s dynamic to factor into it. After the intensity of the time we had spent together I didn't want to come across as disrespectful, but I had no intention whatsoever of letting it go like I was some kind of wilting flower. But what to do?

By the end of the working day I still had no clue.

I decided to send a casual, non-shrewish, text.

Hey you, you've been really quiet since we got back from the weekend. Hope all's OK, will try ringing tonight.

I didn't get a reply. In my heart of hearts I wasn't expecting one, although I still had no fucking clue why.

The clichéd depiction of break-ups is that once you have been spurned by your beau you sink into the pit of despair with some high-quality ice cream and cheesy pop rock of the 70s and early 80s. If that works for you, then great. But for me, to paraphrase Billy Ocean, when the going gets tough, the tough get baking.

I rang James twice that night and it went to voicemail both times. Then I switched on my PC and, thanks to the joys of social networking, found that he'd been online in various places that evening, happy to talk even if he apparently didn't have the inclination to do so with me. By the time I'd hunted down a post he'd made to an obscure music website, asking for help with his speakers – 'I'm lying here with an aching heart and a pounding head wondering what on earth's going on and you're re-cabling your living room?' – I knew it was time to step away and do something else.

I'm not a natural cook. Living alone makes anything other than ready meals a lot of hassle and waste, and I'm usually bored of the prospect of eating anything I make part way through the cooking process anyway. But baking, baking I love. Partly, I guess, because biscuits and cakes and all that stuff are good comfort-type foods, but partly because I enjoy the straightforwardness of it. If you weigh the ingredients out correctly, if you cream the butter and sugar to the right consistency, if you bake it the right length of time, you can create something lovely – and you can give the fruits of your efforts to the people around you in silent apology for walking around permanently close to tears and with a face like a smacked arse.

It was 1am when I decided to start baking ginger short-bread. I don't know why ginger appealed specifically, but I was convinced. By this point I had already drunk most of a bottle of wine, so driving wasn't an option. I pulled my coat on and walked to the twenty-four-hour petrol station with attached shop to buy what I needed there.

Now, I've never been the sort of person who buys petrol – or indeed anything else – at a petrol station fore-court late at night. But it turns out that they lock the doors and instead serve you through a glass window with a grille, not unlike visiting someone in prison, passing things underneath the – very small – gap in the bottom of the Plexiglas screen. This made explaining my late-night bak-ing needs rather more complicated than it would have been otherwise.

To start with the bloke behind the counter was adam-ant that unless I wanted fuel, cigarettes or condoms he couldn't sell me anything else. After listening to me argue for five minutes he grudgingly told me he thought they had some flour he could get me. Once he'd cracked and got that it didn't take much wheedling to get some sugar out of him, but by the time I was asking him to hold up packs of butter to see if I could ascertain which was unsalted there was a look of loathing in his eyes. He gave me short shrift when I asked if they had any ginger – I admit it was unlikely, but heartbreak and drunkenness hadn't dented my optimistic streak – and instead sold me a bar of fruit and nut chocolate to break up in lieu of chocolate chips. By the time I had fed the cash for my overpriced grocery shopping under the gap and he had passed through a carrier bag and then each individual item for me to pack into it, I was so effusively grateful that my eyes were filled with tears at his kindness. As I stumbled away home I think his probably were too, albeit tears of relief that the mental woman buying baking ingredients had sodded off to leave him with late-night petrol buyers and stoners with the munchies.

I woke up the next morning on my living room floor having passed out watching DVDs while waiting for the second load of shortbread dough to chill in the fridge before baking.

If it seems tough waking up with a hangover after being dumped (if that's what this was; it was hard to tell when the person I was dating – well, almost – was such an emotional fucktard that I wasn't entirely sure), then waking up in a furnace – the oven had been on all night, obviously – to find a kitchen in chaos is worse. There was flour on the floor, butter on the cupboards from my overenthusiastic greasing, and every bowl and wooden spoon I owned seemed to have been used and dumped on the side. It was like I'd been burgled. By bakers. Combine that with a banging red wine hangover, sleep deprivation and – as I found when I dragged my sorry self up to the shower – dough in my hair, and I felt awful.

I went into work, still not really there (although the batches of shortbread did much to minimize any co-worker snarking about me not pulling my weight). I tried not to think about James. But thinking about not thinking about James probably didn't count.

In the weeks that followed my colleagues, friends and family did well out of my heartbreak. I made endless variations of golden shortbread, only moving on to Victoria sponges when our assistant editor raised concerns about all the butter having an effect on his cholesterol. I made carrot cake, rock cakes, cookies, and as I beat the eggs, stirred the dough and waited for everything to cook, I went over every element of my relationship with James, the smutty and the not-so-smutty. It made me cry and it made me wet and more than anything it made me angry. I couldn't work out whether everything that had happened between us had been founded on the lie that he was as interested in me as I was in him, or if he had just got bored with me, or if I'd done something to piss him off or what. However I weighed it up, he had thrown away something that, from my end at least, seemed quite special. He had thrown me away. It sounded pathetic – made me feel pathetic – but I was bereft and I wanted to weep. James still hadn't got in touch, although a mixture of stubborn pride and embarrassment made me stop contacting him. I knew he was alive and well, and over and above that all I knew was that he didn't want to talk to me. And that meant I didn't want to talk to him. I'd be buggered before he realized how much he'd hurt me.

I was part way through grating cheese for a batch of three-cheese scones when Thomas rang. He asked how I was. I said I was fine as I was long-since bored with trying to explain the ridiculous depth of my feeling to anyone else. And then he shocked me out of slicing lumps off a truckle of Wensleydale.

'Bollocks are you fine. You're not fine.'

I didn't know what to say for a second; there was such fury and frustration in his tone. I went to say I was fine – by this point it really was my default response – and tailed off as it would appear we both knew I wasn't.

'It's enough moping, Sophie. More than enough. I'm sorry you're hurting and he's a fucking idiot but no more crying and no more bloody baking. Charlotte and I are coming round this weekend. We're bringing DVD box sets and wine and we're going out for actual non-bakery-related food. No arguments. In fact, I'm going to bring the paddle and if you don't cheer up then I will use it.'

I smiled my first unforced smile for weeks. We both knew he had no intention of doing any such thing, that our sexual relationship had moved on, but it still made me smile, made me feel reassured, that there was a support network of people I could rely on, even if – Thomas and Charlotte aside – no one really had any idea of what I was mourning.

'Bloody hell, I'd best make an effort then.'

There was no putting them off. Even my follow up call, where I told Tom I was fine and didn't need anyone worrying about me, fell on deaf ears. The closest we came to a discussion about the trip was a debate over the DVDs he was bringing – we plumped for explosions, political intrigue: nothing that was going to leave me weeping into my wine glass like some kind of kinky Bridget Jones.

In the end, it was brilliant. I suddenly realized I'd bored myself with grief. Life in the doldrums is exhausting, depressing and really bloody dull after a while, and when the force of nature that is Thomas and Charlotte blew into my flat, waving booze, box sets and expensive chocolate, I was suddenly ready to shake it off. Or at least to begin trying. The wine and Pringles helped, as did the most ludicrously plotted action TV show I'd ever seen, made ever more amusing by wine. They arrived on Friday night. We started watching TV early – Thomas remained one of my best friends but he was a bloke and as soon as he saw that a mention of James had my lip wobbling, he was happy to just stick with TV small talk and avoid any tidal wave of tears. After finishing several disks (and several bottles), I let Thomas and Charlotte nab my bed and crashed on the living room sofa, ready to resume watching the next morning – although I'd promised them we'd hunt for a fry up first.

When the doorbell went at 8.30am on Saturday I stifled a groan. I was expecting a delivery from Amazon so I knew I had to run to open it, but it was early, I looked like I'd been dragged through a hedge backwards, and I knew the ringing of the bell had probably just managed to scupper Charlotte's and Thomas's lie in.

When I opened the front door, though, it wasn't the postman. It was the man I least expected to see on my doorstep ever, ever again. I knew I must have looked surprised, but fury ... fury was the main feeling that surged through me. He had the decency to look embarrassed, but he took a step back as though he was also a little scared. James always was a bright man.

'Hi. Sorry to ring so early.'

I actually wanted to swing for him, but in the end I crossed my arms over my t-shirt and made do with glaring instead. As a journalist I'm fully aware of the power of silence. I said nothing, taking the time instead to look closely at him. He seemed tired, but was still sexy enough to make me feel a pang. Not enough that I didn't want to kick him in the shins, though. I couldn't decide if this was a good thing or not.

After a few seconds he cracked. 'I bet you didn't expect to see me.'

Brilliant. I've waited weeks for that? I actually wanted to punch him. Not in any sexual, playful way; in an exacting-physical-violence-that—made-him-wince way. It took all my effort to sound blasé.

I aimed for a carefree shrug. 'I ordered some books for my brother for his birthday. I figured you were delivering them.'

'It's your brother's birthday?'

'No, not yet.'

'Oh. Obviously.' A long pause. 'I'm not delivering any books.'

My jaw was clenched so hard it hurt. 'I guessed that.'

He lapsed into silence. We were floundering, but I suddenly realized I had no inclination to help smooth the path of the conversation. He was finally willing to talk?

Well, he could fucking well talk then. But he wasn't. Or couldn't. His eyes were staring intently into mine, looking for answers in a way that reminded me so much of how he looked to see whether I could stand any more punishment. It made my heart hurt.

The moment was punctured as Thomas swung open my bedroom door and wandered out into the hall, pulling a t-shirt on over his boxer shorts. 'Sophie, is everything OK?'

For a split second the world stopped. Then James spoke, his voice sharp, ugly for the first time since I'd known him. 'Oh. Sorry, I didn't realize you had company.'

I felt a surge of anger, of injustice, firstly that he'd immediately thought the worst, and secondly that he felt he had any right to be pissed off anyway. He'd been lovely and filthy and sexy and mean and once I'd fallen for him he dumped me without telling me why, turning me into a heartbroken baker, and he had the temerity to be hacked off with me when he thought that I'd moved on already? Was he really so oblivious to how much I'd liked him? I couldn't stop myself.

'What's it to you?' He flinched at the fury in my voice. 'Seriously. What is it to you, James? If there's one thing the last month has made painfully obvious it's that you're not interested in continuing to explore what was happening between us. That's fine. You can't fake a connection, although, I actually thought you were emotionally capable enough that if you wanted us to stop seeing each other you'd at least let me know.' A flush formed on his cheeks. He opened his mouth, and for a minute I thought he was going to speak, that I'd finally get some kind of explanation. But his eyes flickered to the doorway behind me, where Thomas had seemingly moved closer. His presence was oddly reassuring even if I couldn't work out whether he was trying to be supportive or actually just leaning closer to hear the gossip. James closed his mouth and swallowed, and did a tiny shake of his head that I assumed meant he wasn't going to be telling me anything now. I felt a surge of rage.

'Do you know what? I don't care. Honestly I don't. You aren't the person I thought you were. I was hoping you were the real deal, someone who complemented me,' I felt Thomas take a step back behind me, diving for cover from the emotional onslaught, 'completed me even if that does sound incredibly lame. I thought you were that person but then I realized you aren't. And now I don't care. I fell for someone who it turns out didn't actually exist. That's my mistake, for being naïve and taking what you said at face value. I'll learn from that. But don't you dare try and guilt trip me. Don't you dare.'

For a second everything was silent. I never lose my temper like that. I couldn't tell you the last time I did. I could see Thomas open-mouthed in my peripheral vision, while James's eyes were wide.

He moved forward, putting his hand out plaintively to touch my arm. 'Sophie, I –'

I moved like I'd been burned, pushing him off with such force I shocked myself and almost knocked him over. 'Don't you touch me. We're done.'

And then I slammed the front door in his face.

As I turned to face him, Thomas's face was a picture. He had never seen me so emotional and he seemed genuinely unsure about what to do. I felt my lip beginning to wobble, and for a moment a look of panic crossed his face, before he steeled himself for the onslaught and moved forward to envelop me in his arms. I cried for a little while, then pulled myself together, slowing my tears and embarrassedly wiping at the damp shoulder of his t-shirt. Then Thomas made a pot of tea for us all – poor Charlotte had been woken by the noise of me slamming the door while bellowing like I was in a soap opera. He told her the full story of what had happened, how amazing I had been and how James had stupid hair. I wasn't sure he was right on either count, but it passed the time until my eyes had got less puffy, and meant we could be sure James had given up and gone before we braved going out for breakfast. I didn't think for a serious second that he would have stuck around, but I still felt a pang, wishing he had despite myself. I had pancakes; it felt like that kind of day.

17

I very rarely lose my temper properly. I'm as prone to a rant as the next woman, but generally I'm fairly easy-going. My confrontation with James was completely out of character, to the extent that both Thomas and Charlotte were a little agog.

They stayed for the rest of the weekend, as planned, but suffice to say there was a James-shaped hole slap bang in the middle of things. Seeing him after so long had left me feeling out of sorts. I was furious, properly furious, at his reaction to seeing Thomas come out of my bedroom. Don't get me wrong, I know it looked unfortunate, but if there was a moral high ground then Mr Hugely-Intense-With-Lord-Lucan-Tendencies didn't get to be on it, not least because – and forgive me if it sounds like I'm harping on about this, but in this instance it felt a reasonable point – he hadn't been in contact for weeks. What did it matter to him what I was doing now or who with? Was he expecting me to be at home alone weeping? I know I had been, but that's absolutely not the point, and I had no intention of letting on that any such thing had happened.

Also, I'll admit it, in hindsight I sort of regretted slamming the door. It felt very satisfying when I did it, and was definitely no less than he deserved. But when the silence had lengthened I suddenly realized that he wasn't going to knock again, and I now had no idea why he'd come round at all. None whatsoever. Dramatic gestures are all well and good in the abstract, but curiosity burned me almost as much as injustice. I still wanted, OK needed, to know why he had disappeared so abruptly, but even beyond that a part of me was intrigued as to why he'd suddenly changed his mind and returned. Of course, my slightly overzealous imagination was running wild, as it had through his silence, but – damn my resumed cynicism – I just wasn't sure he'd returned because he was missing me and had suddenly realized he couldn't do without me. In fact, if the expression on his face when I'd first opened the door was anything to go by, I'd have guessed he'd come round because he'd left his second favourite pair of jeans here or something. There was definitely no look of urgency on his face, just a slightly pained expression. At least until Thomas appeared.

I was so confused. When did a man having a surge of jealousy – I wasn't being an egotist, that really was how it had seemed – become a good thing? When did it become the closest I might get to a sign that he cared? What kind of fucked-up nonsense was this? This kind of emotional high drama was absolutely the last thing I wanted in any kind of relationship – so why did I even care about him anyway, especially after everything he'd done?

My brain kept spinning, even while we watched DVD after DVD. I didn't say much, though. The rest of Thomas's and Charlotte's weekend at the flat passed so inoffensively as to be anticlimactic. After breakfast we headed back for more DVDs and a lot of tea, before heading out for dinner at a great curry house round the corner from my flat. I like to think I was carrying off a carefree and light-hearted demeanour, but I caught Charlotte and Tom exchanging concerned glances at several points so perhaps I wasn't. Overall, I was doing OK. Getting everything off my chest felt oddly cathartic, and had helped draw a line under everything. And I didn't even feel like making a batch of scones, which had to be progress.

Of course, good friends see through the façade. As I was dragging my blanket out for a second night on the sofa, Charlotte touched my shoulder.

'Sophie, you don't have to sleep on the sofa if you don't want to.'

I looked up at her, confused. The things we'd done felt like they'd happened in another lifetime, a lifetime I didn't regret but definitely didn't want to revisit. What was she saying? I cleared my throat, trying to think of a way to say no tactfully, and she suddenly seemed to understand the cause of my misapprehension and shook her head.

'No, I didn't mean that way. I just thought we could make room for you in the bed. Don't sleep in here alone tonight.'

I eyed up my lumpy sofa, mindful of the lack of sleep I'd had the night before, even before the early-morning wake up call. I smiled. 'OK.'

Thomas harrumphed from behind me. 'This is all well and good and lovely, but it's not the biggest bed in the world, and I bet I'll be the uncomfortable one.'

Charlotte smacked him on the arm. 'Shut up and be

nice. It's her bed after all. You can take the sofa if you'd rather.'

Thomas's rapid reply – 'No, darling, you're completely right' – made me laugh, and for the first time since that morning it didn't feel forced.

I woke up the next morning feeling surprisingly well-rested. Charlotte was curled up next to me, both of us firmly tucked under the covers in our pyjamas. As I opened my eyes I saw Thomas pressed into the wall, his hand clutching a postage stamp-sized corner of duvet. It made me grin and I felt a surge of affection for my unconventional friends.

They left later that afternoon, and I sheepishly had a bit of a cry after they'd gone – when you only lose your temper properly once every couple of years there's an emotional hangover to be had and once I was in the flat alone I really couldn't seem to shake it. I lay in front of the telly, hoping crap reruns and tea would help me get the melancholy out of my system. I was hopeful it had worked – if nothing else, after so many weeks of angst I'd pretty much bored myself out of it now. At least that's what I thought until I woke up the next morning and checked my phone.

Hey, I know you had company yesterday, but could we get together? Just to talk? – J xx

I read and reread the text. Two kisses? That suggested something, right? But what? And did I even want to know? Was it worth risking it? What was stopping him from pulling the same stunt a few weeks down the line? And what the hell did he think 'company' was? Did he think Thomas and I were sleeping together? Why didn't he seem bothered about that? Did he think I wasn't available now? Was he relieved? Commitment phobic? Would he even tell me if he was? Did I even really care? Irritatingly, the only question I definitely knew the answer to was the last one and, ironically enough, I really wished I didn't.

There were two different schools of thought, summed up neatly by Thomas and Charlotte. Tom thought the best thing I could do was refuse to meet James, in his charming words tell him to 'cock off and die', draw a line under everything, and start moving on. Charlotte thought I should go along, be friendly but unflirty, wear a killer outfit and leave him regretting what he'd given up. After a couple of days of dithering – no more replying to texts within half an hour now – I decided to go with the latter strategy. Which, yes, may be proof of my masochistic tendencies.

So I found myself heading into the City for drinks, wearing an outfit with arguably a little more cleavage showing than normal. And why? I'm not entirely sure even now. I just felt that I needed to know what had happened, to try and understand. I needed, if such things were available outside of cheesy American talk shows, to have some kind of closure.

We met. He was solicitous. We ordered coffee, making polite small talk, firstly about what the best kind of coffee was, then my brother's birthday, his parents' anniversary. Everything but the elephant in the room. As the minutes passed I began to feel like I wanted to laugh – here we were, sat here like nothing strange had happened. It was surreal. I felt exhausted and even more confused by my own emotions and behaviour than by him. What on earth was I still doing here?

But it seemed I wasn't the only one not exactly capable of explaining what was going on in my head. Finally, James said something non-relative related, seemingly intent on fiddling about with his coffee spoon as he said, in a voice not dissimilar to one discussing the weather, 'I don't know if you noticed me cooling off quite abruptly.'

My mouth gaped open at the understatement and then, I couldn't help myself, I laughed. It sounded bitter, and he flinched a little, but still he kept going. Bravery or lunacy? At that point I wasn't sure.

'I know, I've behaved badly. And I couldn't have explained why to you, didn't really know what was going on, which sounds stupid, I know. But something clicked for me. And I didn't even realize it till the weekend.'

And then he told me. He told I was amazing and that intellectually he thought I was one of the most intelligent, interesting people he'd met for ages, that I made him laugh, that he really enjoyed spending time with me – all lovely things I've mentally filed away for retrieval during those crap days where I feel rubbish about myself. But then, as my inner monologue was gearing itself up for the 'but' that explained why, despite all this good stuff, he'd hotfooted it away like the hounds of hell were after him, he told me something that made me look up, confused, thinking I'd misheard him.

'The more I like you, the more time we spend together, the harder it is for me to dominate you, Sophie. To hurt you. When we first played, seeing the apprehension in your eyes, hearing you whimper, made me hard. But now, it's upsetting. And I'm sorry.'

He was sorry? I was outraged. He didn't sound sorry, but he was going to soon.

'You're an idiot, you know that?' He looked up, surprised. I'm not sure how many people had ever called him that. I wondered if that was part of the bloody problem. 'For someone so insightful, who can second-guess my reactions in a way unlike anyone I've ever known, who prides themselves on understanding what makes me tick, how could you be so bloody stupid? How could you possibly not know that what you did, by being thoughtless and gutless and silent, was going to hurt me more than anything you did with your hands, or anything else you could physically hurt me with?'

He shook his head. 'I know. I do know. I just . . .' He tailed off.

What do you say in that situation? Well, after my initial explosion I said very little, in part because if I'd sat down and written a list of possible reasons for what had happened between us, this wouldn't have been in the first hundred. It felt insane. Later I'd feel a grudging respect for the fact he'd managed to come up with something that even I – with my overactive imagination – had never even conceived of, but in that moment I was quiet. Stunned. And as he kept talking and apologized over and over again, so embarrassed you'd think he was admitting he was suffering from premature ejaculation, my first instincts of fury and bitterness abated until I felt sorry for him. He genuinely looked like he needed a hug, and someone to tell him everything would be all right.

We were silent for a little while, before my brain finally kicked in enough to ask why it hadn't been a problem before.

Running a hand through his hair he told me he'd never dominated anyone in person as violently as he had me. That he respected me more than anyone he'd played with previously in the sense that I was more capable, more equal to him, and while on an academic level dominating me turned him on, hence him talking a good game via email, in person he increasingly found it difficult whether I was glowering up at him or had my eyes filled with tears. And then he apologized some more. Lots more. To the point where I did just give him a big hug and we drank our coffee. I was still furious, not least because he seemed incapable of understanding that his behaviour over the last few weeks had hurt me more than anything he could have done with the crop, a wooden spoon, or anything else he threw my way, and because, thanks to his behaviour, things had changed between us in a way that I wasn't sure could ever be repaired, but at least now I knew. I could begin to understand.

He'd been staring into his cup for a little while before I finally got my thoughts in order enough to speak. I wasn't even sure whether my words would or should make a difference, but felt more than ever that the final piece of the puzzle had dropped into place, and that maybe James needed to hear what I had to say, even if it was difficult for me to say it. Suddenly I was the one swallowing back nerves, feeling tentative. It felt crazy, to have never really said these basic things in person, but to have felt the things I'd – we'd? – felt. I'd honestly never felt more vulnerable – not when I was crying, powerless, being pushed to my limits. Finally I spoke, my voice soft and, ridiculously, shy.

'When you hurt me I like it. I crave it even. I don't know whether you can tell that when I'm glaring at you, when my eyes are filled with tears, when I'm blushing, even when I can't quite hide my expression of fear at the thought of whatever fiendish thing you're going to do next. Being so completely on the back foot, being demeaned, being hurt, diminished, does it for me. Feeling your hands at my wrists, at my throat, or in my hair, feeling you overpower me, master me, makes my breath quicken. It makes me wet. I lie in bed at night thinking about it sometimes.'

I took a big gulp of coffee – this was way harder than begging for orgasm and, somehow, felt like one of the most important conversations of my life, no matter what happened. I continued, peeking over my cup to see his reaction.

'Yes, you hurt me. But you do it with my permission. I beg you to do it, literally sometimes. Hurting me isn't a bad thing in this context. The fact that you're you – kind, intelligent, polite, lovely James – is what makes me feel confident and safe enough for you to do that. I wouldn't give any old person that power over me. I give it to you. In fact, I've never given any other person the level of power over me that I've given you, not even Thomas. And I give you this power because of the vanilla you. If you were as merciless and harsh all the time as you are when you're choking me then I wouldn't want to play with you.

'Don't get me wrong, when you're doing that, when you're cocking an eyebrow at me, when you're making me whimper, it's hot enough to make my breath catch just thinking about it. But I like the paradox. I like both sides of you. I like the fact I can trust you to hurt me, to take pleasure in having the power to make me cry, and yet still be thoughtful and lovely enough afterwards to give me a hug, make sure that I'm physically and mentally OK, get me a glass of wine or some juice. That is a good thing. These two sides of you aren't contrary to each other. They fit together perfectly, and both show a considerateness and awareness of other people's needs. Hurting someone who wants to be hurt is not only not a bad thing, it's practically a cathartic kindness.'

He was sitting completely still. I put my hand on his arm, trying to make him understand, fearing that actually my words weren't going to be enough, which all things considered is pretty bloody ironic.

'As I said, I'm hoping you know this already. And don't worry, I'm not telling you this because I'm trying to wangle my way into a relationship with you.' I suddenly realized I was sounding aloof by accident and tried to clarify. 'Don't get me wrong, I'm not saying I wouldn't be interested in trying one – it's not every day I get to meet someone like you. I have so much fun and enjoy being with you, in and out of bed. But I don't know that you're in the right place for a relationship now even if you were interested in pursuing one with me specifically – and I'm not assuming that either. But if nothing else happens between us except us exchanging moans via email and meeting for an occasional beer, I think you need to hear this anyway.'

I put my cup down. 'Yes, you're sadistic. And maybe you need to get your head round that, to figure out whether you're happy being that person. But for me, I'm happy with you being both the man my mum would want me to bring home and the one she'd warn me about, all in one complex, fascinating package. And I'm happy being me – needing to be hurt, craving it, loving being challenged and being pushed and sometimes pushing back.'

We sat in silence for a little while. When it became apparent he wasn't ready to speak again I decided it was time to brave the traffic home. I picked my handbag from the floor and my coat from the back of the chair. 'If you figure out that you're happy with who you are in the same way I am, then give me a call.'

And then I left. Because suddenly it all made sense, even in the context of the fucked-up, messy emotions of whatever was happening with James and me. If he was my soulmate, the person I was to end up with, my dom, my partner, then it would happen as a result of this conversation. And if he didn't, well, I'd been honest with him, and I knew what I was looking for now.

And I knew it was worth waiting for.

Epilogue

It's been one of those weeks.

One of those weeks where I haven't been able to switch off, where the trials and tribulations of day-to-day life have been so overarching that sex has been the last thing on my mind and just getting through without my brain imploding has felt like a real stretch. I've been juggling long, busy and stressful work days with evenings spent writing to finish this book in time for my deadline. I've been thinking more about my nature – submissive and otherwise – than I ever have before and trying to put it into words that are both sexy and truthful, even when sometimes the self-awareness that comes out of that brings me up short. Ironically, all this has meant my orgasms have been grabbed purely to bring on the blessed relief of sleep.

So when I came into the room and saw him sitting at my PC, reading through a chapter I'd cast aside a few days before, I didn't see it as a prelude to an afternoon of shagging.

But as every sub knows, often it's not down to you to decide.

Getting into the sub mindset comes easier sometimes than others. And right now, with my head filled with the myriad of shit that's been going on for the last week or so, I'm light years away from my obedient submissive best – and let's face it, I have a problem with the obedient part at the best of times. If only he didn't look so damn sexy. It definitely makes what is going to happen next pretty much a forgone conclusion.

'You're nearly done with the book, then.'

I nod. 'Just a few bits left to tidy, here and there. I'm getting there.'

He smiles. 'It's an interesting read.'

I blush. 'Thanks. Surely it's a bit weird reading all these things that aren't you?'

He grins and waggles his eyebrows before taking pity on my slightly worried frown. He beckons me over and as I lean in he kisses me, softly on the forehead and then, harder, on the mouth. 'Not at all. I'd say it was research, but where you're concerned I don't really need to read the manual.'

His smugness makes me laugh. He makes me laugh. I'm the happiest I've ever been. But then, as I stand looking at him, something in his eyes changes. Lust flares, and a little bit of menace. His voice takes on the timbre which makes the butterflies start. 'Get down on your knees.'

I don't move immediately. It's been a long week, and while this is fun and everything I'm not in the right headspace. Irony of ironies, I know, but I'm really not. Of course, kneeling in front of him while he's sitting in the chair means I would have a really great view. Sod it, I think to myself and sink to the floor.

The thing is, I'm still crap at hiding anything. And being half-arsed about this stuff is just opening yourself up to trouble.

'You rolled your eyes then.'

'No I didn't.' Shit. Why the hell am I arguing? That was a mistake too. Shut up. Bugger it.

'Yes, you did. And just then, that sounded like you answering back.'

I swear to god I am actually chewing on the words to argue that I wasn't answering back. I just about manage to keep them in but it's touch and go. And I'm fairly sure he can tell, although he looks more amused than pissed off. But then he's back to business.

'Take your clothes off, except for your knickers, and get back down on your knees.'

My movements are economical. This is no striptease: I'm conscious I'm in quite enough trouble already so I obey quickly, keeping my gaze down as I drop to the floor so no real or imagined eye-rolling can get me into any more hot water.

His groin is just a few inches from my face. My hands clench at my sides with the effort of not moving, of not touching him.

'Pinch your nipples for me. Hard. Show me your breasts. Come on.'

I start to pull and squeeze my nipples, lifting the weight of my breasts up. Being naked, on display in front of him, when he's fully dressed and looking like he's ready for a trip out for dinner, is the kind of little humiliation he revels in and something, even now, I find difficult to deal with. I close my eyes at the embarrassment of it, can feel myself blushing a little, even as my knickers start feeling damp between my legs.

His hands slap mine away and he grabs and twists my nipples. My eyes open in shock and I can't stop a yelp at the pain, as he pulls my breasts high, making me kneel higher to try and ease some of the tension.

'Your pinching is pathetic. This is what I mean.' He twists viciously to punctuate his point and I breathe deeply to try and process the wave of pain. 'Now do it properly. And keep your eyes down.'

Now, I don't know if this is something anyone else with submissive tendencies finds, but I am fine withstanding pain dished out by someone else – I'd even go so far as to say when I'm in the zone I have a fairly good tolerance for pain. But asking me to inflict it on myself? Somehow it's harder to withstand. I can't wax my own legs because the thought of the pain leaves me incapable of ripping the wax strips off. He's mightily pissed off now and so I twist my already red and sore nipples harder, eyes on the floor.

I honestly don't know how long we stay there. The room is still but for the movement of his hand as he strokes himself just outside of my peripheral vision. I am desperate to see him, but stare resolutely at a knot on the hardwood floor between his feet.

'It's a great view. I don't know where to come though. It seems a shame to come in your hair when you've just washed it. Maybe I should come across your breasts. What do you think?'

I sneak a peek to see whether I'm supposed to reply, see him looking at me and am back staring at his toes before he finishes barking the command for me to look down. My voice is hesitant as I try to work out how to say

I want him to come in my mouth. I love having him in my mouth. But with my equilibrium off I feel uncertain of the best way to say it and it ends up sounding like a question, which amuses him if nothing else.

Kneeling here in front of him, staring at his feet, my mindset is shifting a gear. The weight of the week is easing, and all I'm aware of for now is how frustrated this gorgeous guy is making me and how desperate I am to please him so that (and I know this isn't the point but forgive me for being self-indulgent) he'll please me. The idea of him touching me, letting me touch him, is something I want so much that in this instant everything else is fading away.

'Stand up.'

I've been kneeling before him long enough that it takes me a couple of seconds to get my balance. He manoeuvres my shoulder so I'm facing the way he wants me to and then his fingers are sliding along my slit, pushing the slick cotton inside me and chuckling at how wet I am. I battle to stand still, looking straight ahead, as he runs his teasing fingers around me. He stops to draw a line down my spine, which makes me shiver, before pulling my knickers down. Thank fuck. I step out of them as they pool around my feet, and as I do so he grabs my hair, which is gathered in a ponytail at the nape of my neck, and pulls on it hard, yanking me to the floor in ungainly fashion. As I scramble to my knees he pulls me back against his hip bone, holding me in place.

'You're still doing things I've not asked you to do. I don't want you to show initiative. Right now, I don't want you to do anything but what I tell you to do when I tell you to do it. When I ask you a question you are to answer it promptly and politely. You're a clever girl, these are simple things. Do you understand?'

I glare at his patronizing turn of phrase. My throat is dry. 'Yes. Sorry.'

The silence lengthens. I am held in place by my hair, leaning against him while he stands over me like some kind of conquering hero.

'Right. What do you think has to happen now?'

I know. God I know. But I don't want to be too specific in how I answer this in case I put ideas into his head. Is he wearing his belt today? Does he remember where I keep my toys?

He tugs on my hair. 'Well?'

'You're going to punish me.'

'Indeed.'

Once again I'm moving, manoeuvred into position against the arm of the sofa. He kicks my legs open, so he can see between them, and then turns his attention to my arse, running his fingers along the sensitive curve of it, making me shiver while I wait for the first blow.

Being on the receiving end of the cane and the belt at his hand have both reduced me to tears before. But when he wants to make an impression even a spanking can be painful. And as the sound of the first blow reverberates round the room and I suck air in through my teeth to help me ride the wave, I realize this is going to be quite painful, not some kind of play-acting spank session.

The thing is, as the blows rain down and I hold my

position, dealing with the pain clears everything else out of my head. I'm not thinking about my crappy week, not wondering about word counts and paragraph breaks. I'm not worrying what I look like naked with my arse in the air. I'm not even thinking about how horny I am (although, for the record, I'm finding it really hot). I am just riding the waves of pain and withstanding the onslaught that he is dishing out, because at this point I know that is all I need to do to please him. And all I want to do right now is please him. My mind is clear and a weight has been lifted and all it has taken is a thorough thrashing of one arse cheek.

He stops for a second and asks how many times he has hit my arse. I can only guess, while trying not to tremble as he runs a finger along my now-hot bottom. He makes me count off the second cheek, thanking him for every blow, and rest assured there is no eye rolling by then; I'm too busy trying to stay upright and in position on wobbly legs.

Once he's finished he steps back and unceremoniously thrusts his fingers into me from behind. The undignified onslaught has me whimpering and bucking beneath him like an animal as he moves his fingers, being sure to bash the edge of my punished arse with his thumb during every thrust too. The sensation is intense. He slips in and out of me easily, pushing me closer to orgasm, harder and harder while he rubs my clit so viciously that the intense pleasure is almost painful. Having stayed faithfully in position during the punishment, the pleasure is too much for me to stand and I end up coming hard on his fingers, sinking down to the floor where I huddle for a second trying to get my breath back. By definition, there's no such thing as a bad orgasm but this one is the perfect release at the end of a hard week. It's like I've been broken down and rebuilt.

As I become more aware of my surroundings, I lift myself up from my supine position on the floor to see him standing over me. As he moves towards me, finally, I move my head towards him to take him in my mouth. But the sting in my scalp brings tears to my eyes as he pulls me back.

'Not until I say you can have it.'

I open my mouth again, this time to apologise, but as I do he grabs the back of my head and shoves himself past my lips, leaving me struggling for a second to accept him without gagging. My mouth starts working on him, and I lick and suck him eagerly, enjoying the feel of him thickening in my mouth, listening as his breathing changes. At that moment the entire focus of my world is him, his satisfaction. Nothing else matters and the simplicity of that feels exhilarating. As he comes I smile to myself. It's a surreal moment of contemplative peace.

Being submissive is just one facet of my personality. But it is a key part of what makes me the person I am, just as much as the importance I place on my friends and family, the way I love my job, my independent stubborn streak, my love of Marmite, even.

Suddenly my shitty week, everything else that felt so urgent and important twenty minutes ago feels a world away. Right now, for this moment, with my arse sore and the taste of him in my throat, he is the centre of my universe. And I fucking love it.

SYLVIA DAY

BARED TO YOU

Our journey began in fire . . .

Gideon Cross came into my life like lightning in the darkness – beautiful and brilliant, jagged and white hot. I was drawn to him as I'd never been to anything or anyone in my life. I craved his touch like a drug, even knowing it would weaken me. I was flawed and damaged, and he opened those cracks in me so easily . . .

Gideon *knew*. He had demons of his own. And we would become the mirrors that reflected each other's most private wounds . . . and desires.

The bonds of his love transformed me, even as I prayed that the torment of our pasts didn't tear us apart . . .

'This is a sophisticated, provocative, titillating, highly erotic, sexually driven read and extremely well done. I enjoyed *Fifty Shades of Grey*, but I loved *Bared to You*' *Swept Away by Romance*

'*Bared to You* has an emotional feel similar to *Fifty Shades of Grey* . . . It is full of emotional angst, scorching love scenes and a compelling storyline' *Dear Author*

'A well written and sexually charged romance with characters who have real depth . . . I would highly recommend *Bared to You*, because it's what *Fifty Shades of Grey* could have been' *The Book Pushers*

'This is an erotic romance that should not be missed. It will make readers fall in love' *Romance Novel News*